From Darkness to the Dawn

From Darkness to the Dawn

HOW BELIEF IN THE AFTERLIFE AFFECTS LIVING

A.R. van de Walle

TWENTY-THIRD PUBLICATIONS
Mystic, Connecticut

First published in English 1984
by SCM Press Ltd
26-30 Tottenham Road, London N1

Translated by John Bowden from the Flemish *Tot
het aanbreken van de dageraad*
© Uitgeverij Altiora, Averbode, Belgium 1981

Translation © John Bowden 1984

North American edition 1985
Twenty-Third Publications
P.O. Box 180
Mystic, CT 06355
(203) 536-2611

ISBN: 0-89622-272-1
Library of Congress Catalog Card Number 85-51083

Cover design by Kathy Michalove

For Ignace

Contents

PART ONE

Reconnaissance

'Simply because of someone else in me,
who never gets used to land or climate,
and constantly keeps asking
whether there is not another land
that he knows much better.'

André Demedts

I

DISCOVERY, BEWILDERMENT AND FANTASY

There is no escaping it. The more you love, the more you are confronted with death. In the midst of life. Human reactions are as varied as the forms in which we encounter death.

It seems easier to accept death as a universal fact, which makes it both abstract and anonymous. There is life – and then it ends. Human beings are mortal and die. All of them. That is the only thing we know for certain about anyone's future.

However, people are constantly terrified – even if only for a short time – by this calm assertion of our inexorable fate, when they hear of the death of someone with whom they have been personally acquainted for a while. Leo Tolstoy described such an experience in an exceptional way. Piotr hears that his friend and colleague Ivan Ilyich has died after days of distressing suffering. As an illustration of humanity in general, his reaction is as revealing as it is disconcerting: 'The thought of the sufferings of the man he had known so intimately, first as a light-hearted child, then a youngster at school, and later on, when they were grown up, as a partner at whist, suddenly struck Piotr Ivanovich with horror. He again saw that brow, and the nose pressing down on the lip, and was overcome with a feeling of dread on his own account. "Three days and nights of awful suffering and then death. Why, it might happen to me, all of a sudden, at any moment," he thought, and for an instant was terrified. But immediately, he could not have explained how, there came to his support the old reflection that this thing had befallen Ivan Ilyich and not him, and it ought not and could not happen to him, and to think that it could meant that he was falling into a melancholy frame of mind, which was a mistake . . . After which reflection Piotr Ivanovich cheered up and began to ask with interest about the details of Ivan Ilyich's end, as though death were some mischance to which only Ivan Ilyich was liable, but he himself was not.'[1]

This discovery that everyone dies turns to bewilderment when we are confronted with the death of someone whom we have deeply loved. We keep hearing the same disconsolate words, 'It's impossible, incredible!' *He* can't be dead. You can't mean *her*. Of course it is a natural event. But it can't happen to my wife, or to our child. My husband, my friend, never! Dead, dead, dead. Every step a person takes is the echo of this fearful, intolerable word.

In our society it seems to be not the thing to grieve publicly. But left alone with someone who has seen part of himself or herself lost in a person they have loved, we will still witness the same eternally human reactions, however much they may differ in detail: collapse, loud weeping, bitter cursing, impotent rage, rebellion. We anxiously keep hearing the same questions, to which no one knows the answer. Why? Why did he die, when he was so young and full of life? Why not one of those much older people, who have outlived themselves in every respect? Many of those who know what it is to have had someone snatched away in the prime of life will certainly recognize part of their own experience in the unburdening of feeling by Maarten 't Hart. He, and no one else, knows that his father, now so full of life, is fatally ill, but unaware of the fact. He tries to come to terms with this: 'My anger went out above all against that old man and the old people in front of the ticket office because they were already older than my father would ever be. I knew that I hated them to the depths of my soul because they were still alive whereas my father was as it were already dead. Who gave them the right to become older than my father? Why was there not simply an age limit beyond which one could not go? . . . I heard the aggression, I longed to express in music that embittered hatred against everything that lived beyond sixty, while the evil tumour continued to grow in my father.'[2]

For some people – perhaps a majority? – the theory that everyone has to die becomes a cruel absurdity only when they come face to face with their own imminent death. Many people find it much easier to cope with the death of someone else, however dear to them, than with their own death. People are so incredibly complicated that when faced with the death of someone they love dearly they often have to repress in the depths of their own heart, with dismay, a feeling of relief: the other person died; I'm still here; I'm alive.

Living people don't believe in their own death. In the novel by Tolstoy I quoted earlier Ivan Ilyich constructs the following syllogism: ' "Caius is a man, men are mortal, therefore Caius is mortal" had seemed to him all his life to be true as applied to Caius but certainly not as regards himself. That Caius – man in the abstract – was mortal, was perfectly correct; but he was not Caius, nor man in the abstract . . . Caius was certainly mortal, and it was right for him to die, but for me, little Vanya, Ivan Ilyich, with all my thoughts and emotions - it's a different matter altogether.'³

However, we certainly know people who find their own death easier to accept and to face than the death of someone else whom they love more than themselves. So it is quite clear that there are people who prepare themselves, or have prepared themselves, for their own death, perhaps after the various phases of what is often a long-drawn-out process, leading, as Elizabeth Kübler-Ross shows particularly well, from disbelief and withdrawal through anger and bargaining and depression to the acceptance of death. It is perhaps easier for someone who has had the chance to grow old and who can look back on a richly filled life and then, as they say, see it blown out like a candle, to accept this than for those who are young and would normally have all the future before them. There will also be people who recognize themselves in what Bernard Shaw makes Father Adam say: 'It is the horror of having to be with myself for ever. I like you (he says to Eve), but I do not like myself. I want to be different; to be better, to begin again and again; to shed myself as a snake sheds its skin. I am tired of myself. And yet I must endure myself, not for a day or for many days, but for ever.'⁴ Simone de Beauvoir made a similar comment: it would be hell if we could not die.

All that is possible. We may even say something about our personal fate. But we must be much more careful about talking about the death of others, especially the death of others who have had more of their share of the suffering and injustice which so dominate this world. People don't talk of death in a society full of old peoples' homes in the way that they do in a military cemetery containing the bodies of thousands of young men who never really had the chance to live.·

We are affected most deeply at a personal level by the shattering experience of having to look on in complete helplessness when someone we love more than anything else dies inexorably with cruel suffering; or when we learn quite unexpectedly that the person who means more than anything to us has suddenly died in an incredibly stupid road accident or of a heart attack.

Should all this be dismissed as the melodramatic reflections of a bourgeois mentality which ought to be forgotten as quickly as possible and condemned as vigorously as possible? Is not all this the result of a despicable individualism in which people are concerned only for themselves and want others to find their own happiness? Is it not megalomania, arrogance, if one longs like a thief for happiness which is impossible for any mortal? Is not Marguerite Yourcenar right when she points out: 'Our clinging to life here on earth is still mixed up with the ridiculous pride which assures us that we actually have the right to remain here.'[5] Must we not convey all this to people in order to help them over their grief as quickly as possible through this insight, in order to point out to them that they need to sacrifice themselves for others who are alive? We have all learned our lesson well and know that we must say, 'You must not let yourself go. Be strong! Don't lose heart! Your children need you. You still have a future to make. Give up this wretched self-pity. Time heals all wounds.' Or should we follow Marguerite Yourcenar in noting this 'healthy human understanding': 'The memory of most men is an abandoned cemetery where lie, unsung and unhonoured, the dead whom they have ceased to cherish. Any lasting grief is reproof to their neglect.'[5a]

Perhaps the first approach is a correct therapy, given a purified insight. However, it does not help everyone nor does it heal everyone. People remain incurably damaged. You cannot forbid someone to grieve, even if you find offensive the way in which that grief is deliberately cherished. You cannot dismiss as futile self-torture any questions which stem from an inconsolable grief. You cannot dismiss any question raised by anyone else because you personally feel it to be unimportant, ridiculous, useless worry, wild fantasy, a waste of energy. Or simply because you do not know the answer. You cannot brush aside any question, regardless of the existential distress which has prompted it, with a theory which declares *a priori* that it is nonsense.

II

FINDING MEANING IN LIMITATIONS

There is one question which cannot be suppressed, and which keeps welling up at the death of someone who means more than anyone else. Is that the end of everything? Has my husband, my wife, my child, simply disappeared into nothingness? Is it really all up with him? Has she really vanished for ever? Is this the absolute end of our relationship, brutally broken off because our partner simply does not exist any more? Is it really impossible to go beyond the boundaries between life and death? For good or ill, everyone tries to cope with this question, and people do so in many, very different ways.

The answer can be: yes, that is the end. This answer can betray resignation, fatalism or a realistic acceptance of the facts.

1. God and meaning

Christians are all too inclined to conclude from this answer that life therefore has no meaning. However, such a conclusion is by no means evident. It is quite wrong to claim that life would be meaningless and absurd if it came to a complete end with death. Of course, we can understand how, because they are convinced that death is the absolute end of all human possibilities and longings, people can feel that there is no point in getting worked up over a life about which one can ultimately do nothing. However, that need not be the case, and there is no logically compelling reason why it should be. A great many people accept death as the absolute end but find their life, indeed all existence, particularly meaningful. Despite everything, it is worth while trying to give shape to our life, with all its possibilities and challenges, and to make something of it, both for the sake of those others whom we try to help and whose happiness we seek and for ourselves. Some people think that it is the limitations on life which provide the deepest and most compelling reason for living this life to the full, for all its limitations, so as to be able to experience it as intensively as possible. Time is short. Their aim is not to enjoy life in a selfish way but to help as many people as possible to make as much as possible of their own lives.

People with such convictions and such dedication often feel that to think in terms of 'another' life, a life after death, is a betrayal of this life, of life before death. History and the humane sciences often justify their view. For generations, people accepted the most intolerable forms of injustice, exploitation and misery, comforted by the thought that true life, real life, began only after death. These people had no future on earth. If there was a future for them, it could only lie beyond the grave. And there are always those who are all too ready to hide their personal inability to change anything in this world, to improve this life here on earth, behind their longing for another life where one day their dreams will come true, dreams which they cannot fulfil anywhere here, because they constantly fall apart and prove to be illusions.

It is certainly possible to accept that life has meaning despite the limitations and the essential transitoriness of any form of creature-liness. Many people show us this by the particularly worthwhile ways in which they live. However, life can also be seen to have mean-ing, on the same terms, when people deliberately put into practice their belief in God.

I shall go on to show in some detail how over a period of centuries Israel lived by a profound belief in a God of the covenant without any expectation of a 'beyond'. In our own time, too, we sometimes find believers who accept death as a final barrier, even though they may believe in God. Although the French Dominican Jacques Pohier was condemned, among other things, because he did not accept a life after death, one can hardly deny that his arguments lent force to a view which is still common among a great many believers. Pohier rightly puts particular stress on the limitations of any creaturely existence. God alone is God. We may not claim for any creature *qua* creature what we affirm of God as Creator. God alone is eternal. No creature is eternal, nor can it be. We are not immortal. That we die is part of our make-up as creatures. I shall be coming back to Pohier's view.[6] I mention it briefly here in order to show that the acceptance of death as a final barrier can evidently be reconciled with a belief in God. In fact we not only know this from the speculations of theo-logians, who are sometimes said to confuse ordinary people, but we also often learn it personally from the lips of people of really deep faith. Face to face with their own death, they have thanked God for the life that he has given them and for the fact that, all things con-sidered, it was not too bad. They have quietly accepted that this God-given existence has now come to an end. I once heard a forty-year-old woman, who had known more grief in her life than one would have thought possible, say: 'I don't know whether there is anything after this life and I don't dare to hope; if there is, all the better, I will gladly accept it, too. But there really doesn't need to be anything. I thank God for everything.' That made me begin to think about my own reasons for believing in a world to come.

What people like this ask about and worry about is not what is to happen to them – they accept death as the end – but what is to hap-pen to those who are left behind. It is worth listening to the words of an old country pastor: 'We still talk much too soon of a life after death, of the beyond, of resurrection. That sort of thing still springs far too quickly to our lips. In my parish I have known many people, especially ordinary, simple people, old and sick people. And I have to say that their real problem was not, "What comes after death?" What they were really worried about was: "Are my children happy? Have I done enough for them? What will happen to my relatives? How will my husband, my wife, cope when I am no longer there?" Or even, "Isn't my illness far too great a burden for others?" Those were their questions. I have known so many people who never spoke of a beyond and never asked about an eternal life, but who had learned to accept their life in all tranquillity and finally met their end well, in patience and with courage. Is that not the really Christian thing? Can anyone do more? Do we still have to talk with these people about another world?'[7]

Everyone will have met people with such deep faith at one time or another. No human being, no single authority can dismiss their testimony, far less condemn it. They gave, they give this testimony surrendering their whole being for others, in gratitude to God their creator. Once we have experienced that, we no longer dare claim that life would make no sense if death were the irrevocable end. That simply does not seem to be true. When we think about it more deeply, we come to the conclusion that the question of meaning is not quite the same as the question of God. People discover a meaning in life apart from God and apart from eternity. So God is not just another word for meaning.

2. People believe

Most people who regard themselves as believers in the Christian sense refuse to see death as the ultimate end. Because of their belief in God they trust in a life after death. However, among them, too, we find rather less confidence about a future life than seems to have been the case earlier. Their questions are far more sceptical. They will not, they dare not, give up this trust, but modern thought and the climate in which we live raise so many inexorable questions that many people find the ground giving under their feet and simply do not know where they stand and where they may put their trust. This uncertainty, this not knowing, this life with the enormous question-marks is no pose in which people adapt themselves to what is usually expected of a 'modern' or 'progressive' Christian. It is almost taken for granted when a believer proves to be open to the questions and needs of the present world, daring to take seriously his or her own life, world, fellow human beings, culture, personal experiences and that of others, with all the knowledge, insights, affectivity, emotions, creativity and social involvement which are involved. Faith is not the possession of unchangeable, eternal truths which need to be preserved undamaged; it is a way of being human, a particular way of living. In some circles people forget the word with which the creed begins. 'I believe'. The creed does not say, I 'have' faith; I put into practice the attitude of the believer. And the 'I' can only do this in a personal, in a unique way, in the quite specific context of its existence in the church and the world. Like the life and the being of people who believe, believing itself is always a contextual event within a limited time and a limited space, within a particular culture. To live in faith is a matter of dialogue, in which the dialogue between God and man affects a specific person in his or her particular world, conditioned as it is by social constellations, economic conditions, scientific insights, irreversible cultural achievements, geographical situations, and so on.

If belief takes place outside this constant dialogue, it degenerates from a creative life to being a barren possession or an esoteric sectarian life. A person's own identity can then only be found by adopting an attitude of opposition as a member of a group.

Perhaps some people do not find this latter position quite so false – though in my view it clearly is –; the only question is whether it can actually be true. Can believers act in such a way as to suggest that there is nothing to it? Can we disregard specific, impressive, serious and burdensome questions because they seem to stand in the way of our self-assurance and above all the tranquillity of our faith? We cannot simply shift the disastrous conflicts between faith and natural science, which had devastating consequences for the faith of a large number of people, into other spheres, in order to stop conflicts, e.g between faith and history, faith and the human sciences, faith and politics. We should learn from history that such conflicts always have a devastating effect on the community of believers. A church *magisterium* which subsequently has to recognize and affirm as true and correct what it had previously warned against or condemned threatens to lose all credibility.

When believers affirm that they no longer believe certain truths of faith it is usually not because they no longer *want* to believe them but because with the best will in the world they can no longer believe them. They would seem quite false to themselves if they did that, because things cannot now be otherwise. They reject a schizophrenic state in which their thought runs directly at cross purposes to what is required by a life of faith. In such a situation no *magisterium* which continually repeats these truths unchanged and requires assent to them can command respect. The conversation must be kept open, the questions must be raised, earlier insights and formulations must be revised, ideas corrected, and new experiences integrated.

When one comes up against believers who say that they can no longer confess and live out particular truths of faith, there are those who raise a finger in warning or reproof or even use their whole hand to strike as a punishment. Facts must not only be looked in the eye but must also be thought through quite thoroughly. The facts which have been produced by scientific investigations about belief in a future world are quite shattering.

In England, statistics from 1947 show the following picture: 84% said that they believed in God and 49% said that they believed in a world to come. In 1968 the ratio was 77% to 38%. In other countries the same ratios are: Sweden 1947, 80% and 49%; 1968, 60% and 38%; France 1947, 66% and 58%; 1968, 73% and 54%; Norway 1947, 84% and 71%; 1968, 73% and 54%.[8]

In the United States a survey in 1944 showed that 68% believed in a life after death; in 1968 it was 73% and in 1973 still 70%. In Germany in 1967, 63% of Catholics believed in life after death and 37% of Lutherans.[9] In the Netherlands in 1966, 57% believed in a life after death and in 1979 only 42%.[10] In Flanders an investigation among members of the Universal Christian Association in 1973 showed that only 42.7 per cent of them believed in a world to come.[11]

It is obvious that one cannot discover any religious truth by counting heads. However, the shattering results of these investigations must prompt us to a thorough investigation of the causes of this state of affairs. How does it come about, what is the position, how can we explain and make comprehensible the fact that such a large percentage of believers claims no longer to believe in a future world?

This is not an investigation that can be undertaken here. I simply want to draw attention to some of the causes.

3. This world and the beyond

We have to begin with the fact of secularization. This represents a clear break in Western civilization. Before secularization, in the West God occupied a central place in thought and action. At that time God was as it were directly and immediately accessible; he could be addressed, and was a direct object of experience. God caused virtually no problems to anyone: he was the origin, the way, the goal. Everything revolved round God and therefore around heaven, which in some way was identified with God.

When after a long and painful process secularization arrived, human beings came to occupy the central point in this *saeculum*, the centre in this world, on earth, here and now. The autonomy, the independence of human thought and action in original freedom, was detached from what was regarded as a centuries-long tutelage of religion, manipulated by the teaching office of the church.

This secularization with its anthropocentric attitude, i.e. with man at the centre of things, does not necessarily lead to unbelief or atheism. On the contrary, one can produce a good deal of material even from the Bible for developing a secularization which recognizes God.[12] God has created man for this world and has entrusted him with the whole of creation. Remarkably enough, we do not read in the biblical creation narratives, as we do in other creation stories, that God created man to serve him, to free God from toil and trouble. No, the God of Israel created man to be fruitful and multiply, to till the earth and make use of it himself. The God of the Bible does not for a moment alienate humankind from their life on earth, nor does he anywhere raise them above their specific history, above time and space. God makes history with his people on earth. We shall see later that Old Testament faith is radically this-worldly: faith is played out within the history of God with his people on earth. I mention this only to make clear that a biblically based secularization which recognizes God is quite conceivable and capable of being lived out.

As it developed in the West, secularization means that God no longer falls directly and immediately within the perspective of humankind. Secularized men and women are no longer *primarily* interested in God and therefore are also no longer interested in heaven. A great many preliminary stages are necessary before present-day people can envisage God and his heaven. Thus e.g. people who sacrifice themselves in selfless love for others must be shown that God is love. God's providence must be demonstrated in active concern for human beings. God's redemption must become concrete in liberating activity for human beings, which does away with all forms of exploitation, enslavement and need. Besides, has God himself ever revealed himself other than in human beings? For Christians he has done this above all and in a unique way in the man Jesus of Nazareth.

Now it is his disciples, people who live as his disciples, who must put others on God's track by their humane way of life.

As a result of all this, Christian religion has a particularly firm interest in this earth and this history. The love of God is experienced in human love. By following the will of God on earth as in heaven, i.e. by living as disciples of Jesus with the means and possibilities appropriate to our age, we seek to realize something of heaven on earth. Heaven is only another word for God himself, and this God is active as a liberator in our human history. So in thinking of heaven we should also think of history. Heaven seeks to bring about righteousness on earth, to produce radical renewal and liberation.

As we have been able to discover, above all as a result of a biblical revival in recent years, Christianity does not alienate us from earth, and it has become increasingly difficult to claim that religion is the opiate of the people. In Latin America it could even be said that religion works like an acid. People are affected by it in a disturbing way. They have to give up their tranquillity; their own security and future are threatened by it, not to mention 'national security'. For most people, liberation by heaven, by God, still means being stood on one's head, so complete a change and renewal that everything familiar is shaken up, so that a new earth and a new heaven come into view.

As a result of this fortunate evolution, Christians today have become less interested in an eternal future, in a heaven beyond the grave. They build the future on earth. They sacrifice themselves completely in order to open up a piece of heaven, here in this world, for as many people as possible. They do this by breaking down all the barricades that people have erected between themselves in an attempt to maintain distinctions as privileges and inherited rights, with violence, with weapons and superior force. They work for peace, righteousness and love.

Some people, including church leaders, find this emphasis with its biblical motivation extremely dangerous, and they warn against one-sidedness, against too specifically political involvement. However often they speak of social justice, they are scared to death about talking politics. As though social injustice would ever come to an end without real specific political power, which works with appropriate structures.

These worried and anxious Christians, who are afraid of seeing Christian identity lost in a social revolution, and who rightly keep on asserting that social and political liberation cannot be directly identified with the coming of the kingdom of God, are clearly blind to another very real danger. We must do everything possible to stop Christianity again disappearing into sheer spiritualism, so that Christians retreat into the impregnable citadel of an inner life in which they can already have a foretaste of heavenly bliss and where eternal rest is anticipated far too early. It is disastrous and clearly false to want to contrast social and political action with a spiritual attitude. It seems to me even more dangerous to proclaim faith above all as an inner event which comes about in a purely spiritual and sacramental praxis, than to see it as the hard way of following in the steps of Jesus who goes through the midst of this world, on the uncertain, dusty roads of this earth, as a means of renewing the countenance of this earth in the power of the spirit of Jesus.

The revolution in our experience of faith in which heaven is no longer exclusively in the future but is already realized in fragmentary form within our human history goes a long way to explain why a vivid interest in the beyond is much less compelling than an active concern to bring about something of heaven on earth. Because people are relatively succesful in the latter, and because they can construct a happier, more just and more human existence for an increasing number of people; because they can make life on earth more attractive through prosperity and welfare; because at least in the West the average life-span is relatively long; in other words, because the offer of happiness and the possiblities for happiness in this world are – thank God – increasingly great, we can understand why people ask fewer and fewer questions about eternal bliss. To ask about such things even seems inappropriate, because it apparently demonstrates the impermissible and insatiable way in which people seek to give an eternal dimension to the bourgeois desires of the consumer society.

This observation that a lessening of interest in what has yet to come follows from the prosperity of a way of life that has already been realized indicates that the content of faith, i.e. that part of faith in which the believer is interested, is always related to a context. We listen to God's word in faith from a particular situation, and we see God's offer of salvation from a particular perspective. The word of God does not exist for itself, but is always perceived by people in faith; and it is always limited people, governed and conditioned by their specific surroundings, who receive, live out and hand down this word.

In noting that there is less questioning about the beyond because of the prosperity of the present, we must at the same time take account of the objection that this is a typically Western attitude. By far the majority of the population of the world does not know this level of prosperity which can write off any interest in a future eternal life as a superfluous luxury. And if we follow through human history, we can understand how desperately few people have ever achieved a truly human existence, and how very many have met an early death as a result of war, violence, exploitation, famine, natural disasters and countless forms of sickness. For all these people happiness beyond death is really not an arrogant desire. Nor is that the case with people who regard themselves as 'successful', who in all honesty can say of themselves: I really need not be like these people who try to reconcile themselves to the desperate misery of all the humiliated and downtrodden of their own human history.

This objection to the 'Western' character of the believer's attitude towards the beyond should not be allowed for a moment to suggest that Christians would be happy to point to the unhappiness of mankind in order to present their beliefs in a more or less convincing way to other people. Christians must be the first to attach supreme importance to removing all forms of human suffering from the world. They may only refer to the significance of faith in a world to come if it already leads to decisive changes here and now. In doing this they must learn to acknowledge that if their own strength is inadequate, the power of God has not yet been exhausted. If we have really done everything possible to give good clothing to a people in rags and have not wholly succeeded, then we can accept an idea of W. F. Hermans: 'But that's what I read in my youth. "The God of a people in rags is not a God." That's a fine thought! But what future is there for a people in rags *without* God?'[13] If believers do all that is humanly possible to make a bit of heaven for people here on earth, and in so doing come up against their own limitations and those of others, then they need not really be confused or ashamed to point to a future heaven which can mean everything for those who are not really helped by social justice, for the less fortunate in body and mind, for the failures, with which no society can cope, for the desperate and the lonely.

It is up to believers themselves to do away with the misconception that faith in a beyond is a betrayal of life in this world. That was refuted in a particularly impressive way in a sermon which was given during the Dutch Pastoral Council: 'What would a child do if you gave him a ball and said, That is the only ball that you will ever get?

What would he do? Not very much, I think. He would anxiously clutch this ball to himself; the ball might fall into a gutter or a hole or land on a roof – it would only be a source of anxiety. But if you gave a child a ball and said, That is a very fine ball, you must learn to play with it well, but if it gets lost or damaged, you will get a much better one, which cannot be damaged – what would happen? An ineradicable misunderstanding holds that this child will then throw the first ball away because he will simply sit down and wait, being interested only in the indestructible ball to come, which is not yet there. I don't find that natural. I would have thought that now for the first time the child could play properly with the first ball. If we are to do something, to be able to play, to be able to live on earth, we need a little perspective, a little expectation, a little hope, a little future.'[14]

III

LONGING AND ILLUSION

We have dealt in quite some detail with a first cause of the obscuring of faith in the beyond, namely the fear of forfeiting the only life we have in a barren longing for another life. A further frontal attack on this faith comes from particular interpretations of psychological facts and the results of psychoanalysis. There are strong warnings from this side against illusions, self-deception, satisfaction with pious consolation.

Ordinary people shrink from regarding their dreams as reality. This critical attitude towards oneself cannot be commended too highly: Why do I believe? Do I believe something just because I want to believe it? Do I take my wishes as reality? Is it not a projection; in other words, in this case do we not project something which we experience in ourselves as longing, primal instinct, an ideal, on to reality and then look on it with gratitude as something which really exists and is given in itself? We dream of a real loving community embracing all people. Clearly there is no place for this on earth: it is

a utopia. Is the invention of a heaven anything other than the creation of a place where our dreams could be realized? In other words,
is this belief in a beyond anything but wishful thinking?

It is evident that this belief corresponds to different, deeply human
longings, which can be established and clarified e.g. by psychoanalysis. Freud was led to point out that there is a remarkably close corres-
pondence between Christian belief in a beyond and what human
beings would want for themselves. But that is hardly an objection to
the validity of this belief, nor do psychoanalysts intend it to be.
Though they may show with their own scientific methods that e.g.
the fulfilment of primal human longings plays an essential role in belief in a future life, their findings still do not contain any value judgment, far less any direct disqualification.

On the contrary, belief in a beyond should disturb us very much if
it did not seem to match up with human longing. Faith can only be
expressed meaningfully and responsibly as a human possibility if it
corresponds with human longings, desires, needs and experiences.
Human beings must be able to understand the word of God. This
word must address us, must offer us something, have something to
say to us. If not, it is not a message for us at all. Faith is a covenant
event, an event of dialogue. So it is not just about God but also about
man, who is involved with all his being, with all his powers; not just
with his reason and his will, but also with his emotions and desires.
If the word of God is a joyful message, good news, which satisfies
man, does that not also mean that it should meet his deepest and
strongest longings and desires in order to satisfy them? Why not
roundly concede that we are made happy by God?.

That does not remove all suspicions of wishful thinking. We can
join Marx in objecting to this view, 'that while this dimension has
emerged from the human side, all of belief in a resurrection and a
happier existence after death is the daydream of an immature humanity, a flight of the tormented human heart from the misery of this
world, an illusion which only serves to keep our head above water
here. That is the last and strongest attack which can be made on
Christian belief because it is so irrational: we are dissatisfied with
this life and therefore we constantly create illusions. But that is not a
proof. The fact that we need the comfort which lies in the resurrection does not prove that it is only fantasy. That is demonstrated only
if we begin from the postulate that any religious expectation must
end up in disappointment. Unbelief is *a priori*, just as faith is.'[15]

The projection theory works with what is certainly an obsolete epistemology, but we cannot go into that here.[16] Another weakness is that critics who make strong use of arguments of this kind must be able to explain how it comes about that we find the same projection over all centuries and all cultures, though it is projected on quite different screens.

Furthermore, fortunately it is not the case that our deepest wishes can never be matched by a reality. It is really not true that what we long for through all the phases of our existence does not relate to anything and can never be matched by anything. Sometimes it happens that a young man dreams and longs to be loved by a particular girl, and this girl actually does love him! Here the burden of proof lies with the prosecution, not with the defence.

We seem to be infected with a remarkable virus which makes us unable to accept normal happiness. The longing for eternity is mocked as individualism. In its place there is praise of a heroism which sounds very exalted and very splendid, but before which a normal person must give in. There is a very fine expression of it in R.Garaudy: 'My life has its eternal dimension not *after* this life or *outside* it, but here and now, when I am so certain that I live by the conviction that love in its highest form does not come to fruition in the relationship between you and me but only in my relationship to everything, through the mediation of the other. Only this love saves us from death. For death is the greatest love: it is the gift of the whole of finitude to the other and through the other to the whole of creation . . . Everything is played out in this history and in this life. Together we form a humanity which does not die, even if we die.' [17] The demand formulated here for complete self-denial, for self-transcendence, shows a good deal of similarity to certain sayings of Jesus. Jesus too speaks repeatedly of losing, of surrendering, of hating life: 'Whoever seeks to gain his life will lose it, but whoever loses his life will preserve it'(Luke 17.33). However, Jesus never makes this harsh demand without at the same time holding out the prospect of the regaining of life in eternity: 'He who loves his life, loses it, and he who hates his life in this world will keep it for eternal life' (John 12.25; cf. Mark 10.29f.). This compensation or reward, the prospect that the sacrifice will benefit not only others but the person who makes it, seems to me to be more human than the egoism which Garaudy represents.

Ernst Bloch, too, uses equally strong language: 'Only one kind of man goes the way to death almost without any comfort: the Red hero. By confessing the cause for which he has lived up to his death, he goes clearly, cold-bloodedly, deliberately, as a free spirit, into the nothingness in which he has been taught to believe. His sacrificial death is therefore also different from that of the earlier martyrs; for almost without exception these died with a prayer on their lips, believing that they had attained heaven. The spiritual atmosphere not only leaves the fear of death far behind, but in many cases (the hymns of the Anabaptists at the stake) even shows insensitivity towards suffering. By contrast, the Communist hero under the Tsars, under Hitler and beyond sacrifices himself without hope of resurrection. His Good Friday is not mitigated, or even removed, by any Easter Day on which he personally will again be raised to life. The heaven towards which the martyrs stretched out their hands in flame and smoke is not there for the Red materialist; nevertheless, he dies, as a confessor, as much above it all as an early Christian or an Anabaptist.'[18]

A heroism of the kind described here compels admiration. Although the Red hero of whom Bloch writes goes freely to death for the sake of an ideal, for the sake of the heaven on earth for others, this does not detract in any way from his heroism as a martyr. But is it really the case that the death of an Archbishop Romero, who knew all too well that he would be murdered if he continued to intercede for his tortured people of El Salvador, was less heroic than the death of the materialistic militants because as a bishop he believed in a personal eternal life? Bloch seems to have a remarkable view of the existential meaning of the certainty of faith. It is never the firm assurance of an evident knowledge; it is never an experience which becomes a firm possession; it is never an unshakeable insight based on absolute guarantees. Faith is always a surrender in trust, and therefore a believer knows himself or herself to be extremely vulnerable, uncertain, defenceless. 'We have this treasure in earthen vessels' (II Cor.4.7); the certainty of faith is very fragile.

The certainty of a conviction seems to me to be stronger. Bloch calls the Red fighters martyrs and heroes, because he shares their convictions. But the Nazis also used to talk about Brown heroes, a number of whom also went willingly and enthusiastically to their deaths as a contribution to the formation of the 'thousand-year kingdom'. And were there not also heroes among those who took the field against Communism in order to save Western culture? Were there not also heroes of the Islamic revolution? In saying this I do not want to disparage the value and significance of real heroism. But who calls whom a hero? And when I hear the word 'hero' I am involuntarily reminded of a song that a friend of mine once tried vainly to teach me to sing: 'Soldiers who want to be heroes, number practically zero; but there are millions who want to be civilians.'

By contrast Christian faith presents itself as a message for ordinary people; Jesus repeatedly speaks of reward, compensation, recompense, and he brings God as a gift. Christian faith is primarily acceptance of an indicative, daring to believe in good news from God: Do not be afraid, for you have found favour, grace has discovered you, God is on your side, his Spirit makes you unconquerably strong. A Christian need not be disturbed that he still trusts in this word of God down to his dying day. For at that moment there is perhaps also something heroic about this trust.

The suspicion of projection which is attached to faith in a beyond and against which reference is made to heroic people who simply accept their limitations and do not give way to an overweening longing for eternity also applies, and in the first place, to belief in God itself. As a refutation of this theory I have already called attention to the masterly investigations of Han Fortmann, who is too little known and appreciated. However, I cannot resist also adding a comment by W.F.Hermans: 'It may perhaps be unbelievable that there is a God. But I would like to ask what would follow from that. The conclusion would be that mankind is the supreme authority in the whole universe, and I think that there can hardly be anything sadder than that.'[19]

IV

KNOWING AND LIVING

1. One-track thinking

We find a third basic reason for the decline in belief in a future life in what in the West is still accepted quite generally as the only model for science, positivism and empiricism. Of course on the purely scientific level this position is thought to be out of date. The more science progresses, the further the frontiers of the universe are pushed back and the greater become the dimensions of the unknown. Nowhere do we come up against the limits of reality or the limits of what can be known. We have joined in a game for which we know only a fraction of the rules. Moreover these rules constantly change, the more our knowledge progresses; so much so, in fact, that we no longer know whether what we have achieved so far is still valid. It is impossible to reduce reality to a series of limited problems, all the elements of which are known. It seems untenable to assert that a question of which we can know nothing is meaningless. On the contrary, it seems meaningless to want to reduce everything to what we can know. [20]

However, a positivistic attitude still continues to have a powerful influence on everyday thought and action. Only what we can establish by experimentation, what we can measure and analyse, is true. In fact this ideal, which was once praised so highly, has to a large extent narrowed our perspective on reality. We have at our disposal now only one wavelength on which to receive the unfathomable riches and the tremendous variety of our many-dimensional reality. We can think only in terms of rationalization, function, utility, efficiency, regularity. Reality is reduced to its phenomena, to its outward dimension. We have some control over this, so we can do something about it. It is impossible to see beyond the appearances. All there is is what we can perceive. And that points nowhere. It does not represent anything deeper, that might be manifested in it. It is not an expression of an inner reality, a sign, a symbol. Reality consists in cast-iron facts.

Our language has become adapted to this. We use only operational concepts, i.e. concepts which exclusively refer to activities. We immediately test any theory for its utility. What can I do with it, what can I buy for it? Any question of meaning is rejected as being quite useless. It is a waste of time, which only romantics and non-committed artists can afford. Anyone who asks Why? and Wherefore? is immediately interrupted by the harsh command to become involved, to do something. We may no longer ask, Why am I alive, what am I here for? The only legitimate question is: What am I needed for, what use am I, what purpose do I serve?

It is clear that this climate strangles any form of belief at birth. For to believe means that we are interested in something which lies outside our immediate surroundings. It is precisely this belief which has always intrigued people. This belief in something outside our immediate surroundings has made people set out, explore, arrive at places where no one had been before. We may not throttle the dream of faith. Without dreaming and believing, everything becomes grey and commonplace. We must continue to look for meaning in and behind the brute facts for the sake of the magic of existence.

Belief in a future life cannot, of course, strike any roots in the climate of empiricism. It is impossible in principle to experience a life after death in this life. If we can only talk about what we have experienced personally, about something that happened in our presence, then we all have to keep silent about a life after death. People who live on this earth cannot experience death and eternal life. However instructive the testimonies of those who have looked death in the eye, who have awoken from a long coma or clinical death, they are and remain testimonies of the living. No one, no individual living person, can experience death and being dead, much less life after death. It does not necessarily follow from this that in that case there is nothing left but to keep silent; rather, that everything we think we can say about this can be expressed only with the utmost restraint, cautiously, with the necessary reticence and with qualifications. It is impossible to use an operational language here. Here we must reach for symbols, images, for a language which is indicative, suggestive, and is more suitable for art and for visions than for a merely informative or functional conversation.

To be able to speak in a symbolic language presupposes that we have acquired an eye for the referential character of the phenomena themselves. Human beings are never condemned merely to look at facts as they are. Human perception of facts is always and at the same time also an interpretation of these facts. 'Do the tears of someone we love mean no more than a perceptible release of moisture around the eyelids? Cannot this release of moisture be the *sign* of various – invisible – realities such as grief, emotion, joy or even hypocrisy? Is it not above all the sign that something is taking place within my friend which I cannot see, something which can only be fathomed by one who not only "sees" but also feels and knows what a weeping person might possibly be experiencing?'[21]

As we can nowhere ever experience life after death directly, we have to look for the signals of this life here on earth. Is there something in our experience which points to such a life? Can we interpret particular experiences in this sense? Can the hypothesis of a beyond perhaps reveal the final sense of my life in this world?

This last question clearly indicates that the interest in another world is not necessarily to be attributed to curiosity, but can be a fundamental search for meaning in and for the present. Every future is important and determinative of the present. In the present we must take account of the future. The future provides orientation. This is true to an even greater degree if it should prove that man has an eternal future. But that in turn must be capable of verification in the present, in contemporary experiences.

I personally believe that one of the most important tasks of Christianity in our time is to open up human experiences and interpret them responsibly as perspectives on an eternity and a heaven which is only to the smallest degree operational (i.e. the result of a human action), however important and compelling in a Christian sense this may be, but which is above all unmerited gift, an unearned present.

Christian proclamation and practice must dare to subject everything to the criterion of eternity. In this light everything is given its true value and is recognized in its true relationships. In this light nothing within the world or within the church is made an absolute. Only God is God, and everything that is not God is recognized and treated as such. All the gods disappear. Our task of following in the footsteps of Jesus and building something of heaven on earth does not become less serious and significant as a result; rather, we carry it out in a climate of greater freedom, without bitterness or grimness. We receive freely and we give freely (cf. Matt. 10.8). If we are not aware of heaven's protection above us or any unmerited divine compensation for our failure, the whole of our life as Christians becomes a 'chilling faith'.[22] We can even endorse the comment of the author whose phrase that is, to the effect that: 'People turn away from the church today and look for their salvation in every conceivable Christian and non-Christian sect, usually not because the church has betrayed the earth but because in their eyes the church has betrayed heaven. Sometimes I think that it has even betrayed both earth and heaven.'[23]

2. Fantasy and conjecture

Contemporary views about humanity, anthropology, cause quite specific difficulties for belief in a beyond. Until recently it was almost universally accepted in the West that human beings were composed of soul and body. This was called a dualism, in which the unity of a person could be divided into two parts. We have inherited this dualism by way of a centuries-long Christian tradition from the Greek philosopher Plato, who lived in the fourth century. So in this anthropology the human being is regarded as a composite of two completely different and separable elements, body and soul. The body is purely material and as such is of course transitory. The soul is a purely spiritual reality and as such is essentially immortal. Therefore death exclusively affects the body and is the consequence of a process of decay which is normal for this body. The soul does not die. As a purely spiritual reality, the soul is not subject to time, becoming and decay.

This Greek dualistic view of humanity deriving from Plato established itself in Christian views of death and resurrection, despite the fact that Thomas Aquinas had adopted the anthropology of the Greek philosopher Aristotle. For the latter, soul and body were not to be regarded as two independent elements which could be separated like the two parts of a box but as two elements which were completely dependent on each other and which could not survive in separation, but only together. Thomas himself had to violate his anthropology in order to rescue what was regarded as official church doctrine about the immortality of the soul.

The dualistic Platonic anthropology of which Christian belief in the resurrection gratefully and naturally made use for centuries, envisaging the resurrection only of the body, because the soul itself is immortal, is now regarded in contemporary anthropology as being hopelessly out of date. Contemporary anthropology generally assumes that a human being is an indissoluble unity and cannot be divided into two independent parts, soul and body. If these two elements are maintained nevertheless, it seems more correct to speak of an ensouled body or an embodied soul. A human being does not *have* a body and something else in addition, the soul. A body is not something that human beings have in common with the biological structure of animals, and in addition a spiritual soul or a spirit which would in turn make them akin to purely spiritual beings. Human beings *are* their bodies. As human bodies they are ensouled and thus are in no way purely biological or animal. The body is simply the presupposition for everything that the human being is as spirit. A human being *is* his spirit, but as a human spirit this always necessarily and inseparably goes with being a human body. Existence in the body is not the act of an independent soul. In developing this view of humanity Thomas is much more usable than Plato.

There is no need to study these problems of anthropology in order to recognize the correctness of modern insights. We all know that our so-called purely spiritual activity, our knowing and willing, our freedom, are essentially conditioned and to a large degree determined by our physical situation. People with severe damage to vital brain cells can no longer think, speak or react as free human beings. Nor need we resort to so extreme an example. When we have a bad headache or raging toothache we are no longer ourselves; we do not act in complete freedom and it is recognized that we are less responsible. In such situations our 'spiritual' capacities often rest on inactivity.

This view of human beings as an indissoluble unity of soul and body lets us see death in all its brutality and as radical absurdity. Death can no longer be seen as something which exclusively affects the body – often still regarded in derogatory fashion as the less important part of a human being – but leaves the real, the important, the most exalted part, the soul, completely unaffected. On the contrary, in this context there is repeated mention of the liberation of the soul from the prison of the body.

The consequence of all this seems to be total death, as many people put it. In that case death means no longer existing. We shall also have to tackle this complex of problems seriously and at length, because at first glance it seems to be so irrefutably and compellingly a scientific insight of contemporary anthropology. Still, in this sphere too, we must avoid a conflict between faith and knowledge. If faith in an immortal soul proves to be scientifically impossible, we cannot maintain its existence as an unchangeable and essential element of faith. We shall be able to demonstrate responsibly that the hypothesis of an immortal soul is in no way rooted in resurrection faith, but in a scientific view of man which is of Platonic origin. This insight, which we must of course establish in detail from scripture and tradition, will allow us to make a number of qualifications, bold yet modest, to a pronouncement made by the Congregation for the Doctrine of Faith on 17 May 1979, which said, among other things: 'The church confirms the continuation and the preservation after death of spiritual elements endowed with consciousness and will, so that the "human I" continues to exist. To denote this element the church uses the word "soul", which has been accepted by the usage of Holy Scripture and tradition. Although it is well aware that this word is given different meanings in Holy Scripture, it is nevertheless of the opinion that there is no adequate reason for rejecting the word and moreover thinks that this verbal means is necessary in order to preserve the faith of Christians.'[24]

3. Imagination and thought

Remarkably enough, the hypothesis of an immortal soul which continues an independent life after the death of the body enormously increases the difficulties of envisaging belief in the resurrection. In that case the resurrection of bodies at the end of time is unimaginable and even seems inconceivable. We may become deeply involved when looking up in silent reverence at the remarkable tympana of the Romanesque churches with which the monks of Cluny adorned the already attractive countryside of Burgundy and feel drawn into the paintings of the resurrection which are so realistically depicted there, but after some reflection we come to the sober realization that these are symbols and pictures, and that such a physical and material event can never be a reality.

However, a great many people continue to be tormented by conceptions of an earlier time. Often these conceptions are infantile as well as materialistic, and were inculcated at an early age through catechetics and preaching; they are associated with all kinds of complex and unassimilated notions which contribute towards the decline in belief in the resurrection. No fantasy was too crazy to find someone to defend it: there were ideas of a resurrection in the valley of Jehosophat in the attractive and pleasing bodily form of sturdy thirty-year-olds, at the sound of a trumpet from which one could choose between different notes; or the sending out of legions of angels, in order to collect the ingredients of millions of bodies which had turned to dust; or the most profound speculations about the state of the disembodied soul.

In earlier centuries, when people still had no awareness of the enormous extension of the human race in space and time and could think on a relatively small scale, such conceptions were evidently still acceptable. Today, however, things are quite different. When we realize that so far approximately seventy-seven thousand million human beings have lived and that countless millions more are still to be expected if life on earth, given food reserves, can continue for four hundred million years, then any conception of a resurrection of the body at the end of time, coupled with some thought of material identity, is sheer nonsense. No reasonable person can hold such a belief any longer. Because such notions seem ineradicable and sometimes are still claimed as the official teaching of the church – though that is not in fact the case – we can understand why on this question many people throw out the baby with the bath water. In other words, these classic accounts of belief in the resurrection make it difficult to believe in the message of the resurrection itself.

In addition, there are all the fantastic ideas about the intermediary period, the state of souls in heaven, in hell or in purgatory. Have these disembodied souls any desire or any need of corporeality? Do they experience their separation from the body as a painful and impatient wait for the resurrection of their body? Has it ever occurred to those who have a particular devotion to a saint that this saint still lacks something? Surely we picture the saints as always being completely happy? In that case, does not the real content of faith, the resurrection of the body, become a superfluous event and a luxury? In other words, is not an article of faith put at risk here simply because of the assumption of an immortal soul, an assumption which does not arise from the resurrection event but simply and solely from more or less convincing philosophical arguments?

In any case, how can souls burn, whether in purgatory or in hell itself? Do disembodied souls still experience time, so that for example they can really spend a certain period in purgatory before they are admitted to the blessed vision of God?

Furthermore, there is the untrammelled imagination of theologians and preachers who, with honest intentions but unaware of their ignorance, above all of history, and often with doubtful taste, often bordering on vulgarity, make use of the future world to depict God's righteousness and anger in a terrifying way. Threats of the future state were more a matter of playing on human fears in a psychologically irresponsible way than a proclamation of good news. The *dies irae*, the day of wrath and divine vengeance, played a much greater role in Christian spirituality than the *in paradisum*, the paradise to which we are welcomed by a procession of angels and martyrs. The very melody of this funeral hymn takes us up into the holy city and fills our present life with an unshakeable trust in God which leaves no more room for fear and trembling.

The declaration of the Congregation for the Doctrine of Faith which I have already mentioned describes how believers are confused by new interpretations of life after death. But this document says equally clearly: 'In speaking of the state of human beings after death we must specifically guard against conceptions which rest exclusively on imagination and arbitrary thinking; for such exaggeration is a major cause of the difficulties which Christian belief often encounters.'[25]

It can in fact happen that believers are shocked by certain statements and theories about resurrection and eternal life. However, we really should not disguise the fact that with the best will in the world, a very large number of so-called ordinary or simple believers can no longer believe what they were once told about the world to come simply because this is not a belief they can take seriously, and because as thinking people concerned for the truth they want to believe in a responsible way in the modern world. Besides, these difficulties are not as new as all that, still less are they the consequences of post-conciliar theological innovations. As early as 1952, Romano Guardini wrote: 'The popular believers know that they are deeply bound up with their dead . . . By contrast the educated have lost that particular concern for the dead, and many views and customs alienate them. That fact is not to be dismissed with the observation that their faith no longer has any power. Popular prayer for the souls of believers is not just faith in the Christian sense: it also expresses the primordial links with the realm of the dead among those who live close to the earth. To have these links is nothing to do with the will of the individual but depends on the degree to which he or she still lives according to the original ordering of existence . . . Educated people have lost their links with the realm of the dead, so the dead are not immediately real to them . . . For educated people, dying has become a biological and a personal event which has largely lost its mystery; so their relationship to the dead is usually not directly religious but personal, moral and spiritual. It is easy for them to feel that concern for the dead, along with the images and customs connected with it, is very strange . . . Now concern for the dead is an important ingredient of liturgical life – one might think of the commemoration of the dead in the canon of the mass and the offices for the dead. So we cannot simply leave it aside or even reject it, but must seek to understand what it is all about.'[26]

4. From darkness to the dawn

This book has been written for the 'educated' people mentioned in the last paragraph, for people who feel an existential problem here as they do in many other areas of their belief. I hope to help them gain a perspective which frees them, enabling them to live in the present with confidence for the future. Our present is determined by whatever it is we can see of the future. Some of this future is in our own hands. However, even for those who shape the future, the

Christian future is always in the first place directed by God, prompted by God and brought by him to a glorious fulfilment.

I want to help those with questions who are trying to formulate their own personal belief. So we shall be going on a long and sometimes laborious journey of discovery through the history of this belief in a future life in the Jewish-Christian tradition. However brief it is, a look at this history can reassure and hearten despairing and hesitant people, for they will recognize that belief in a life after death was never an unchallenged certainty, a generally affirmed truth which has always found unanimous assent, but that this belief was fought for in a struggle with God for God's sake.

That also explains the title of this book. I have taken it from the splendid story of Jacob's fight with the angel (Gen.32.23-33). Jacob wrestles with God in the darkness. He cannot see him or recognize him, but he guesses who his opponent is and asks for his blessing. God does not show himself. He disappears before the dawn. We do not know the meaning of God, heaven or eternal life, all of which are synonyms for God. We are involved with them, we struggle with them, groping in the darkness. Now we have only his blessing, but we hope that one day we shall see him face to face, when the sun rises. In the meantime we are left with a struggle for insight, a struggle to grasp the one who gives us no rest because he holds us in his grasp. This is a struggle with God for God until the dawn.

What I offer here is a kind of theological survey of thinking about the future life, what is called eschatology, that is, the doctrine of the last things, the ultimate final future and purpose of man and the world.

In the bibliography I have listed the literature which I have used – in addition to the commentaries on the various books of the Bible. This bibliography is by no means complete. I could have filled a thick book with it. I have limited myself to mentioning works which might be accessible even to the non-specialist reader and which can be understood without an enormous amount of effort. I have listed more technical works in the notes.

This book is a working document. It does not set out to be a complete treatise, but it offers some elements which could be developed further. I could not devote the same amount of space to all the elements of eschatology which are important to it. That would have made the book too long. However, at some points I did want to go into more detail, with the deliberate intention of giving ordinary people, the theological laity, a glimpse into the theological workshop. It may make you dizzy for a while to breathe the thin air which prevails there or to follow through the complex procedures with which we work, but I hope that you will soon be able to breathe again as it becomes clear to you that theologians do not simply invent problems for themselves on their own initiative or in order to show off to people, 'People, who will not endure sound teaching, but having itching ears they will accumulate for themselves teachers to suit their own likings' (II Tim.4.3). Throughout we shall be concerned with theologians whose pastoral commitment is as great as their academic knowledge and who therefore seek to investigate the real problems presented to them by their fellow human beings as a result of particular difficulties in belief. They seek to give a responsible answer on the basis of scripture, tradition and academic criticism. That obliges them above all to make a thorough investigation of the sources of faith, where they have come from, by whom and when they were discovered, in what circumstances and through what channels they have been handed down and how we can still use them today. Here we must work with what has been produced by the application of new methods of scholarship.

The result of theological research is never complete and cannot be claimed as binding doctrine. No theology can lay down the future lines of faith, proclamation and Christian life.

Whether theologians can convince anyone to revise earlier views is another matter and largely depends on whether the arguments they produce are clearly irrefutable, and on the freedom in which believers confess what they believe. Such a freedom is presupposed in any formula of faith, on the basis of the insight that faith never stands or falls by a formula but relates to a further reality, to an undefinable person to whom the formulas unerringly point. However, theologians can work to undermine certain deeply entrenched arguments which are wrongly used to defend a standpoint adopted earlier.

I do not aim to go beyond my capabilities, and simply offer an approach, a guarantee, reassurance. Things can be expressed in this way; things can be looked at in this way; this is in fact the case; this seems to be quite responsible. At any rate, I feel that this is the way in which we should describe the content of our faith or the reality to which it refers: less as a 'must' and more as a 'may' or a 'can'. It has to be described less as law and more as grace. People keep claiming that the content of Christian faith is good news. An ordinary person is all too ready to believe this. But it is certainly wrong to *compel* anyone to be healthy, happy and free. That is a privilege, a grace, which may and can belong to everyone. Morality may sometimes seem harsh to sinful people, but that cannot be the case with the gospel.

Jesus of Nazareth has brought us good news from God. God wants to see people happy as they live on earth, God's own creation, in a history which God unfolds along with human beings and for them. God wants people to be successful, even in their plans for the future, as they dream of infinite happiness. God himself brings his people and his creation to fulfilment. We can confidently trust in this God of promise, the God who has made one covenant for all times: for his grace lasts for ever.

That is not a message which anyone can be forced to accept. When we hear it, we can hardly believe our ears. It is too good to be true. People simply do not dare to believe it for fear that it might prove to be an illusion. People cannot believe it, because there is so much which makes this promise incredible. But they would like to believe it. However, above all else they want to be true, they do not want to fool themselves and they will not be taken in by anyone. People prefer truth and honesty to a doctrine to which we can no longer assent because of our concern for truth, however much they may want to and however much they may envy those who still have this faith.

Is that not the situation of very many Christians, certainly when it comes to belief in eternal life? These people cannot be helped by being given unchanged the traditional notions of faith and being told that they are still binding and obligatory. Besides, if their problems are real, they are to a greater or lesser degree the problems of the theologians themselves, the catechists, those who proclaim faith and hold office as teachers. So all together must look for an answer with which they can honestly live.

People must help one another to proclaim the reality of faith in a credible way and to present it as a liberating message and a redemptive praxis. So that those who think, those who search, may dare to accept and be able to accept a truth that makes them free.

PART TWO

The End in View

Eternity is meaningless
unless it garbs you
with all the glory
portrayed in the Apocalypse.

Gerrit Achterberg

A. Old Testament Variations on a Theme

I

FUTURE FOR HUMANITY

1. 'The heavens are the Lord's heavens, but the earth he has given to the sons of men' (Ps.115.16)

If we begin to read the Old Testament to gain information about a life after death and another world, we very soon see that we have picked up the wrong book. Only at the very end do we find anything about that, and by then we have come very close to the Christian era, when Israel already had a centuries-long tradition of faith to look back on. In the Old Testament there is seldom, if ever, any reference to a life for human beings after their death.

Israel's faith is radically this-worldly, i.e. it is exclusively interested in the history of people on earth. Yahweh plays the main role in it. He chooses his people on earth and gives them rich blessings on earth. He makes a covenant with this people which is in force here on earth. Yahweh liberates his people. He goes to war with them and brings them victory and salvation. He chastizes the disobedient, the unwilling, the unbelieving people, here on earth, in the course of their history. Yahweh brings down and raises up. He gives life and leads people into the realm of the dead.

Israel knows that its God is with his people. It discovers Yahweh in what happens in and with the people. God manifests himself in history and nowhere else. He wants to see people happy in history, in their own lives, as they are.

It is Yahweh's will that human beings should live. There is not much reflection on death. It seems to be part of life, even more than suffering, since people wrote about suffering earlier and at more length than about death. For centuries Israel took human death for granted; it was simply bound up with human creatureliness. Man is man and not God. God alone is eternal. All that is not God is transitory, not as punishment for some misdeed or sin but because it is a creature and not God.

To begin with, Israel had no cult of the dead. That is striking, because this people lived in the midst of other cultures, including Egypt, where the cult of the dead produced some sublime pieces of art. Perhaps this remarkable fact can be explained simply from the original nomadic existence of the tribes. Nomadic people cannot worship their dead in the places where they were buried. Later, when Israel settled in Canaan, there were fixed burial places and everyone dreamed of being laid in the family tomb.

'The breath of the Almighty gives me life' (Job 33.4)

The fact that Israel was not particularly interested in the fate of the dead is connected with its anthropology. That is, if we can talk of anthropology at all. Israel did not think in such abstract categories and did not arrive at a unitary conception of being human. Israel thought of human beings as they could be seen, so its view of them was not particularly elevated. Certainly mankind is created in the image of God, like God (Gen. 1.26,27). That means that God created mankind as his partner, as his counterpart, as someone whom he could address and call, to whom he could entrust things, with whom he could conclude a covenant, whom he could make responsible, whom he could protect and rescue. Human beings are the image of God, like him, not because of some essential human characteristic, their reason, their will, their freedom or immortality, but simply because God made them his partner with whom he could deal on equal terms. Human beings owe all their higher characteristics exclusively to God's relationship with them, the relationship which God wills to enter into with them, of which he makes them capable and to which he summons them. The Israelite never ceased to be amazed at this: 'When I look at thy heavens, the work of thy fingers, the moon and the stars which thou hast established; what is man that thou art mindful of him, and the son of man that thou dost care for him? Yet thou hast made him little less than God, and dost crown him with glory and honour' (Ps.8.4-6; cf. Ps.144.3).

Only much later, in the middle of the first century before the Christian era, could an otherwise unknown teacher in Alexandria, which at that time was a focal point of Hellenistic culture (a man who was under the influence of Greek dualism which I have already mentioned), write: 'God has created man for incorruption, and made him in the image of his own eternity' (Wisdom 2.23). Here being in the image of God no longer consists in the fact of being human, with mankind as God's partner, but in a particular human property: not in what human beings are but in what they have, namely immortality.

All in all, using an anachronistic term, we might call the Israelite understanding of humanity a materialistic one.

Human beings are taken from the dust and by a normal process they return to the dust (Gen.2.7; 3.19; Ps.90.3: 'Thou turnest man back to the dust, and sayest: "Turn back, O children of men" '). Human beings must go the way of all earthly things (Josh.23.14; I Kings 2.2; Job 16.22), they perish like a flower of the field (Isa.40.6; Ps.103.15). 'All living beings become old like a garment, for the decree from of old is, "You must surely die" ' (Sir.14.17). 'We must all die, we are like water spilt on the ground, which cannot be gathered up again' (II Sam.14.14). Human beings are dust, a piece of earth which comes to life only because God breathes his own breath of life into them (Gen.2.7; Job 27.3; 33.4; 34.14f.; Ps.104.29f.; Isa.42.5; Ezek.37.1-14). We should not attach too much significance to this breath of life, *ruah* as it is called in Hebrew. It is simply the stream of air which human beings breathe in and out and which is thus indispensable to life. After all, we still speak of dying as 'breathing one's last'. Besides, human beings have this breath of life in common with animals (Gen.6.17; 7.15,22; Num.16.22; 27.16; Ps.104.30).

From this perspective there is nothing mysterious about either life or death. When God gives the breath of life, then dust comes alive; when he takes this breath back again, all life returns to dust (Job 34.14f.; Ps.104.29; 146.4; Prov.3.19;12.7).

In Hebrew a different word from *ruah*, *nephesh*, is used to describe a living being as such. However, we may not interpret this word in a spiritualistic sense any more than the term *ruah*. The Greek translation of the Bible renders it *psyche*, which we in turn translate as soul. This can lead to difficulties. Thus the Israelites, too, see people as being composed of both soul and body. But if we translate *ruah* as spirit, we end up with more than Hellenism had to offer: soul, body, spirit.

The Greek translation is responsible for this misunderstanding. *Nephesh* does not mean an immaterial soul, but has almost the same content as the term *ruah*. Perhaps we can say that *nephesh*, i.e. specific life, man or woman as a particular living being, is the result of *ruah*, as a principle of this life. Thus we read in the creation story:

'The Lord God formed man of dust from the ground, and breathed into his nostrils the breath of life (*riah*); and man became a living being (*nephesh*)' (Gen.2.7).

Thus *nephesh* stands for living being, life itself (Gen.19.17; Ex.21.23,30; I Sam. 19.11; II Sam.19.6; Job 2.4; 33.18). But in that case we are still not talking about life in a universal abstract sense but always about life bound up with a body, the life of the man who exists in his own body, someone's life (Gen.9.5; Lev.2.1; 4.2; 5.1; I Sam.18.1; Job 9.21) or the life of several people (Ex. 1.5; Deut. 10.22; I Chron. 5.21; Ezek.1.18; 17.17). So here according to our terminology we can regard *nephesh* as a synonym for what we call person.

Nephesh not only stands for physical life, where the term is immediately connected with the blood as the seat of this life – which is why blood may never be drunk – but also points to all forms of psychological, emotional, moral and religious life. In this context *nephesh* is not to be understood as the designation of *one* aspect of being human but as a designation of being human generally, seen from one particular aspect.

Yahweh, who himself is *nephesh* (Jer.51.14; Amos 6.8), can take away *nephesh* just as well as *ruah* (Gen.9.5). The *nephesh* can die and be killed (Lev.24.18; Num.31.19; Job 36.14; Ps.22.21; 35.17). That even the dead can be described with the word *nephesh* (Lev.19.28; 21.11; 22.4; Num. 5.2; 6.6; 7.10; 9.6, which refer quite specifically to corpses) is perhaps not so amazing when we remember that *nephesh* also has the meaning of 'someone' or person. In that case the reference is always to someone's body.

All this should be enough to demonstrate that in the Old Testament view of humanity we are not dealing with precise concepts which we can immediately and exactly take over into our own arsenal of concepts. [1]

I have already pointed out that the Israelite thinks of a human being as he perceives him or her, as an indivisible unity and totality. All the terms, body – for which there is really no adequate expression in Hebrew – *ruah* and *nephesh*, do not refer to independent elements in a human being but to the one, total, indivisible human being.

'Man is like a breath, his days are like a passing shadow' (Ps.144.4)

In every respect of their humanity men and women are completely dependent on their creator and God. They owe their life to him, and they also accept death from his hand. God is the sovereign Lord over life and death (I Sam.2.6; II Sam.12.15-24; Job 14.5; Ps.39.14; Eccles.3.2).

For a long time death was not connected with sin. Death was the normal result of a process – terrifying, but unavoidable – which takes place in a human being who as a creature is transitory and mortal.

The pious are given a prosperous and a long life (Gen.15.15; 25.8; 35.29; I Chron. 29.28; Job 42.17), and this earthly life is regarded as a supreme blessing (Job 2.4; Prov.3.16; Eccles.9.4); it is the only reward for an obedient existence in accordance with God's word (Deut.5.16; 16.20; 30.15-18; Ezek.3.21; 18; 20; 33).

Only a premature death is quite generally regarded as a punishment (I Sam.25.38; 26.10; II Sam.3.33; Job 15.32; 22.16; Ps.55.24; 102.24f.; Jer.17.11), although there are vigorous protests against the universality of this view (Isa.57.1f.; Wisd.4.7-15).

Because from this perspective death intervenes as a premature event in the midst of a full life, which also happens when death casts its shadow at the noontide of life in the form of sickness, suffering and persecution, in the lamentations and thanksgivings of Israel to be saved from these different forms of suffering is also presented as a rescue from death. We shall have to return to that.

In addition, death abroad is also experienced as a punishment for sin (Jer.20.6; 22.11f.; 42.16; Ezek.12.13; Amos 7.27).

In that case, what are we to make of the creation narrative in Gen.2.4b-3.24, where death is clearly connected with human sinfulness? If we read a causal connection between sin and death out of this report – as we do under the influence of the view of St Paul as formulated in Rom.5.12 – then we are not reading it accurately. When Yahweh forbids Adam and Eve to eat of the tree of the knowledge of good and evil, he does not threaten them just with death, but with immediate death: 'In the day that you eat of it you shall die' (2.17). Now it is very striking that this does not happen: Adam lived to be 930 years old (Gen.5.5)! Death is not mentioned once in the sentence that is actually passed (Gen.3.14-20). Here death appears more as the end of an existence which is vitiated by sin and in which human beings are at variance with themselves, with their God, their fellows and the whole of creation. The suffering caused by this lack of harmony is a punishment for sin. Death is held out, rather, as the prospect of the end of this punishment. Mankind's hard work never finds an end, an eternal rest, the *requies aeterna* of which we sing in the Latin Requiem. After their wearisome existence human beings may again return to the dust. In his punishment Yahweh shows himself far more merciful than the Greek gods, who subjected rebels like Tantalus and Sisyphus to eternal torment.

The account of the Fall is not a historical account but must be read as what is called an aetiology. Here the author projects the actual condition which he experiences in his own body, the specific situation in which he himself is writing, on to an earlier period of history with the aim of either giving the cause or the explanation of what now lies in the past or of making clear through a pictorial representation that what is happening now has really always been the case. Aetiologies follow the pattern 'because then . . . so now' or 'as now . . . so earlier'. People seek to gain an insight into complex situations. The aetiology is an attempt to cast some light on the mysterious forces which are evidently at work through history, beneath the historical facts which can be perceived clearly. In this way we come up against structures. It can be noted that particular facts keep emerging in one and the same or in an equivalent mutual relationship. The one produces the other, not simply in a causal connection but in such a way that the one fact can only be explained from the other. Only the reciprocal connection makes it possible to understand the facts. We simply cannot say anything about one without talking about the other. We do not see the one at all unless we have an eye for the other.

We have a structure of this kind in the story of the Fall and its sequel. This speaks not only of sin but in the same breath also of a divine promise of deliverance and of divine protection (Gen.3.15, 20f.). In this way the author seeks to gain an insight into his complex situation. Here he experiences a basic disharmony. He lives in a disrupted relationship with his God. This causes him problems. He sees his fellow human beings only as threats, hence his aggressiveness. He is deeply offended at the resistance of the world around him. He is hemmed in on all sides. But this is only one aspect of his experience. For remarkably enough, in a way which he cannot explain fully, there lives on in him an unquenchable hope that everything might be different. All these distorted relationships could be put right again. Yes, again. Human beings have the impression that once they were different. Perhaps they need this conviction as a spur to their attempts to make whole again what was shattered. Things are different because they once were different. Be this as it may, this recollection is not an incapacitating force. It works like dynamite. It drives men and women incessantly on, to renew the past in a future which is offered and presented to them by a God. In fact the believer interprets this inexplicable hope as God's presence in and with him. His God is a God who promises deliverance and who stays close to human beings on their way to the future, to paradise, protecting them and shielding them.

This was the experience of the author himself and his fellow believers. What he presents in the story of paradise is quite simply an attempt to come to terms with these contradictory experiences. He simply wants to make clear that these contemporary experiences are not at all new. Things have always been like that. People have always been the same as they are now, full of contradictions, living out a failed existence which never gives up hope. They are constantly under threat of drowning but can always keep their heads above water. The believer calls the power to withstand this, constantly to begin again in hope, his God.

I have spent rather a long time on this story of the Fall because the traditional explanations which regard sin in a historical and realistic sense as the cause of death present insuperable difficulties. Some people drew from this the obvious conclusion that had Adam not sinned then no one would ever have died. What a problem that would have caused in terms of surplus population! Others found this all too foolish and imagined that had Adam not sinned human beings would have died without pain and grief, passing over from temporal to eternal life without any problem. This has been expressed with the image of changing horses for the stage coach, in order to continue the journey unhindered.

Furthermore, the Old Testament itself never alludes to a causal connection between the sin of Adam and the universality of death. The allusion to that is very late and brief (Sir.25.24; Wisd.2.23f.). However, this causality was to play a major role in the Christian tradition, as I have said, above all under the influence of what Paul writes in Romans. Still, Paul himself is not so concerned to depict the Fall as a historical event. Granted, he takes over a view of this account which already existed in his time in order to stress and to explain both universality and solidarity in sin. But he does this only in order to refer to the universal significance of the redemptive death of Jesus. No one can pass over this redemptive event because all without exception need it. Just as all men are in fact caught up in the sin of Adam as a result of their personal sin, so Christ opens up to all men a solidarity in redemption.

Thus generally speaking it must be said that the Old Testament regards death in a matter-of-fact way as part of human life, since human beings are essentially transitory. Anyone who has completed his days goes to rest with his fathers (Gen.25.8; 35.29; 49.29; Num.20.24,26; I Kings 2.10; 11.43; 14.20,31; 15.8,24; 16.6,28; 22. 40,51; II Kings 8.24; 10.35; 13.9,13; Sir.47.23). At death men and women are gathered like sheaves at the harvest (Job 5.26).

Such a view of death as being a normal part of life also leads to a degree of fatalism. So we read: 'Since one fate comes to all, to the righteous and the wicked, to the good and the evil, to the clean and the unclean, to him who sacrifices and him who does not sacrifice. As is the good man so is the sinner; and he who swears is as he who shuns an oath. This is an evil in all that is done under the sun, that one fate comes to all; also the hearts of men are full of evil, and madness is in their hearts while they live, and after that they go to the dead' (Eccles.9.2f.). At another point we find: 'Do not fear the sentence of death; remember your former days and the end of life; this is the decree from the Lord for all flesh, and how can you reject the good pleasure of the Most High? Whether life is for ten or a hundred or a thousand years, there is no inquiry about it in Hades' (Sir.41.3f.).

'He walked with God' (Gen.5.24)

Thus Israel accepted death without too many problems; however, in history there are two accounts of people who did not die. We have to take note of them because these stories were later to play a major role in connection with resurrection and glorification. They were used as models for expressing a glorified life with God.

Noah's great-great-grandfather Enoch lived to be only 365 years old; he 'walked with God; and he was not; for God took him' (Gen.5.24). Since all the other patriarchs lived to be about 900 years old, people were obviously concerned to understand Enoch's early death. However, the length of his life in years amounted to the number of days in the solar year, which again refers to a complete life cycle.

Equally mysterious is the transportation of the prophet Elijah. While he was walking along, talking to Elisha, a chariot of fire suddenly descended and they were separated. Elijah was taken up to heaven in a storm wind (II Kings 2.11).

We find similar ascension stories in Babylonia, and in Greek and Roman literature.[2] People were taken up to the gods to live with and among them in a state of blessed joy. Here there is no mention of dying. Thus both Bible stories are most likely to have arisen under the influence of these mythologies from surrounding cultures. It is possible that the origin of the legends simply goes back to the fact that nothing was known about the end of either Enoch's or Elijah's lives. They did not even have known tombs; not a trace of them was left. On the other hand, it could hardly be assumed that they had simply disappeared. They had been taken from the earth by God and received up into his glory.

Both stories are so striking and strange in the wider context of the Old Testament and play so small a role elsewhere in it that it would be irresponsible to interpret the legends as a first deliberate allusion to a belief in immortality in Israel. Later, shortly before and immediately after the Christian era, these stories, above all that of Enoch, were to play a major role in thinking about eternity.

'In Sheol who can give thee praise?' (Ps.6.5)

Although it is therefore abundantly clear that the Israelite was interested above all in the history of the living God with earthly human lives, we also find reflection about the fate of the dead. The dead remain in Sheol. This concept, which is originally connected with desolation, emptiness, depth, earth, dust and tomb, the underworld, is comparable with the Greek Hades.

Sheol lies under the earth (Num.16.33; Deut.32.22; Ps.55.16; Isa.14.9,15), under the waters which support the earth (Job 26.5). It is a place – or rather a non-land – to which all the dead go without distinction, both righteous and sinners, rich and poor (Josh.23.14; Job 3.13-19; Ps.89.49; Eccles. 6.6; Sir.8.7; 14.17). The inhabitants of this wretched place are called *rephaim*, shadows with a ghostly existence (Job 26.5; Ps.88.11; Prov.9.18; Isa.26.14,19). They have a miserable fate, closer to not-living than to real existence.

Faithful Israelites lament that in Sheol there is not even any contact with Yahweh (Ps.6.6; 30.10). Yahweh himself seems to be helpless towards those who live there: 'Dost thou work wonders among the dead? Do the shades rise up to praise thee? Is thy steadfast love declared in the grave, or thy faithfulness in Abaddon? Are thy wonders known in the darkness, or thy saving help in the land of forgetfulness?' (Ps.88.11-13; cf. Ps.115.17; Isa.38.11,18).

In Sheol people know nothing of what happens on earth. They are forgotten by all and have nothing more to hope for; all is finally over

(Job 14.21f.; Ps.88.13; Eccles.9.5f.). There is only darkness (Job 14.21f.; Ps.88.7,13; Lam.3.6) and silence (Ps.94.17; 115.17). It is a land of no return (II Sam.12.23; Job 16.22; Ps.12.6), closed in by doors (Job 38.17; Isa.38.10) which are firmly bolted (Job 38.10; Jonah 2).

Sometimes Sheol is also imagined as a monster which opens its maw to swallow people up into the realm of the dead (Num.16.30,34; Prov.27.20; Isa.5.14).

As I have said, Yahweh has nothing to do with this land of forgetting and darkness. He is a God of life and light. However, for a believing Israelite it was hard to think this through consistently, so there are a few texts which seem to suggest that Yahweh does have power over this realm of the dead. 'Yahweh brings down to Sheol and raises up' (I Sam.2.6; Tobit 13.2; cf. Amos 9.2). 'If I ascend to heaven, thou art there! If I make my bed in Sheol thou art there! If I say, "Let only darkness cover me, and the light about me be night", even the darkness is not dark to thee, the night is as bright as the day' (Ps.139. 8,11f.). Moreover, Yahweh can pursue his enemies when they have fled to Sheol to escape his anger, to bring them up and take vengeance on them (Amos 9.2; Wisd. 16.13-15).

However, when reading and interpreting these latter texts we must note that the Israelite can also use the term Sheol in the figurative sense. In that case he speaks of people who are in the distress of death, who are persecuted, who are tormented by bitter suffering, whose fate is so lamentable that they might as well be already dead (Ps.18.5,7,17-19; 22.30; 116.3,8; 143.3f.,7).

This shadowy existence is presented as a very weakened form of physical existence. That is suggested by texts which show that this shadowy existence is dependent on the fate which befalls the body or the bones. The body or the bones are as it were the earthly substrate for existence as shadows. Thus the Jews abominated the Moabites who had burnt the bones of the king of Edom to chalk (Amos 2.1), because in so doing they had robbed the shade of this king of any possibility of existence. The burning of a body was therefore one of the most serious crimes and punishments that could be envisaged in Israel (Gen.38.24; Lev.20.14; 21.9; Josh.7.25). You did not do that even to an enemy; they had a claim to orderly burial in the earth (Josh.8.29; 10.26f.; II Sam.21.13f.).

If this shadowy existence is somehow seen as a continued existence after death, we can understand the desire to go to rest with the fathers, still to share with them some form of community. People sought to achieve this by providing for their burial in their own land (Gen.23), where their fathers had been buried (Gen.49.29f.). Joseph dies in Egypt but wants his bones to be buried in his own land (Gen.50.25; cf. Josh.24.32). If it is at all possible, people want to be buried in the tomb of their fathers (Judg.8.32; 12.7; 16.31; II Sam.19.28; II Kings 9.28; 12.22). To be buried in a common grave was usually regarded as a scandal and a punishment (Jer.26.23; II Kings 23.6).

All this has very little to do with belief in eternal life. For this presupposes a form of real life and expects a more intensive form of existence. By contrast, the life of the shadow does not even merit being called life. However, these very conceptions would be used later to express belief in an eternal life and a resurrection experience. Thus, for example, we hear Jesus say that the form of body with which one dies determines physical life in heaven or hell: 'It is better that you lose one of your limbs than that your whole body go into hell' (Matt.5.29f.).

2. 'Their bodies were buried in peace, and their name lives to all generations' (Sir.44.14)

Israel did not have much difficulty in incorporating death into its belief in God. How can this be explained in the light of the understanding of faith with which we are familiar and in which we take it for granted that the existence of God and an eternal life go together like sun and warmth?

Faith is a contextual event. The insights of faith are never experienced in complete purity and do not come down directly from heaven. Faith is achieved and seeks to express itself in the universal human context in which it is experienced. The historical context, determined by social relationships, economic conditions, cultural involvement, political interests, and views of man and the world provide the inevitable perspectives from which we gain the glimpse of a God and in which God's word is perceived and heard. Human beings speak of God, and God cannot be spoken of other than by human beings. Human beings speak of heaven and eternity in the context of the earth and its history. Thus specific human experience always and unavoidably plays a part in any talk of God. And this human experience is always time-conditioned and determined by the possibilities and the limitations of the culture in which one lives.

The Israelite view of humanity which I mentioned is therefore not really revealed by God, any more than any other such view. It is simply the view of all primitive people about humanity, which identifies the reality which they see simply and naturally with reality as it is. They do not see anything in mankind that might be eternal; they note that the human beings they see and know die. Their faith says that God is deeply involved with this: he gives the breath of life and he takes it back again.

It is above all the social context which makes it possible to involve oneself in the death of the individual.

To begin with, Israel thought and lived out its faith in Yahweh in a very strong tribal alliance, as a tribe, a family, a clan, a community, a people. Nowadays we would call this a collective. The individual is completely incorporated into the tribal alliance. A person is nothing in and of himself or herself. He or she is everything as a member of the community, the people. Yahweh is not there for the individual, but for the community as such. He does not necessarily reward and punish individuals, but he intervenes positively or negatively in their family, in their descendants. Hence we can understand what we read of him: 'I am a jealous God, visiting the iniquity of the fathers upon the children to the third and the fourth generation of those who hate me, but showing steadfast love to thousands of those who love me and keep my commandments' (Ex.20.5f.; cf. Ex.34.7; Num.14.18; Deut.5.9f.; Jer.32.18).

If we combine the two factors of primitive anthropology and collectivist social thinking and living we can immediately understand how in this context there were no questions about an individual life after death, a future after the death of the individual. But this made the desire and the sacrifice for the future of the clan, the group, the family, and the people all the more intensive. All expectations for the future are exclusively directed towards the future of the people within the limits of earthly history.

The individual cannot do anything but submit himself to his inevitable end. Job describes this existence without illusions in imagery which still strikes one more than any other language into which eternity is translated (see e.g. 14.1f., 5-12).

'The righteous will be remembered for ever' (Ps.112.6)

Although the hope of Israel primarily concerns the future of the people as people, we come across different forms of longing for a continued personal existence.

First of all there is a widespread conviction that man lives on in his children and in all his descendants. Abraham, the nomadic cattle-rearer without children, is given a promise by Yahweh both of his own land and of descendants (Gen.12.1f.; 15.2-6). Abraham himself will live in his descendants. Only these descendants will take possession of this promised land (Gen.12.7; 13.15; 15.18; 24.7; 26.4; 28.13). God's promise to Abraham is fulfilled in his descendants, who receive as their possession the land which is really promised to Abraham. So one could say that Abraham himself – as the subject of God's promise – lives on in those in whom Yahweh brings his promise to fulfilment.

It remained a comforting thought among Jewish people down the ages that a man lives on in his children. 'The father may die, and yet he is not dead, for he has left behind him one like himself; while alive he saw and rejoiced, and when he died he was not grieved; he has left behind him an avenger against his enemies, and one to repay the kindness of his friends' (Sir.30.4-6). That explains the institution of levirate or kinship marriage (Deut.25.5-10). If brothers live together and one of them dies without leaving behind a son, then one of the surviving brothers takes the widow as his wife and the first son of this marriage is regarded as the legitimate son of the dead man (see Gen.38; Ruth 1.11f.; 2.20; 3.12; 4.5,10; cf. Matt.22.24-28). In this way the name of the dead man lives on and he himself continues to live in his name.

The individual also survives in family history through the patriarchal blessing. Through the patriarchs Yahweh blesses the whole tribe. In giving his blessing before dying the patriarch hands on God's promise as a gift, in such a way that he cannot revoke this blessing and give it to another. In and through this blessing he hands on that which has given content and colouring to his personal life, namely his dealings with Yahweh. So in the blessing he hands on the nucleus of his own existence. In this way he transcends his own death (see Gen. 27.27-30; 48.15-20). After the exile there are pious or wise men who hand down this divine blessing in the form of admonitions, guidelines, proverbs and discourses. In this way they hand on to their disciples as a possible life-style the content of their own communion with God, which has been expressed in knowledge and wisdom. Thus the wise, too, continue to live in those who follow them in wisdom and insight.

A very clear form of a personal hope for immortality is the continuance of a good name. Thus the name of the tribal patriarch lives on in the tribe. Hence the form of blessing which Israel utters over his son Joseph: 'And in them let my name be perpetuated, and the name of my fathers Abraham and Isaac' (Gen.48.16). At another point we read: 'But those were men of mercy, whose righteous deeds have not been forgotten; their prosperity will remain with their descendants, and their inheritance to their children's children. Their descendants stand by the covenants, their children also, for their sake. Their posterity will continue for ever, and their glory will not be blotted out. Their bodies were buried in peace, and their name lives to all generations' (Sir.44.10-14).

The worst thing that can happen to anyone is for his name to be blotted out and forgotten. Everything possible must be done to gain a good name: 'The mourning of men is about their bodies, but the evil name of sinners will be blotted out. Have regard for your name, since it will remain for you longer than a thousand great stores of gold. The days of a good life are numbered, but a good name endures for ever' (Sir.41.11-13; cf. Prov.22.1; Eccles.7.1).

It is also horrifying when sons are killed and therefore the name dies out (Ps.109.13; Isa.14.20-23). This is taken to such an extent that Yahweh can even give pious eunuchs the following comfort: 'I will give in my house and within my walls a monument and a name better than sons and daughters; I will give them an everlasting name, which shall not be cut off' (Isa.56.5). For others, too, a memorial can make up for the lack of living descendants and so as it were give material form to the permanence of the name (II Sam.18.18).

The desire to live on in worthy remembrance is often also to be seen in the same perspective (Ps.112.6-9; Sir. 37.26; 39.10f.; 40.19; 44.10-15; 46.12; Wisd.4.1-19; 8.13; I Macc.2.51; 6.44; II Macc.6.31).

These various forms of the longing for eternity – if we can use this important word as early as this – do not suggest in any way that there was such a thing as a future life which was conceived of or dreamed of as a personal life after death. The longing which we have now tracked down is bound up with the hope for the future of the people. It is in this that people want to live on. These two aspects of a hope cannot be completely separated in the faith of Israel. Certainly because of their specific context different traditions can over-illuminate one aspect and neglect another, but the God of Israel is never only the God of the individual; he is always the God of the people, even if at a later stage of the history of Israel there is a further development of the conception of the relationship between person and community.

The thought and action, the sense of solidarity, bound up with family, tribe and people, increasingly gives way before what we might call the rise of personalism. This development can be dated quite accurately. In the reign of King David (about 1000 BC) the central government increasingly took over the authority and the initiatives from the tribes, or, more accurately, the clans. As a result the solidarity of the group and within the group began to function less as a necessary normative principle. The connection between the members of groups became looser. Whereas earlier the clan formed a network of mutual relationships, now everything went through a single channel to the central government. Once the group means less as a group, there is increasing opportunity to act as an individual. This political constellation with important social consequences gave birth to a certain form of personalism.

Faith immediately experiences the influence of this change and now stresses quite different points. Yahweh himself is seen differently. Later, the prophets were even explicitly to attack a view of Yahweh's righteousness which had arisen from the notion of solidarity: 'In those days they shall no longer say: "The fathers have eaten sour grapes, and the children's teeth are set on edge." But every one shall die for his own sin; each man who eats sour grapes, his teeth shall be set on edge' (Jer.31.29f.; cf. Ezek.18).

Moreover, within a personalistic way of thinking, it becomes increasingly difficult to see a causal connection between personal guilt and suffering on the one hand and personal righteousness and reward on the other. This connection is questioned above all in the book of Job, and even denied outright in an unparalleled way. Ecclesiastes reacts in a less desperate way. He becomes more cynical: 'Then I saw the wicked buried; they used to go in and out of the holy place, and were praised in the city where they had done such things. This also is vanity. Because sentence against an evil deed is not executed speedily, the heart of the sons of men is fully set to do evil. Though a sinner does evil a hundred times and prolongs his life, yet I know that it will be well with those who fear God, because they fear before him; but it will not be well with the wicked, neither will he prolong his days like a shadow, because he does not fear before God. There is a vanity which takes place on earth, that there are righteous men to whom it happens according to the deeds of the wicked, and there are wicked men to whom it happens according to the deeds of the righteous. I said that this also is vanity' (8.10-14).[3]

However, the very real problems which Job and Ecclesiastes present seem to contradict a centuries-long tradition to such a degree that at a later stage, even in the first years of the second century before Christ, we still find an attempt to defend the traditional doctrine and to restore it in an honourable way (Sir.2.9-11; 3.6-9; 4.11-19; 7.1; 11.20-22).

3. 'God will ransom my soul from the power of Sheol, for he will receive me' (Ps.49.16)

This is above all a prayerful reflection on the mystery of the prosperity of sinners and the persecution and suffering of the righteous which arouses the suspicion that God's love and righteousness are not limited by what happens in this world. There are some psalms which seem to be relevant to such an interpretation. Earlier exegesis here offered to dogmatics, the academic reflection on the content of faith, arguments from scripture to justify belief in a personal life after death, which dogmatic theologians were happy to accept. Contemporary exegesis shows clearly that these psalms do not point quite so unequivocally to belief in eternal life.

It seems natural to see Ps.16 as an expression of belief in the resurrection. There we find literally: 'Thou dost not give me up to Sheol, or let thy godly one see the Pit. Thou dost show me the path of life, in thy presence there is fullness of joy, in thy right hand are pleasures for evermore' (vv.10f.). But this verse is no evidence for belief in eternity. The first verse of the psalm does not allow such exegesis. 'Preserve me, O God, for in thee I take refuge.' The pious person is obviously in danger and asks God for deliverance. It might be that this danger really consists in a threat of death. In that case the prayer here would specifically be not to have to die, not to be handed over to death and the tomb. There is no mention here of a life beyond the tomb. Nevertheless, this very psalm is already quoted in Acts as a reference to the resurrection of Jesus from the tomb. To achieve this Luke, the author of Acts, had to manipulate the original text of the psalm to some extent. Where the psalm says that the pious man will not be afraid of the tomb because he is confident of escaping the imminent danger of death by the help of God, in Acts we find that the holy one will not see 'corruption' (2.25-28,31; 13.35). In fact Jesus saw the tomb, but not corruption.

Another two psalms are usually mentioned in connection with this problem, Pss. 49 and 73. I shall begin with the latter, because its support for an argument in favour of a belief in resurrection seems less convincing than might be the case in Ps.49.

Ps.73 is a text which is particularly complex. The psalmist has reflected intensively on the mystery of retribution and therefore on God's justification. His experiences make him doubt almost everything. He knows that he despises the prosperity of the evil (vv.2-12). He himself is chastized all day long, although he can attest that he keeps his heart pure and can wash his hands in innocence (vv.13f.). He thinks deeply about all this, and it is a torment to him (v.16). He feels embittered (v.21) until he realizes that despite everything he is guided by God. In the midst of his nagging doubt he knows that God is still with him. God holds his right hand firmly (v.23). God gives him an insight into his discouraging experiences by showing him the end that awaits the godless. God casts them down into the abyss. It is a shattering fall. Nothing is left of them, not even their name. Quite a different fate awaits the faithful: God later takes them to glory (v.24). God will take them to himself.

Exegetes differ as to the real significance of v.24. According to some it expresses the expectation that the faithful will be taken up into God's glory before his death along the lines of the ascension model which we have already discovered in the accounts of Enoch and Elijah. Others read into this verse, given its immediate context, an explicit hope of rescue from the kingdom of the dead, in other words, a belief in the resurrection.[4]

Verses 25f. seem to me to be particularly important for a correct interpretation of the psalm: 'Whom have I in heaven but thee? And there is nothing upon earth that I desire beside thee. My flesh and my heart may fail, but God is the strength of my heart and my portion for ever.' After all his complaints and doubts the pious person eventually realizes that nothing is more important than a right relationship to God. That is a blessing in itself. Nothing more needs to be added. It is all up to God. Apart from God the pious man requires nothing else on earth, and without God even heaven means nothing to him. What is said here culminates in what is said in Ps.63.3: 'Because thy steadfast love is better than life.' If one can trust in God's love, then though suffering and misery assail a man, he is founded on a rock. He retains God, and that is his good fortune, the nearness of God (v.28).

Can we go further? It does not seem to me irresponsible, taking

account of all the inevitable differences and adding all the necessary
qualifications, to claim that here in prayer there is also an inkling of,
a trust in, resurrection from the dead. Because of his own intimate
contact with God, the person who prays has more certainty about
God's truthfulness and faith than he can demonstrate from his own
grievous experiences. Thus anyone who prays and expresses all his
disappointments and despair in the presence of God is perhaps convinced that God cannot abandon his covenant with those who keep
faith with him to death. Otherwise evil would have the last word,
and that is quite impossible. The last word is spoken by the one who
also spoke the first word by which everything came into being: Yahweh, God. However, at the same time we must reckon with the possibility that the interpretation we put forward is more a matter of
reading in a later belief than interpreting the text itself.

The problems of Ps.49 are almost the same as those of Ps.73. Here
the sinners are presented as rich men. Their prosperity is a challenge
to all those who are pious. The theme of the psalmist is the transitoriness and the ultimate uselessness of riches and possessions. No man
is rich enough to pay God a ransom for his life; the price of his life is
too high, since his riches are not enough for eternity (vv.8f.). 'Man
cannot abide in his pomp, he is like the beasts that perish. This is the
fate of those who have foolish confidence, the end of those who are
pleased with their portion. Like sheep they are appointed for Sheol;
Death shall be their shepherd; straight to the grave they descend, and
their form shall waste away; Sheol shall be their home' (vv.12-14).
The pious man is convinced that another future awaits him: 'But
God will ransom my soul from the power of Sheol, for he will receive
me'(v.15).

Here the ascension model is again used, but this time it is more
clearly coupled with a belief in the resurrection than in Ps.73. The
exaltation takes place after death, and points to a liberation from
Sheol.[5]

Here the psalmist is perhaps the first to see the possibility of a retribution after death. As one who prays he sees it more in a vision. As
a doctrine it seems strange to him. He understands that it must seem
mysterious to others. Therefore he resolves to express his own intuition in poetry, with music: he discloses his secret with the sound of
the zither (vv.4f.).

What is handed on here, then, is not a generally affirmed insight of
faith. Here we have the dawning of something completely new, an
insight which speaks to the heart (v.4). However, it is remarkable

that this new vision of the Godness of God emerges in the reflection of prayer. The intuition arises in prayer, in which the vision of a future beyond death comes into being. Here prayer precedes the articulation of faith by a long way. First of all there is an experience of God, and only then comes doctrine. Prayer itself becomes the event of revelation which later looks for expression, for images and concepts. In prayer with God it becomes clear that everything depends on a communion with God in love. This relationship with God is more real than death. It is inconceivable that it should be devoured by death. The actual experience of the love of God is quite simply the end. The end of life takes place on a different level and has nothing to do with it.

4. 'Many of those who sleep in the dust of the earth shall awake' (Dan.12.2)

Only later does what originally was guessed at and hoped for become a more general conviction. As far as our theme is concerned this happened in a context in which the people of Israel *qua* people were still familiar with the same experiences as the people at prayer whose voices we have heard in the psalms. In both cases the focal point is the faithfulness of God which is maintained even in the midst of unmerited suffering from which one can only stare in bewilderment at the good fortune of the godless. This suffering over God, which prompts cries of anguish in Job, provokes the scepticism of Ecclesiastes, and makes the faithful in the psalms wail and hope, is only experienced in all its perplexity when it has to be noted not only that the righteous must suffer but also that they are persecuted precisely because of their righteousness, because of their faithfulness to the law of Yahweh.

That became a crude and cruel reality in the reign of Antiochus IV Epiphanes (175-63 BC). For political reasons, this king of the Seleucid dynasty, who ruled over Syria and had annexed Palestine after 198, sought to carry through Hellenization in Jerusalem with all the power at his disposal. He tried to change the identity of Judaism, which was primarily determined by religion and tradition, replacing it with Hellenistic culture which in many areas offended the deepest convictions of the Jews. Antiochus could count on the collaboration of leading Jewish circles in Jerusalem. In their struggle with one another to control the high priesthood, a number of these Jewish aristocrats were prepared to make political, financial and religious concessions to the king. In this way they retained the high priesthood. Those Jews who remained faithful to the law, to be found above all in the lower strata of the population, were dismayed and bewildered. They offered resistance. The rebellion under the Maccabees, which began in 166, was to become the climax of their revolt which had already been brewing for a long time. In this struggle many victims among the revolutionaries fell. After all the disappointed hopes that the Jews had experienced during and after the exile, the death of those resistance fighters who had remained faithful to the law was a thrust at the heart of the faithful believers of Israel. Was Yahweh now showing his impotence in handing over to death and destruction followers of his whom he should have taken under his protection because of their faithfulness to his law and his word? This hopeless struggle, in which the most pious and faithful of the Jews were the ones who perished, deprived the people of all hope of a change in their fortunes, of happiness after tribulation, of reward for merit. In what seemed to be the closing phase of a long-drawn-out tragedy the only alternatives were for Jewish faith to perish with the people themselves or for the God of Israel to show himself stronger than death. Belief in this ultimate supremacy of God was to help them surmount the complete collapse of their hopes in disappointment and despair.

'Those who are wise shall shine like the brightness of the firmament' (Dan.12.3)

The book of Daniel came into being in this period. Here we find the first indisputable testimony to a belief in the resurrection.

> At that time shall arise Michael, the great prince who has charge of your people. And there shall be a time of trouble, such as never has been since there was a nation till that time; but at that time your people shall be delivered, everyone whose name shall be found written in the book. And many of those who sleep in the dust of the earth shall awake, some to everlasting life and some to shame and everlasting contempt. And those who are wise shall shine like the brightness of the firmament; and those who turn many to righteousness, like the stars for ever and ever (Dan.12.1-13).

These verses clearly reveal the religious context in which they arose. Among the persecuted Jews of that time, *apocalyptic* came into its own. I shall investigate it in detail in section B. All that need be said here is that apocalyptic is a complex of ideas with strongly dualistic thinking. Here we find two worlds and two spheres in which the God who makes history is active. The general expectation was that God would soon intervene to destroy this visible world, corrupted as it was by sin, and to replace it with a new one. Or it was expected that God would put an end to this history lying under the sway of evil in order to introduce a new and final phase of history in which he would implement his plans for his people without hindrance. Ideas about how and when this would happen are as different as they are complex. These last events are revealed to certain people (the Greek word 'apocalypse' means uncovering or revelation) in visions and dreams which they communicate in strange and often bizarre imagery.

At all events, the text of Daniel in which we are interested here is concerned with the ending of the first phase of history. As we saw, the historical situation of Israel was such that its political role seemed finally to be played out. Against the background of this history it was impossible to see a point of light on which trust in a historical restoration in the future could have been oriented. But Yahweh would intervene. In a devastating judgment he would exterminate the enemies of Israel. He would then begin a new history with his elect in which he would bring his plan of salvation to completion.

Interpreted in this way, the expectations which are formulated here by Daniel would be very much in line with Jewish prophecy. For methodological reasons I shall discuss this prophecy rather later. It expresses more of a future expectation for the people as a whole than for an individual hope of life after death, a problem which still concerns us for the moment. Or, to put it another way, we discuss prophecy when we are talking of general eschatology, whereas we are now very much concerned with individual eschatology. This prophecy looks for a change in history, on this earth. It does not think at all in dualistic terms, as is the case with apocalyptic.

If the text of Daniel may be interpreted along the lines of Israelite prophecy, then the term eternal life which is mentioned in v.2 still does not have the meaning which it received later and which is still to be found in the emotional sense in which we use the word. For us, eternal life represents a transhistorical and meta-historical reality, i.e. it is concerned with a life which takes place above and outside actual life on earth. We usually interpret eternal life in terms of transcendent eschatology, i.e. of a future expectation in which the future is thought of as beginning only after this life and after our human history, as an event which really stands above them or outside them. We must note that one can also speak of a historical eschatology in which a future is expected within this history and on this earth. The distinctions between these two different views of the future, the one apocalyptic and the second prophetic, must be recognized quite clearly. In the apocryphal and/or pseudepigraphical writings[6] it is not always easy to hold them both apart.

I mention these works already at this point; we shall be coming back to them later in more detail. I want to use one of them so that we can gain a better understanding of the term 'eternal life' in this text of Daniel. It is Ethiopian Enoch, or I Enoch. Some fragments of the work are earlier than the book of Daniel or come from the same period. I Enoch speaks of the just who are saved at the last judgment. As a reward they receive a long life on earth, in the same way as their fathers did. Evidently this reference is to the patriarchs, all of whom had a life-span of nine hundred years before the flood (cf. Gen.5.5-21). During this long life those righteous who have been saved experience no more suffering or tribulation and they delight in blessedness. Nothing in the book of Daniel seems to demonstrate convincingly that the content of 'eternal life' could have any significance other than a long life on earth, of which Enoch speaks. So Daniel would have nothing to do with a life after history or above history.[7]

You will have already been struck by the fact that Daniel speaks of the awakening of 'many' of those who sleep in the dust. Not all? The most plausible explanation would in fact seem to be that only the righteous arise.[8] Chapters 11 and 12 speak of great wars. A great many people lose their lives in these wars. Those who 'are numbered in the book' (12.1; cf. Isa.4.2f.) remain alive. In the destiny of the righteous we must therefore distinguish between those who escape death during the wars of persecution (12.1) and those who had died earlier and will now be raised at the last judgment (12.2a). By contrast the godless are destined to the reproach of eternal shame. During the war all the godless will perish and those who had died earlier will not rise; in this way they will be delivered over to the eternal shame of death and oblivion.

If this interpretation is correct, this first explicit confession of belief in resurrection in the Old Testament writings argues for an exclusive and positive content for the concept of 'resurrection'.

Resurrection will happen only to the righteous. Resurrection is a reward.

The event of resurrection is called an 'awakening' of those who 'sleep' in the dust of the earth. At the same time that indicates that the expression 'rise' is not to be understood literally. That would be possible only if the dead in fact sleep. If they sleep, they can awake, they can be awoken, rise, arise. So here we clearly have pictorial language.

There is no description of the long resurrection life. But we are told that in this final phase of history 'the wise' will shine like the splendour of the firmament, and 'those who turn many to righteousness' will shine eternally and for ever like the stars. The 'wise' are perhaps the religious leaders of the anti-Hellenist resistance movement, or the apocalyptists, the seers themselves. In common with those who helped the people to withstand the trial of their faithfulness to the law they will now take over the role of Antiochus Epiphanes, the shining one.

In all this we should not overlook the fact that the author is primarily concerned to encourage his contemporaries. He wants to help them to remain faithful to the faith of the fathers. They are not to be made to despair by the straits in which they find themselves. The prospect that even the dead will have a share in the life of coming history, which will be the definitive time of salvation for ransomed Israel, plays a tremendously important role in motivating the courage of the martyrs.

'The King of the universe will raise us up to an everlasting renewal of life because we have died for his laws' (II Macc.7.9)

II Maccabees takes a substantial step forward in working out the problem as experienced in the diaspora situation of a Jewish community, perhaps in Antioch.[9]

In ch. 7, in this connection we find a vivid account of the fate which those martyrs who have been faithful to the law expect after their death. In it we have something of a theology of the resurrection, with the story of the martyrdom of the seven brothers and their mother simply serving as a framework for early-Jewish[10] belief in the resurrection. The figures, who remain anonymous, represent all those who prefer to die in the time of Hellenistic persecution rather than transgress the law of the fathers (v.2).

During the macabre scene of the martyrdom of their spokesman we hear the brothers and their mother encourage one another with the words: 'The Lord God is watching over us and in truth has compassion on us, as Moses declared in his song which bore witness against the people to their faces, when he said, "And he will have compassion on his servants"' (v.6). The trust of the martyrs is nurtured by a saying from the Torah, the law, and this runs: 'Yahweh will vindicate his people and have compassion on his servants, when he sees that their power is gone' (Deut.32.36). According to this view Yahweh changes the fortunes of his people for the better when he sees the suffering of his servants. He cannot as it were continue to look on this suffering and intervenes to punish the enemies of the people and free the faithful. So we read: 'Praise his people, O you nations; for he avenges on the blood of his servants, and takes vengeance on his adversaries, and makes expiation for the land of his people' (Deut.32.43).

Early-Jewish belief in the resurrection therefore refers primarily to a basic fact of the law: Yahweh does not allow his people to be utterly oppressed, but vindicates them in his faithfulness and in his mercy.[11]

In this trust we can perceive the expectation: 'The King of the universe will raise us up to an everlasting renewal of life, because we have died for his laws' (v.9). That is said to the king of Syria. While he can kill people here and now, he has to face the King of the universe, who gives his servants 'eternal life'. In view of the contrast which is deliberately drawn in this verse, here, in contrast to Daniel, 'eternal life' is doubtless meant to be a transcendent, heavenly life, and not a historical eschatology.

This heavenly life is thought of in physical terms: 'I got these hands from Heaven, and because of his laws I disdain them, and from him I hope to get them back again' (v.11; cf. 14.46). How this will happen remains an open question and is quite irrelevant here.

As he dies, the fourth brother cries out: 'One cannot but choose to die at the hands of men and to cherish the hope that God gives of being raised again by him.' But to the king he says: 'But for you there will be no resurrection' (v.14). As in Daniel, so here resurrection is a term with positive connotations. It is a 'resurrection to life'. Sinners are excluded from it. Verses 17, 19, 34-37 give us the clear impression that the godless Antiochus will be punished on earth by a premature death and by what happens to his descendants. So for them there is no resurrection, but the shame of an eternal death. He is not even granted a further life in and through his descendants.

The author makes the mother give a theological explanation of the trust in the resurrection which is attested here. She speaks of the origin of man and of his creation, and concludes from this that God also has the power to recreate those martyrs who have died for the sake of his law. The miracle of human creation makes her conclude that a new creation must be possible in heaven: 'I do not know how you came into being in my womb. It was not I who gave you life and breath, nor I who set in order the elements within each of you. Therefore the Creator of the world, who shaped the beginning of man and devised the origin of all things, will in his mercy give life and breath back to you again, since you now forget yourselves for the sake of his laws' (vv.22f.).

Thus the resurrection is seen in terms of the creative power of God. God, who has created all things from nothing, has not exhausted his possibilites when martyrs are killed for the sake of his law. He creates life anew from this nothingness. The miracle of creation stems exclusively from God who called all things into existence by his word; the miracle of the second, the new creation equally derives from the same voice of God. Therefore the mother says to her youngest: 'I beseech you, my child, to look at the heaven and the earth and see everything that is in them, and recognize that God did not make them out of things that existed. Thus also mankind comes into being. Do not fear this butcher, but prove worthy of your brothers. Accept death, so that in God's mercy I may get you back again with your brothers' (vv.28f.).

This last notion seems rather to take up the expectations of a historical intervention by God. It is not entirely clear. In the wider context of the text one might perhaps say that if God raises the martyrs to an eternal life, i.e. if he gives them a new heavenly mode of existence in his glory, he will then also change the destiny of his people for the better in a definitive way.

Before he dies, the youngest brother says: 'And if our living Lord is angry for a little while, to rebuke and discipline us, he will again be reconciled with his own servants. For our brothers after enduring a brief suffering have drunk of everflowing life' (vv.33, 36). This is a new argument for belief in the resurrection: the faithfulness of God's covenant guarantees an eternal life. The martyrs share in this immediately after the brief suffering of their martyrdom. So the brothers have eternal life even before the death of the youngest.

As well as this instructive story about the death of the martyrs in II Maccabees we have three other texts dealing with life after death.

According to the account in 12.38-45, the Jewish resistance fighters who perished in battle had worn pagan amulets. To atone for this sin on the part of the fallen, money is collected for the offering of a sacrifice. Judas sent money 'to Jerusalem to provide for a sin offering. In doing this he acted very well and honourably, taking account of the resurrection. For if he were not expecting that those who had fallen would rise again, it would have been superfluous and foolish to pray for the dead. But if he was looking to the splendid reward that is laid up for those who fall asleep in godliness, it was a holy and pious thought. Therefore he made atonement for the dead, that they might be delivered from their sin' (vv.43-45).

This is an expression of the confidence that the living can do something for the dead. So these latter are not completely dead. It is nowhere said here that their 'soul' would live on, and it seems difficult to presuppose such an idea in an author who stresses the physical resurrection so strongly. What the author was thinking about when he wrote about this praying for the dead remains quite obscure. All we can conclude from it is that the dead live with God and that therefore something can be done for them by the living, even beyond the bounds of death.

In 14.37-46 we find an attempt by a certain Razis to commit suicide. This man was highly regarded by the Jews because in the period before the great rebellion he had risked life and limb for the Jews. When there was a danger that he might be taken prisoner, he hurled himself from the wall of a tower. 'Though his blood gushed forth and his wounds were severe he ran through the crowd and, standing upon a steep rock, with his blood now completely drained from him, he tore out his entrails, took them with both hands and hurled them at the crowd, calling upon the Lord of life and spirit to give them back to him again. This was the manner of his death' (vv.45f.).

This story is not appetizing, and I would never have quoted it had I not seen here yet another expression of faith in a physical resurrection in which, as in ch.7, the resurrection body is identified in material terms with the body which dies. This faith rests on trust in the power of the creator, who is here called the Lord of life and breath.

Finally, there is mention of a life after death in the vision of Judas in 15.12-16. In a dream Judas sees the former high priest Onias who was murdered because of his faithfulness to the law (cf. Dan.9.26; II

Macc.3-4) praying in heaven for the Jewish people. Jeremiah also appears in this vision as glorified in heaven. In this connection it must be remembered that according to a Jewish Christian tradition Jeremiah died a martyr's death in Egypt. So this vision is concerned with the heavenly glorification of two Jewish martyrs.

The resurrection faith expressed in II Maccabees is there based on God's faithfulness to his covenant: 'The Lord will vindicate his people and have compassion on his servants' (Deut.32.36). The problem arises out of a quite specific situation. How does God's righteousness and faithfulness apply to those martyrs who die for the sake of his law? Their resurrection is envisaged here as happening immediately after their martyrdom. This resurrection is clearly seen as something which happens to the whole person, existing in the body. This specific person, whose body is tortured for the sake of the law, arises in his body in the glory of God. This physical resurrection immediately after martyrdom is seen as a new creation, a recreation of what was destroyed by martyrdom. This new creation takes place in heaven and therefore has nothing directly to do with the material body which dies. A new miracle of creation takes place.

Nothing more is said about this in the book. It is important that belief in the resurrection is expressed here in the context of trust in the God of the covenant and in the creative omnipotence of the same God.

So the book of Maccabees recognizes the life, the resurrection, of martyrs after their death.

5. 'God created man for incorruption, and made him in the image of his own eternity' (Wisdom 2.23)

Finally we must look briefly at the Book of Wisdom, a work written in Greek and dating from the first century before the Christian era. It, too, arose in the Jewish diaspora, this time in Alexandria in Egypt.

The problem which is of interest to us is discussed in the first five chapters of the book from the familiar perspective of the suffering of the innocent and the righteous. Here these are usually described as being mocked, persecuted and killed by the godless, who do not understand them.

By his conduct the wise man is a living reproach to the godless. These resolve: 'Let us test him with insult and torture, that we may find out how gentle he is, and make trial of his forbearance. Let us condemn him to a shameful death, for, according to what he says, he will be protected'(2.19f.)

The author retorts with his judgment: 'Thus they reasoned, but they were led astray, for their wickedness blinded them, and they did not know the secret purposes of God, nor hope for the wages of holiness, nor discern the prize for blameless souls; for God created man for incorruption, and made him in the image of his own eternity, but through the devil's envy death entered the world, and those who belong to his party experience it' (2.21-24).

Here we are clearly in a very different climate from that of the authors of the books of Daniel and II Maccabees. The author of the Book of Wisdom is already steeped in Hellenistic dualistic thought about man. From this perspective he gives a commentary on two factors from the two creation narratives in Genesis. He declares that man is the image of God in and through the immortality of the soul. Historically that is not at all correct. Man is the image of God not by virtue of his properties but precisely in being human. The author then interprets death as a consequence of sin, which came into the world on the urging of the devil. I have already commented on this (see pp. 39ff.).

In this view the death of the body is a pseudo-problem. Everything depends on the life of the soul. The souls of the righteous attain life in full only after physical death, which in the eyes of the godless is final: 'But the souls of the righteous are in the hand of God, and no torment will ever touch them. In the eyes of the foolish they seemed to have died, and their departure was thought to be an affliction, and their going from us to be their destruction; but they are at peace. For though in the sight of men they were punished, their hope is full of immortality. Having been disciplined a little, they will receive great good, because God tested them and found them worthy of himself' (3.1-5).

Here again the positive content of eternal life is striking. Only the souls of the righteous have a part in it. The godless 'will become dishonoured corpses, and an outrage among the dead for ever; because he will dash them speechless to the ground, and shake them from the foundations; they will be left utterly dry and barren, and they will suffer anguish, and the memory of them will perish. They will come with dread when their sins are reckoned up, and their lawless deeds will convict them to their face' (4.19f.).

The purpose of these chapters from the Book of Wisdom is the same as that in Daniel and II Maccabees: to encourage believers at the time of the Hellenistic oppression, when they became very bewildered over the happiness and success of the godless and faithless Jews. The motive for faithfulness to the law despite all persecutions is now no longer the prospect of a resurrection but the fact that people appeal to the immortality of the soul. However, that holds only for the righteous. Therefore we cannot directly assume that the Book of Wisdom shares the Hellenistic view of the immortality of the soul as a spiritual reality. Rather, it is righteousness which is immortal. So we explicitly find: 'Do not invite death by the error of your life, nor bring on destruction by the works of your hands, because God did not make death, and he does not delight in the death of the living. For he created all things that they might exist, and the generative forces of the world are wholesome, and there is no destructive poison in them: and the dominion of Hades is not on earth. For righteousness is immortal. But ungodly men by their words and deeds summoned death' (1.12-15).

Eternal life therefore applies only to the righteous (cf. 5.15). 'But ungodly men by their words and deeds summoned death; considering him a friend, they pined away, and they made a covenant with him, because they are fit to belong to his party' (1.16). These godless will perish finally and without praise when God uses all the powers of the universe to unleash his wrath upon them and to wipe them off the face of the earth (cf. 5.17-23).

Here we see clearly that Jewish thought is influenced by Hellenistic anthropology. That is inevitable. Cultures are not separated like islands, nor do they pass by one another like ships in the night. Cultures permeate one another. However, Hellenistic dualism was not accepted readily. When Koheleth hears talk of an immortal soul which is said to go to heaven after death his scepticism leads him to make the following comment: 'I said in my heart with regard to the sons of men that God is testing them to show them that they are but beasts. For the fate of the sons of men and the fate of beasts is the same; as one dies, so dies the other. They all have the same breath, and man has no advantage over the beasts; for all is vanity. All go to one place; all are from the dust, and all turn to dust again. Who knows whether the spirit of man goes upward and the spirit of the beast goes down to the earth?' (3.18-21). Furthermore, as I have already pointed out, the Book of Wisdom, too, does not simply take over the Greek concept of the soul. So the book clearly does not know any pre-existence of the soul. It was evident to Hellenism that the spiritual soul exists in eternity. As a punishment for some crime it is given a temporal punishment in a physical prison. When this time is up the soul is freed and returns to its origin. Only derogatory comments are made about the body in this context. We find nothing of this in the Book of Wisdom.

'Let thy salvation, O God, set me on high!' (Ps.69.30)

In this first chapter I have said something about what one might call the individual expectation of the future in Israel or individual eschatology, i.e. the ulimate destiny of the individual.

This lengthy and somewhat dry analysis provides the arguments by which I justify the conclusions which I shall now draw.

To begin with, Israel was little interested in another world. What I have said makes it quite clear why this should be the case. However, at a very early stage we can find evidence of a longing for eternity. There was a desire to live on in the people, in one's own name. The explicit longing to be able to live eternally with God is first expressed in the context of prayer. That this might be possible appears more as a vision than as a clear doctrine of the spirit. Only when there no longer seems to be any future for the people, so that one can no longer desire meaningfully to live on in their history, is there a longing for a final saving intervention on the part of Yahweh in favour of those who have remained faithful to his law, who are tortured and killed for this faithfulness. In this perspective we have the conception of an individual resurrection of the martyrs. They arise after their death as they are, with a body. This corporeality does not consist in the identity of material ingredients. God, who has created everything from nothing, will also recreate the destroyed bodies of his martyrs – i.e. these martyrs in their totality – in heaven, in his glory.

Nowhere in the Old Testament is there mention of an immortal soul in the Hellenistic sense of this term. Even if there is a reference to the idea – as is clearly the case in the Book of Wisdom – the word does not have the same content as in Hellenism.

In the Old Testament there is no allusion to a general resurrection. Resurrection, as far as this term is used after and alongside the term 'exaltation', always, like that term, has an exclusively positive content. It is a reward, a rehabilitation of those who did not have a fair deal here.

This faith rests on God's faithfulness to his covenant, and it is made credible and understandable by a reference to the miracle of the creative power of God. Retribution for wickedness seems to come on this earth or consists in an absolute death.

Thus historically, belief in the resurrection arose from a situation of extreme distress and was regarded as the only possible way of saving belief in Yahweh itself. It was precisely for the sake of God that people came to posit an eternal life in the authentic sense of this word.

This belief in a beyond is quite the opposite of a flight from reality. Because there is a life after death, one must hold fast to Yahweh's word here on earth and fulfil his law faithfully. Belief in the resurrection proves to be the strongest motivation for active resistance to the emergence of Hellenism. It gives courage, the capacity to resist and faithfulness in this life.

As we have already noted, this individual expectation of final salvation is closely bound up with the longing for final peace and happiness for the people as such, and even with the dream of universal salvation for all peoples, each chosen for their relationship to God's own people. The promise to Abraham was never forgotten: 'I will bless those who bless you, and him who curses you I will curse; and by you all the families of the earth shall bless themselves' (Gen.12.3).

The way in which at this stage I have detached individual eschatology from the universal eschatology in Israel has been an artificial move which I can justify only on methodological grounds and for the sake of clarity. In reality, in the life of Israel, these two aspects of a future expectation belong indissolubly together.

II

FUTURE FOR THE WORLD

In this second chapter our attention will be directed explicitly towards the universal aspect of Israel's expectation of the future.

In the course of its national history, Israel had clouded all its future prospects. It lost its unity, its prosperity, its freedom and independence. Social injustice prevailed. Some of the people were made slaves by those who themselves had once been slaves but had been freed by the powerful arm of Yahweh. Foreign gods were worshipped. People trusted more in the worthless help of secular powers than in the omnipotent help of Yahweh. The nadir of this wretchedness was reached during the exile (587-538 BC). The period which followed was to make all remaining hope disappear, as an illusion.

In a situation which became increasingly hopeless, it was above all the prophets who sought to keep up the courage of the people. They interpreted these many forms of wretchedness as divine punishments for Israel's faithlessness and sin. But precisely because Yahweh had a hand in it, the situation was not entirely hopeless. If the people are converted, Yahweh will again have mercy on them. Many prophets expected an imminent intervention from Yahweh.

1. 'After two days he will revive us, on the third day he will raise us up' (Hos.6.2).

A kind of collective expectation for the future developed on the basis of this prophetic proclamation. By its evocative force, the imagery which is used in prophetic language provides the material from which later concepts were forged to produce belief in the resurrection.

Thus conditions of depopulation, exile, alien rule, oppression and persecution were often depicted as so many shadows cast by death in the midst of life. Yahweh himself had placed this veil of death over the sinful people. By contrast, the future visions of freedom, numerical increase and religious revival were seen from this perspective as resurrection, as a return to true and authentic life.

So a call to conversion by the prophet Hosea is answered with these typical words: 'Come, let us return to Yahweh; for he has torn, that he may heal us; he has stricken, and he will bind us up. After two days he will revive us; on the third day he will raise us up again, that we may live before him' (6.1-2). This passage is clearly not concerned with the revival of individuals but with that of the people, on the 'third day'. This third day is not to be taken literally as a chronological indication. It is a favourable, appropriate, suitable time. There is often mention in this connection of 'qualitative' time. In the Bible the third day proves to be the day of the saving intervention of Yahweh in which he puts an end to trials and suffering in order to achieve final salvation. Thus Abraham is ready to sacrifice Isaac, but on the third day he is spared this sacrifice (Gen.22.4). On the 'third day'

Yahweh also appears on Sinai (Ex.19.11,16). In connection with the appearance of great figures in the Old Testament, the third day means the dawning of God's salvation, as with Joseph in Egypt (Gen.42.18), with Esther (5.1) and with Jonah (2.1). Thus God will also raise Jesus from the dead 'on the third day, according to the scriptures'.[12]

In this text Hosea produces a literary image of the revival of the people which is to be depicted in detail in the larger-scale vision of Ezekiel (Ezek.37.1-14). This is a metaphorical description of the national restoration of Israel, who, during the exile, saw itself already delivered over to annihilation and death. Isaiah similarly speaks of a resurrection of the people and depicts it with the same pictorial material. The great Isaiah apocalypse in chs.24-27 is always mentioned in this context.[13] This is really quite a late, independent passage, which could form a separate book in the Old Testament. It is in fact an apocalypse, the description of a revelation about the end of the world, the annihilation of death and resurrection. 'The earth is utterly broken, the earth is rent asunder, the earth is violently shaken. The earth staggers like a drunken man, it sways like a hut; its transgression lies heavy upon it, and it falls and will not rise again' (24.19f.). However, finally Yahweh will take away the veil of mourning which has covered all peoples like a shroud and will set up a banquet for all people upon Mount Zion: 'And he will destroy on this mountain the covering that is cast over all peoples, the veil that is spread over all nations. He will swallow up death for ever, and the Lord God will wipe away tears from all faces' (25.7f.). The enemies of the people are finally destroyed: 'They are dead, they will not live; they are shades, they will not arise; to that end thou hast visited them with destruction and wiped out all remembrance of them' (26.14). By contrast the dead of Israel arise: 'Thy dead shall live, their bodies shall rise. O dwellers in the dust, awake and sing for joy! For thy dew is the dew of light and on the land of the shades thou wilt let it fall . . . and the earth will disclose the blood shed upon her, and will no more cover her slain' (26.19,21).

It cannot be denied that we find typical apocalyptic features in this text: the cosmic event, the judgment on all nations, the annihilation of death and the resurrection of the dead. The texts which I have quoted here will certainly already have evoked reminiscences of the Daniel text which we discussed earlier. Here too only the righteous are raised.

However, it is perhaps better to interpret these texts symbolically.

In that case this would be the resurrection of the people humiliated in and through the exile and not an apocalyptic, eschatological event affecting all mankind and the whole cosmos. In fact this text alludes to Israel's small and unpopular neighbour Moab (25.10f.), which is the object of the annihilating wrath of God; it also refers to the particularly difficult circumstances in which Israel looks for help, to the fact that Jerusalem remains unpopulated (27.8-12). As a result of all this the vision of the future seems to be related more to the final restoration of Israel (27.6,13), to the lasting peace (25.3,12) of the people, than to events which would make an end of history and the world.

With this interpretation I am putting the so-called Isaiah-Apocalypse on the same footing as the prophetic expectations of Deutero-Isaiah, who prophesied a time of prosperity and paradisal happiness for his people after all their catastrophes and disappointments, 'a new heaven and a new earth' (65.17; 66.22). Here the author is not thinking of the disappearance of this earth nor of the end of this history but of a complete transformation and renewal of all existing conditions, a transformation which would be so radical that 'former things shall not be remembered' (65.17).

This creation of a new heaven and a new earth – for the Hebrew word for creation is in fact used here – is a new creation, a miraculous renewal of the existing reality of 'heaven and earth', i.e. of everything. So this is not a new creative act of God to be taken literally, one which would follow a catastrophic annihilation of existing reality or the first creation. In the general context of these prophecies of salvation there is in fact no mention anywhere of cosmic catastrophes which suggest an end of the world. In the outline of the time of salvation to be expected after the creation of the new heaven and the new earth there is no allusion to a radical disappearance of the first creation. Yahweh will simply make the inhabitants of Jerusalem rejoice: 'For behold, I create Jerusalem a rejoicing, and her people a joy. I will rejoice in Jerusalem, and be glad in my people' (65.18f.). So the new creation clearly refers to existing Jerusalem and Judah and brings about an intensification of earthly happiness (65.19b-25).

2. 'Why would you have the day of Yahweh?' (Amos 5.18)

In the account of the final and decisive saving intervention of Yahweh there is repeated mention of the 'Day of Yahweh'. Here initiatives taken earlier by Yahweh in history for the benefit of his people are projected on to the future. Yahweh will soon take such an initiative on 'his day' when he annihilates the enemies of his people and gives his people unhoped-for joy. For Israel itself this expectation includes an ethical revival; otherwise the day of Yahweh will be primarily a condemnation for Israel, a day of wrath and vengeance. Amos was to make this clear in unmistakable words: 'Woe to you who desire the day of Yahweh. Why would you have the day of Yahweh? It is darkness and not light . . . Is not the day of Yahweh darkness, and not light, and gloom with no brightness in it?' (5.18,20).

Zephaniah, along with many other prophets, will have inspired the *Dies Irae* when he wrote: 'The great day of the Lord is near, near and hastening fast; the sound of the day of the Lord is bitter, the mighty man cries aloud there. A day of wrath is that day, a day of distress and anguish, a day of ruin and devastation, a day of darkness and gloom, a day of clouds and thick darkness, a day of trumpet blast and battle cry against the fortified cities and against the lofty battlements. I will bring distress on men, so that they shall walk like the blind, because they have sinned against the Lord; their blood shall be poured out like dust, and their flesh like dung. Neither their silver nor their gold shall be able to deliver them on the day of the wrath of the Lord. In the fire of his jealous wrath, all the earth shall be consumed; for a full, yea, sudden end he will make of all the inhabitants of the earth' (1.14-18).

The term 'day of Yahweh' was possibly taken over from earlier holy wars [14], when Yahweh set forth as War God to annihilate the enemies of his people and to win victory after victory fighting for his people – the day on which Jericho fell (Josh.7.2-5), the day on which Yahweh delivered the Amorites into the hands of the Israelites (Josh.10.12), the day when he gave the Midianites into Gideon's hand (Judg.7). The term is an expression which was to play a very important role in eschatology and apocalyptic. It is a day of vengeance (Isa. 2.11-22; 13.6-9; 61.2; 63.4; Jer.46.10; Ezek.7.19; 13.5) on which Yahweh punishes Judah for its sins (Joel 1-2) but also affects all nations (Isa.34-35; Ezek.30.3; 38-39; Joel 4; Zeph.2.1-15; 3.8; Zech 9.1-8; 12.9; Mal.3.1-5). It is a day of wrath against Midian (Isa.9.3), against Babylon (Jer.51.29-33), against Egypt (Jer.46.10), against the Philistines (Jer.47.4), against Egypt and its allies (Ezek.30.4), against Edom (Obad. 1-16), against all neighbouring peoples who have ever attacked Jerusalem (Joel 4.9-14; Zech. 12.3-14).

At the same time this day brings Yahweh's salvation and final deliverance for the pious and faithful among his people, for the 'holy remnant' (Isa. 4.3; 6.13; 11.10f.; 49.8; 61.2; 63.4).

Thus the day of Yahweh unmistakably has a significance within history. It brings a decisive turning point in the future of Israel and thus of all peoples.

Yahweh's intervention on 'his day' has cosmic elements. Yahweh has the whole cosmos at his disposal both for his judgment and punishment and for his reward and deliverance. Thus we have in Joel 2.1-11, as a precursor of the coming day of judgment, all the typical themes which can already be found in Isa.3.9-13: the devastation of the earth, the eclipse of sun, moon and stars (cf. Joel 3.4; 4.15; Amos 8.9; Zeph.1.14-18), the shaking of heaven and earth (Jer.4.23f.; Nah.1.5).

These cosmic catastrophes mean relief for Judah (Joel 3.4f.; Zech. 13.1-14; Mal.3.2-6, 19-24). They are terrors which bring deliverance to Jerusalem (Joel 4.16-21). If in Isa.13 the shaking of heaven and earth are phenomena accompanying the final judgment (cf. Hag.2.6,21), then it is clear that judgment on the powers of the world which are hostile to the world and on sinful history is a necessary prelude to the time of salvation for the just who survive. The darkening of sun, moon and stars symbolizes Yahweh's victory over the gods of Babylon. Moreover the punishment of Egypt is symbolically represented in Ezek. 32.7f. as the darkening of the sun and the lights of heaven, which were also worshipped in Egypt as deities.

The comprehensive descriptions of cosmic catastrophes on the day of Yahweh contain a warning to reckon with a God who has such power at his disposal. Thus the sole concern of the prophets is to summon people in the present to conversion and to constant trust in faith, with the expectation that God will come to judgment in the future. All the powers are at his disposal for this.

The day of Yahweh must reveal the power of Yahweh, the final triumph of his righteousness and faithfulness. Cosmic catastrophes are only images to express the terrifying omnipotence of God in his judgment, in order to bring the people and all nations to repentance.

Here – as I noted in connection with the expression 'the creation of a new heaven and a new earth' – there is no thought of the day on which Yahweh will put a final end to the first creation in order to begin something completely new. Even when we read that the day of Yahweh seems to put an end to the seasons – 'And there shall be continuous day (it is known to the Lord), not day and not night, for at evening time there shall be light' (Zech.14.6; cf. Isa.30.26), it is clear that we do not have something that is to be taken literally but that this is metaphorical language. That is evident when we hear: 'The sun shall be no more your light by day, nor for brightness shall the moon give light to you by night; but the Lord will be your everlasting light and your God will be your glory. Your sun shall no more go down, nor your moon withdraw itself; for Yahweh will be your everlasting light' (Isa.60.19f.). This elimination of the alternation of day and night merely serves as an image to indicate the final victory of Yahweh over all darkness, the darkness which is the symbol of chaos, hostility, sin and evil.

From this analysis of texts which seem to presuppose an end of the world, I think that we can conclude that the Old Testament nowhere contains a real doctrine of the end of the world.[15] We should not expect that if we take into account the mentality of the Semites. The Semites did not work with theories and spectacular outlines, but thought very specifically in terms of direct action. They were not concerned with an abstract end-time but with the immediate future. This future can only be seen as an event within this history, on this earth.

Here the vision of the future is given its specific content by strongly idealized remembrances of the past; here above all the key figures are King David, the victorious warrior king, and King Solomon, with the peace and prosperity which prevailed in his reign.

This last assertion can be verified from the messianic expectation of the future. Although what I have described here as eschatological hope was originally dependent on a messianic view (cf. Isa.2.1-5; Micah 4.1-5), just as conversely the messianic expectation originally did not include any universalist and cosmic dimensions (cf. Jer.23.5-8), these two trends gradually influenced each other and to a large degree came together. That this was possible is perhaps to be attributed to the constant role played by reminiscences of the time of David.

It would take us too far from our real subject to go into the problem of messiahship further here. One text may suffice to clarify the role of David within this model of expectation: 'Behold, the days are coming, says the Lord, when I will fulfil the promise I made to the house of Israel and the house of Judah. In those days and at that time I will cause a righteous Branch to spring forth for David; and he shall execute justice and righteousness in the land. In those days Judah will be saved and Jerusalem will dwell securely. And this is the name by which it will be called: "The Lord is our righteousness." For thus says the Lord: David shall never lack a man to sit on the throne of the house of Israel' (Jer. 33.14-17; cf.23.5f.; Isa. 16.5).

So while we can affirm responsibly that in the Old Testament the future expectation is always and above all within this world, and historical, on the other hand, in our investigation we came across an imagery on the basis of which it is easy to conceive of a vision of a transcendent future, a future after this history. This was to happen in the early Jewish period which I have already mentioned. In this period we find a hope and an expectation which also dares to look beyond the world and outside history. We have already come across such attempts in the visions of the future for individuals in the books of Daniel and II Maccabees. In the period which we shall be considering next, the expectation of the future for man and the world is for the most part transcendent.

B. Apocalyptic Visions

We find the heyday of apocalyptic in the period from about 200 BC to AD 100. Apocalyptic is a term which is not at all easy to define accurately. I use it to denote a particular kind of piety and a particular mentality. According to a number of scholars it will have flourished especially among ordinary people and will therefore have been a kind of popular piety; however, in the view of others it will go back to a kind of teaching authority which was exercised at this time by scribes and Pharisees.

This piety found expression in a whole series of writings by anonymous authors who appealed to secret 'revelations' (apocalypse is the Greek word for revelation). They presented their ideas under the auspices of great names from Jewish history and sent them out into the world on their authority.[1]

Apocalyptic literature is extremely complex, often hard to decipher, and very bizarre. Scholarly interest in it is quite recent. However, we find in these writings a great many ideas which also recur – sometimes word for word – in New Testament writings. We often get the impression that the New Testament is really shaped more by what we read in these apocalyptic writings than by the canonical books of the Old Testament.

This assertion brings us directly to a problem which is still much disputed: is apocalyptic a further development of Jewish prophecy, with the expectations of the future which that contains, or does it have another, alien origin? I want to discuss this briefly in the chapter which now follows.

I

PROPHECY AND APOCALYPTIC

We must note that the apocalyptic writings are little known in Christian circles. They are really familiar only to scholars who are professionally concerned with them. The scholarly study of apocalyptic is a prime example of the view that academic activity is never unprejudiced. Bultmann once affirmed this in a convincing way in connection with exegesis,[2] but it is true of any academic approach to reality, particularly in the sphere of history and the human sciences. A matter is investigated from a particular perspective, and this means already adopting a standpoint before the investigation begins. This standpoint, whatever it may be, is and remains determinative for the results of the investigation. Purely objective science is a fiction based on a false view of man. Human beings are never merely dispassionate observers of a reality which passes before them. Humanity and reality are completely interrelated one with the other.

I can clarify these last remarks by means of what I am going on to say, very briefly, in connection with the academic investigation of apocalyptic writings.

That apocalyptic is a further and legitimate development of Old Testament prophecy is a theory which is defended above all in Anglo-Saxon circles. Through their writing, their symbolism and their expectations, the writing prophets are said to have collected all the material from which the apocalyptists forged their own ideas. Thus prophecy is said already to have contained all the ingredients of apocalyptic, whether in nucleus or explicitly.

Apocalyptic arose at a time when the Jewish people had no prospect of a political revival. To expect any change in the world situation, after all the disappointments and failures, was simply self-deception and vanity. However, that was not taken to mean that even trust in God was an illusion. God remained the same, even over his faithfulness to the covenant. As a result of the completely changed political situation, the people of the covenant were obliged to review and investigate the substance of this covenant in the light of the radically new situation. In this way they began to discover other aspects of the covenant. God would fulfil the promises of his covenant in the future. Whereas the prophets could still imagine this future in this-worldly terms, that seemed no longer to be possible in view of the utter helplessness of the people in every respect. Hope, even hope in God, has to find some anchorage somewhere in human experience. Hope for a restoration of the people on this planet, within this history, had no support whatsoever in the period of which we are now speaking. Yet the hope with which the prophets had infected the people as with an ineradicable virus remained, and persisted despite everything. The future is and remains God's future. He will rescue his people in this future. But this future can no longer be regarded in historical terms. It will be realized and made manifest only after this history, in another age, another aeon.

That is one way of looking at apocalyptic, championed – as I have said – above all in Anglo-Saxon circles. There it is also recognized that apocalyptic also assimilates authentic Old Testament material and thinks it through further, now under the influence of Persian religion.[3]

By contrast, earlier German-speaking exegetes and those involved in the study of the history and tradition of religions refused to recognize apocalyptic as a legitimate child of Old Testament prophecy. It is not improbable that this is to be explained by the influence of rabbinic Judaism and later Jewish orthodoxy, which generally rejected apocalyptic.

The rabbis devoted themselves above all to the study of the Torah and the oral tradition connected with it. They rejected apocalyptic because they believed that it was a direct inducement to the nationalistic Jewish rebellions which had failed so tragically, one of them leading to the fall of Jerusalem and the destruction of the second temple in AD 70 and the other, under the leadership of Bar Kochba in 132-135, having been violently suppressed by the emperor Hadrian.

In addition, apocalyptic had firm roots in the young Christian communities. The first Christians found that apocalyptic, with which they had perhaps grown up, provided a great many ideas and expectations to which they could evidently give or transfer direct Christian content. So we can see clearly that Christian ideas were later incorporated into existing apocalyptic traditions and writings. Moreover there is also a specifically Christian apocalyptic literature.

Taken together, all these factors explain the negative attitude of official Judaism towards apocalyptic. Only after a number of years have Jewish scholars too begun to devote themselves to an intensive study of this literature. On the other hand, we must not make the gulf between apocalyptic and orthodox rabbinic Judaism too wide. Although apocalyptic literature was rejected by the rabbis and therefore was not incorporated into the Tanach, the rabbis paid tribute to the traditions handed down by word of mouth in which apocalyptic ideas were common currency.[4]

On the basis of the derogatory attitude of orthodox Judaism, but above all under the influence of the study of history and the tradition of religion, German exegesis, at least until recently, has tended to see apocalyptic as a marginal phenomenon and a stepchild of Old Testament prophecy. Its origin is thought to be in Persia, in Babylonian mythology or in a broader Hellenistic and Oriental syncretism.[5] Therefore it is supposed that its influence on the New Testament was small and can virtually be left out of account.[6]

In the last twenty years there has been a change of opinion in many areas of German-speaking exegesis and theology. In Germany now apocalyptic is even revered as the mother of all Christian theology.[7]

In French-speaking circles the study of apocalyptic developed late.[8] Current interest in apocalyptic there sees the origin of apocalyptic in prophecy and finds a contextual rather than an essential difference between the two trends. It is generally assumed that apocalyptic had a particularly great influence, if not on Jesus himself, at least, beyond question, on the first generation of his followers.[9]

These different and often diametrically opposed interpretations of the meaning and influence which apocalyptic had on the writings of the New Testament are so striking that we must spend some time on these apocalyptic writings. Obviously we are doing this only in the light of the problems with which we are concerned in this book.[10]

II

FUTURE FOR HUMANITY

It is quite impossible to give a clear and systematic account of the ideas in apocalyptic. The writings come from various groups and traditions, from different periods, and are often written or compiled by very different authors. A single book sometimes contains a number of independent traditions which have nothing at all to do with one another, and even present conflicting views, but are skilfully woven together and then appear under the pseudonym of a single author. The fact that one and the same book contains contradictions at least indicates that these were not felt to be such by the person who composed the writing as a single volume. The apocalyptists did not proclaim a doctrine but offered illustrations as so many aspects of one great vision. They were not concerned with connected insights but with perspectives showing a reality which can never be grasped within the contours of firm concepts. The apocalyptists did not trouble to dispel the mists which lie over the future. They followed broken guidelines.

In what follows I shall try to indicate these broken lines with the aim of investigating whether what we have here are really ideas which are determinative for views of the future within the New Testament writings.

1. Belief in resurrection

All the apocalyptic writings presuppose the resurrection as a matter of course or speak explicitly of the resurrection event itself. Scholars sometimes differ in interpreting texts, but all recognize that these writings contain a belief in the resurrection.

Only the righteous rise

What we have seen in the books of Daniel and II Maccabees, that resurrection only happens to the righteous, is also the predominant view throughout apocalyptic literature.

Only the righteous are raised to participate in the life of the messianic kingdom to come (I Enoch 22.11; cf. 91.10; 92.3; 100.50). In this view the death of sinners is regarded as final. Their real punishment is that they are completely forgotten: 'The destruction of the sinner is for ever, and he shall not be remembered when the righteous is visited (by God). This is the portion of the sinners for ever. But they that fear the Lord shall rise to life eternal, and their life shall be in the light of the Lord, and shall come to an end no more' (Ps.Sol. 3.12-16; cf. 14.2-4; 15.13).

The same view can also be found in the Testaments of the Twelve

Patriarchs, in LAB 19.12; 21.4; 23.13; 51.4 and in II Bar. 30.1-5. It seems also to have been the view in the Qumran community.[11]

According to certain critics some texts from I Enoch 37-71 may be interpreted as a reference to a view which thinks in terms of the immediate resurrection of the righteous at death. Now they already live in heavenly dwellings with the Son of man and form a heavenly community around him. At the end of time this community will be made manifest by descending from heaven in order to experience the messianic kingdom on earth with the elect who have survived (cf. 39.4-13; 41.2; 48.1; 60.2,8; 61.6-14; 70.1-4; 71.5,16).[12]

According to LAB 50.7, too, dying is a progress from this world to God. There we also find that the man Moses now already lives with God (32.9).

In this connection the exaltation model plays a major role. That is the case in LAB 48.1ff. and above all in IV Ezra. There we read of the author himself: 'But you will be taken up from among men, and will remain with my son and with those who are like you until the times are ended . . . Then Ezra was caught up, and taken away to the place of those who were like him' (14.9.49; cf. 7.28). Evidently, a number of people have already been taken up to God, those who are like Ezra. Baruch is also told: 'Because you have incurred the fate of Zion, you will be preserved till the times are ended' (II Bar. 13.3; cf. 43.2; 46.7; 48.30; 76.2ff.).

Here I should recall that apocalyptic predominantly sees the resurrection as something which happens only to the just; according to certain texts they do not even need to wait for this event, since it takes place at death. Other texts use the model of exaltation to speak of a life over which death has no power.

In all this, the political context is determinative. Pious Jews who are faithful to the law are persecuted for their faith. Apocalyptists seek to encourage them and urge them to persevere. And so they make use of the model of resurrection and exaltation. Those who now fail to receive their due, exclusively and precisely because of their loyalty in belief, for the sake of their God, will have what they lack made good in the future. In view of the political situation, which is looked on realistically, this future can be conceived of only in transcendent, heavenly terms.

This faith is no tranquillizer, but an encouragement to persevere, to have courage, to remain true to God.

General resurrection

I have already commented that apocalyptists are not afraid of contradictions. So alongside this view we also find the view of a general
resurrection. In that case resurrection no longer has just a positive
content, as an entry into an eternal life, as a reward; resurrection is
now also necessarily thought of as recompense. Death and ultimate
oblivion are no longer sufficient punishment for sinners. The
unrighteous, too, will rise at the end of time to receive retribution:
'In those days the earth shall give back what was entrusted to it and
Sheol also shall give back what it received and hell shall give back
what it owes. For in those days he (the judge) shall choose the
righteous and holy from among them; for the day has come when
they are to be saved' (I Enoch 51.1f.). 'The earth shall restore those
who sleep in her, and the dust those who are at rest therein, and the
chambers shall restore the souls that were committed to them. And
the Most High shall be revealed upon the throne of judgment: then
comes the end and compassion shall pass away, and pity be far off,
and longsuffering withdrawn; but judgment alone shall remain,
truth shall stand, and faithfulness triumph. And recompense shall
follow and the reward be made manifest; deeds of righteousness
shall awake and deeds of iniquity shall not sleep. And then shall the
pit of torment appear, and over against it the place of refreshment;
the furnace of Gehenna shall be made manifest, and over against it
the Paradise of delight. Then shall the Most High say to the nations
that have been raised: Look now and see him whom you have denied,
whose commandments you have despised. Look now before you:
here delight and refreshment, there fire and torments. He will speak
these words to them on the day of judgment'(IV Ezra 7.32-38; cf.
LAB 3.10; II Bar. 42.7; 50.2). In the Testament of the Twelve Patriarchs, all the patriarchs only teach a resurrection of the righteous.
The Testament of Benjamin is an exception. According to this work,
first the patriarchs arise to take part in the earthly kingdom (10.6),
then the twelve sons of Jacob, each at the head of his own tribe
(10.7), and 'after that shall all men arise, some to glory and others to
shame' (10.8). In the New Testament the role of the twelve sons of
Jacob in the final judgment is assigned to the 'Twelve' among the disciples of Jesus (cf. Matt.19.28; Mark 10.29; Luke 18.29; 22.30).

The resurrection event is looked on quite generally as something
which takes place at the end of time, except in some texts which can-

not be ignored and which can be interpreted in terms of a resurrection at death. We should also remember the exaltation model.

If resurrection only takes place at the end of the times, we necessarily encounter ideas about an intermediary period between the death of the individual and the partial or general resurrection.

2. Between death and resurrection

In the canonical books of the Old Testament we read that all the dead went down to Sheol. There they all, without any distinction, led the same shadowy existence. This Sheol was a final state for everyone. That is no longer the case if one envisages a resurrection at the end of time. The kingdom of the dead then becomes an intermediary stage, a transitional state.

Almost all the apocalyptists describe this intermediary period in detail. Qumran seems to be the exception, perhaps because the end of time was thought to be so near that any speculation about an intermediary period seemed to be a superfluous luxury.

Retribution or recompense already plays a role in this intermediary period. According to I Enoch 22 all the dead remain in the underworld in four different caves. Three of these are completely dark; one is brightly lit and has a spring. Sinners remain in the dark caves and are tormented by a vicious thirst (there is a direct allusion to this in the story of poor Lazarus and the rich man, Luke 16.19-31, v.24). The righteous are refreshed in the illuminated cave. All the souls of the dead remain in one of these caves till the day of judgment. For the righteous this intermediary period ends with the resurrection. It is not immediately clear whether that is also the case for sinners. Perhaps their souls remain permanently in the dark caves of Sheol.

The author of the Testament of Abraham speaks of two gates through which the souls of the dead are brought in: 'This narrow gate is that of the righteous; it leads to eternal life and those who go through it enter paradise. The wide gate is that for sinners; this leads to destruction and to eternal punishment' (8.10f.; cf. Matt.7.13; Luke 13.24).

If reward or retribution come immediately after death, a last judgment is simply the final sealing of the fate of the souls in the underworld (cf. II Bar.30.4f.).

The abode of the souls

Apocalyptic literature often speaks of rooms or dwellings in which the souls of the righteous have their abode (I Enoch 39.4-13; 41.2; 61.6-13; 70.1-4; 71.26; LAB 23.13; 32.13; IV Ezra 4.35,41; 7.78, 101; II Bar. 21.22-24; 30.2).

In his farewell discourse Jesus alludes to the many dwellings in his Father's house where he is going to prepare a place for his disciples.

The 'underworld and the chambers of the souls are like a womb' (IV Ezra 4.41; cf. Luke 16.33, where it is said that on his death Lazarus is taken by the angels 'into Abraham's bosom'). They are above all places of rest. There the souls enjoy undisturbed rest, something that is not granted to the souls of sinners: 'Such souls shall not enter into habitations, but shall wander about henceforth in torture, ever grieving and sad' (IV Ezra 7.80).

That the chief thought is of rest for the souls of the righteous follows from the conception of death as sleep. We have seen that the Old Testament already had the ideal of going at death 'to sleep with one's fathers'.

The liturgy of the requiem has its origin in this literature. The Catholic doctrine of an individual judgment at death, of immediate reward or retribution, is prepared for here.

In fact the souls do not just rest in their rooms. They are rewarded and taken to God: 'When the decisive decree has gone forth from the Most High that man must die, as the soul from the body departs that it may return to him who gave it, to adore the glory of the Most High first of all . . . Of those who have kept the ways of the Most High this is the order, when they shall be separated from this mortal shell. Earlier, when they still lived in it, they painfully served the Most High, and were in jeopardy every hour, that they might observe the law of the Lawgiver perfectly. Therefore they have this promise: first of all they shall see with great joy the glory of him who receives them; then they shall rest in seven orders' (IV Ezra 7.78, 88-91).

All this applies only to the souls of the righteous. The souls of sinners go to the place of torture.

Hell and hell fire

This place of torture for souls is often called Gehenna (I Enoch 90.26ff.; IV Ezra 7.36; II Bar. 59.10; 85.13; and above all in rabbinic literature).[13] This word comes from the Hebrew Ge-hinnom, i.e. the

Valley of Hinnom. This was a place south of Jerusalem (so called in Josh.15.8; 18.16; II Chron.33.6; in another place it is called the valley of Ben Hinnom, the valley of the son of Hinnom: Jer.7.31f.; 19.6; 32.35; II Chron.28.3). This valley was thought to be cursed because children had once been sacrificed there, burnt in honour of Moloch (II Kings 16.3; 21.6; Jer.7.31; 19.6; 32.35). In Jer.7.32; 19.7, too, we learn that this valley is to become a place of judgment. There all the sins of Jerusalem will be punished, so that the valley of Ben Hinnom will be called :'the valley of slaughter'.

When we remember that Yahweh has an oven in Jerusalem (Isa.31.9) and that there is a place of cursing near to Jerusalem to which the inhabitants of this city go to see the condemned whose worm does not die and whose fire is not quenched (Isa.66.24), and when we further note the role of fire on the day of Yahweh, we can immediately understand how apocalyptic designated this valley an eternal place of torment, full of fire.

The New Testament also knows this place. Whereas apocalyptic speaks of a place of torment for souls, the New Testament gives the impression that the whole of a person can enter it (cf. Matt.5.22,29; 10.28; Mark 9.43; Luke 16.24). The historical origin of our term hell shows that in this context there is always mention of fire and flame: 'In those days they (the godless) shall be taken to a fiery abyss' (I Enoch 10.13): 'I saw how an abyss full of fire opened up in the midst of the earth . . . All were judged and thrown into this fiery maw' (I Enoch 100.9); 'Woe to you sinners, for you will burn in glowing fire' (I Enoch 103.8).

Christians are familiar with this imagery, but for a long time it was not always recognized that these are indeed images and not hard facts. The material I have summarized here relating to this imagery should finally prevent anyone from interpreting hell fire literally.

Repentance in the intermediate period

We already discovered in II Maccabees that prayer and sacrifice for the dead were thought to be meaningful. This view also appears in other apocalyptic literature. According to the Apocalypse of Moses angels pray for Adam (35), and even sun and moon intercede for him (36). In the Testament of Abraham we learn that souls are tested twice, once by fire and once by means of a balance. Furthermore the seer discovers a kind of intermediary class among souls. These are the souls of men whose merits and sins balance one another out. The prayers of the righteous for these souls can bring about and hasten their entry into eternal salvation (ch.14).

However, the majority of apocalyptists are convinced that no change is possible after death. That is expressed most sharply in the following text: 'There shall not here be again a place of repentance, nor a limit to the times, nor a duration for the hours, nor a change of ways, nor place for prayer, nor sending of petitions, nor receiving of knowledge, nor giving of love, nor place of repentance for the soul, nor supplication for offences, nor intercession of the fathers, nor prayer for the prophets, nor help of the righteous' (II Bar.85.12; cf. IV Ezra 7.102-15).

3. Apocalyptic anthropology

What I have said about rooms for souls and the torments of hell after death and before the resurrection will already have made it sufficiently clear that apocalyptic has quite a different anthropology from that of the Old Testament. Here the influence of Hellenism is very obvious: everywhere there is a distinction between soul and body.

There is repeated mention of souls as part of human beings, their spiritual element (LAB 23.13; 32.13; 33.4; 62.9; IV Ezra 4,35,41; 7.32, 87,80,88).

Although the term soul is sometimes used as a synonym for spirit, it cannot be denied that here we find the influence of Hellenistic dualism. Thus death is explicitly seen as a separation of soul and body (LAB 43,7; 44.10; IV Ezra 7,78,88,100).

However, that does not mean that the negative Hellenistic attitude towards the body was taken over as it stood. For the apocalyptists the body remains a gift of divine creation. Whenever we read that at death the soul may be separated from this mortal shell, it does not mean that people are happy to be able to shake off the body as something evil or bad, or to be allowed to leave it as a prison; it is an indication that those who served the Most High in this body did so only with great difficulty and were exposed to danger every hour (cf. IV Ezra 7.88f.). In other words, the difficulties lie not in bodily existence as such but in the historical circumstances which must be endured here on earth. The pious are so persecuted for their faithfulness in this earthly existence, in their bodily life, that they may long for death as liberation from bodily suffering, rather than from the body as such.

The fact of a hope for resurrection of the body, and the fact that the souls in their abodes are full of longing for the end of the world, when they will rise as human beings, is sufficient evidence that here we do not have a contempt for the body and the glorification of an immortal soul.

Nor is there any mention of a doctrine of an immortal soul; all hope is directed towards the physical resurrection.

The view of the resurrection body is dependent on the idea which the various apocalyptists have of the final kingdom of salvation. That is what this chapter is about.

If this final kingdom is imagined as life on earth, then the resurrection body is thought to be more physical and material. We find this idea in the earliest writings, though not only there. We have already found it in II Maccabees. In the Sibylline Oracles we read: 'Then God himself shall fashion the bones and ashes of men, and shall raise up mortals once more as they were before' (IV, 181f.).

If the final kingdom is thought to be transcendent, a life in heaven, then the resurrection body, too, is envisaged more in spiritual terms. At the resurrection 'the righteous and elect shall have been clothed with garments of glory. And these shall be the garments of life which come from the Lord of Spirits' (I Enoch 62.15f.). The author of II Baruch stresses very strongly that at the end of time the righteous will be raised from the dust of the earth and appear in the physical form in which they died, without any change in their outward appearance (50.2). The author obviously intends this to be apologetic: those who now deny the resurrection must, if they themselves survive to see the final judgment to come, be able to recognize the dead who are raised, so that they are really certain that they are risen. But after that, the text continues: 'Then shall the aspect of those who are condemned be afterwards changed, and the glory of those who are justified. For the aspect of those who now act wickedly shall become worse than it is, as they shall suffer torment. Also as for the glory of those who have now been justified in my law, who have had understanding in their life, and who have planted in their heart the root of wisdom, then their splendour shall be glorified in changes, and the form of their face shall be turned into the light of their beauty, that they may be able to acquire and receive the world which does not die, which is then promised to them' (51.1-3; cf. II Enoch 22.8f.)

This 'spiritual' body is often described as clothing. 'Go and strip Enoch of his earthly garments. Clothe him with the raiment of my glory' (II Enoch 22.8). It is also said that Enoch's body must be replaced with a heavenly body like that of the angels (II Enoch 22.9; cf. Matt.22.30; Mark 12.25; Luke 20.36). A connection is generally seen between the physical body and the spiritual body in which people will rise. This latter is depicted as a transformation of the former (I Enoch 108.11). It is the body, buried in the earth, which on the day of resurrection is raised to be a glorious body (cf. I Cor.15.42ff.). The author of II Baruch asks what the resurrection body will be like: 'Will they then again resume this form of the present and put on these entrammelling members . . . or will you change these things which were in the world as also the world itself' (49.3; cf. I Cor.15.35). We have already heard the answer. People rise in exactly the same form as they had when they died, and even old physical deformations or other typical characteristics will be clearly recognizable (cf. Matt. 5.29f.; Matt. 18.8f; Mark 9.43-46). Once the judgment has been given, however, the bodies of the righteous will be gradually transformed into purely spiritual bodies.

However, this spiritual body is clearly thought of as the physical body. Enoch's spiritual body needs no food, nor anything else from this earth (II Enoch 56.2). As we have already seen, he is like an angel. But when he returns to earth for a period of thirty days, evidently in his heavenly body, he is not only recognized by his friends but allows the whole assembly to approach him and to kiss him (64.2f.; cf. John 20.27). In other words, the spiritual body is the physical body, but completely adapted to another environment, a new world, transformed reality, heaven.

Thus the conception of the resurrection body is closely bound up with the view that people have of this world and history. In the view of some apocalyptists the final kingdom will come on this earth, whereas according to others this world has become so corrupt through sin that it must disappear completely. Not because this material world is intrinsically bad, but because the sin of man has utterly spoilt it. Therefore people look longingly to the end of this historical world and the beginning of a new heaven and a new earth.

III

FUTURE FOR THE WORLD

When the apocalyptists dream of a new earth and a new heaven, i.e. when they dream of everything being made new, they fill out this longing for everything to be different in various ways.

The content of their longing is not directly, nor always, a transcendent reality, heaven, but usually relates to a completely different phase of our history. Many long to be able to begin a second life; but for that to be possible, a completely different scene is needed. The world must be transformed.

1. On earth or in heaven?

It cannot be said outright that apocalyptic has only one pattern of expectation. Usually a quite different, a quite new future is expected. This can come about either on a radically changed earth or in heaven.

The author of I Enoch dreams of a messianic kingdom on earth. Israel's enemies must first be completely exterminated, and the despised and scattered Jews must be brought together again. The temple will be rebuilt in all its splendour in a free and prosperous Jerusalem. Then follows the resurrection of the righteous who, together with the survivors, will enjoy the blessings of a patriarchal age: 'Let the plant of righteousness and truth appear . . . the works of righteousness and truth shall be planted in truth and joy for evermore. And then shall all the righteous escape and shall live till they beget thousands of children, and all the days of their youth and their old age shall they complete in peace. And then shall the whole earth be tilled in righteousness . . . And all desirable trees shall be planted on it, and they shall plant vines on it; and the vine which they plant shall yield wine in abundance . . . And the earth shall be cleansed from all defilement, and from all sin, and from all punishment, and from all torment . . . throughout all the generations of men' (10.16-22). This description makes it clear that this longed-for final kingdom is sometimes called Paradise, with a clear allusion to 'earthly paradise' which is the way in which the Greek translation renders

Garden of Eden. The New Testament also often speaks of paradise in this sense (cf. Luke 23.43; II Cor.12.3; Rev.2.7).

This vision of Enoch's could just as well have been portrayed by an Old Testament prophet. Not all apocalyptists look in this direction. For some of them, this earth, with all its evil, its suffering and grief and sin, is so completely corrupt that it can never be a suitable place for the messianic kingdom to come.

So in another tradition of the same book of Enoch it is first taken for granted that the earth has to be completely changed. Quite simply, there must be a new world. This world comes from above. At the end of time the messiah will come from heaven to earth with the righteous who are already with him, in order to change this earth completely. Heaven and earth become one. In this context, for the first time this world is presented as the world of unrighteousness and sin. The new world will therefore be quite different from this world (cf. I Enoch 37-71).

Slavonic Enoch offers another approach. Here the final consummation clearly takes place in heaven as a transcendent reality. We find the earliest confirmation that heaven is the ultimate future in this work (II Enoch 65.8-10). In reality this notion is a direct inference from the notion of souls, or even of people enjoying heavenly blessedness immediately after their death or at their exaltation. This is the least that they can accept at the final time of salvation, and it is never achieved on earth. If the happiness of souls begins in heaven after their death, we must suppose that universal and ultimate blessedness takes place in heaven.

So here we quite clearly find a different view of reality from that to which we have been accustomed by Jewish thought, which envisaged reality more as history. The future was something still to come. In II Enoch, reality is not thought of in successive stages but in various levels. There is a lower and an upper level: a lower reality, earth, and an upper reality, heaven. Now and then we get a glimmer of this conception in the writings which we have analysed so far, but here we find it clearly formulated for the first time.

The author of II Baruch begins from a compromise. First of all there is a messianic kingdom on earth, and then an eternal heavenly kingdom. It is said of the Messiah: 'His kingdom will last for ever, until the world of corruption comes to an end' (40.3). 'That time is the consummation of that which is corruptible and the beginning of that which is not corruptible' (74.2; cf. I Cor.15.42, 50; Rom.8.21). Incorruptible life is lived out in heaven.

IV Ezra also speaks of an eternal kingdom of the Messiah on earth, which is followed by an eternal kingdom either on a transformed earth or in heaven. This latter cannot be established so simply. God has created two ages: this age or period (in Latin *saeculum*) is transitory, and the age to come is not. The time of the Messiah and the last judgment are described like this: 'For behold, the days come, and it shall be when the signs which I have foretold shall come to pass, then the city that is now invisible shall appear, and the land which is now concealed shall be seen. And anyone who is delivered from the predicted evils, the same shall see my wonders. For my Son the Messiah shall be revealed, together with those who are with him, and shall rejoice the survivors four hundred years. And it shall be, after these years, that my Son the Messiah, shall die, and all in whom there is human breath. Then shall the world be turned into the primaeval silence seven days, like as at the first beginnings; so that no man is left. And it shall be after seven days that the age which is not yet awake shall be roused, and that which is corruptible shall perish. And the earth shall restore those that sleep in her, and the dust those that are at rest therein, and the chambers shall restore the souls committed to them. And the Most High shall be revealed upon the seat of judgment' (7.26-33).

Mention of a messianic kingdom established by the Messiah on earth who is accompanied by those who were already his followers immediately reminds us that heaven is at present an invisible city which descends to the earth. This allows us to make a direct connection between these views and what the Revelation of St John says about the thousand-year kingdom with its famous first resurrection (20.1-6).

All this emerges from the fact that apocalyptic offers two rival views of the world. On the one hand, the apocalyptists are heirs of the optimism about creation found in the Old Testament, so that they talk of a change in this world, a transformation of this creation in the age to come (I Enoch 45.5ff.; II Bar. 49.2), a renewal of the world (IV Ezra 7.75; II Bar. 32.6), or simply of 'a new creation' (I Enoch 72.1; Jub.1.29; 4.26; IV Ezra 7.75). On the other hand, they are pessimistic about everything that exists, not because it is evil in itself, but because the original goodness in everything has been vitiated by the sin of humankind. Therefore all that exists must be destroyed before something completely different can begin (I Enoch 91.14; IV Ezra 7.39-42).

Here we find two different views of reality. For the most part, reality is still thought of as history, as event, but under the influence of Hellenism to some degree it is increasingly seen as consisting of various parts or spheres. In the former case we have two eras following each other in time, and in the latter two worlds, one visible and transitory, and the other at present still invisible, hidden, but permanent.[14]

These two different views of reality, each of which has its own terminology – one is expressed in historical categories and the other in ontological categories – are not always clearly distinguished, whether in this apocalyptic literature, the writings of the New Testament or in the history of theology. Thus the doctrine of two aeons can relate either to two successive stages of history or to two completely different worlds. In this latter case the one world can already penetrate the other, visible world; or the existing world which is now already hidden is thought of as a world which is to be manifest in the future, after or at the end of the world, which now exists visibly.

We shall come up against this doctrine of two ages time and again in the New Testament: this age (Matt.12.32; Luke 16.8; 20.34; Rom.12.2; I Cor.1.20; 2.6,8; 3.18; II Cor.4.4; Eph.1.21); the present world (I Tim.6.17; II Tim.4.10; Titus 2.12); the present evil age (Gal.1.4); this world (I Cor.3.19; 5.10; 7.31; John 8.23; 11.9; 12.25,31; 16.11; 18.36; I John 4.17); the age of this world (Eph.2.2); this time (Mark 10.30; Luke 18.30); the present time (Rom.3.26; 8.18; 11.5; II Cor.8.13); the coming age (Matt.12.32; Eph.1.21; 2.7); the age to come (Mark 10.30; Luke 18.30; Heb.6.5).

2. When and how?

All apocalyptic writings share the conviction that the final time of salvation is near – no matter how it may be imagined, whether on earth or in a transcendent heaven. All apocalyptists, including the community of Qumran, are convinced that they live at the beginning of the end-time.

Often this end-time is immediately preceded by a holy war in which God takes vengeance on the enemies of Israel (cf. I Enoch 91.12; 95.3-7; Jub.23.30; 1QM 12.10-143). In the War Rule of Qumran the final battle is portrayed as a forty-year war between Israel and the nations of the world; finally the sinful world itself is annihilated through all kinds of natural catastrophes.

It is not so easy to decide what is meant in these writings when they talk about the end of days and 'the world to come'. These terms are not always used with one and the same meaning. Their content must in each case be read out of the context in which they appear. Thus they can refer both to the end of this world generally and also to the end-period proper, interspersed with war and devastation, and the period of salvation which follows. This confusion in terminology is connected with the two views of reality which I have already mentioned and which are constantly intertwined.

The end of the world is characterized not only by divine vengeance but also by human cruelty and the increasing activity of Satan. The whole world is caught up in this process: 'In the days of the sinners the days shall become shorter . . . all things on earth shall change and shall not appear in season; no rain shall come, the heaven will retain it' (I Enoch 80.2); 'The earth shall perish, for there will be neither seed nor wine nor oil, because the action of men is full of faithlessness' (Jub.23.18). According to one work from Qumran our earth will be annihilated by earthquake, fire and storm: 'The foundations of the wall shall rock like a ship upon the face of the waters; the heavens shall roar with a noise of roaring, and those who dwell in the dust as well as those who sail the seas shall be appalled by the roaring of the waters' (1 QH 3.13). 'While the rope beat down in judgment and a destiny of wrath fell upon the abandoned and a venting of fury upon the cunning. It was a time of the wrath of all Satan and the bonds of death tightened without any escape. The torrents of Satan shall reach to all sides of the world. In all their channels a consuming fire shall destroy every tree, green and barren, on their banks; unto the end of their course it shall scourge with flames of fire, and shall consume the foundations of the earth and the expanse of dry land. The bases of the mountains shall blaze and the roots of the rocks shall turn to torrents of pitch; it shall devour as far as the great Abyss. The torrents of Satan shall break into Abaddon, and the deeps of the Abyss shall groan amid the roar of heaving mud. The land shall cry out because of the calamity fallen upon the world, and all its deeps shall howl. And all those upon it shall rave and shall perish amid the great misfortune. For God shall sound his mighty voice, and his holy abode shall thunder with the truth of his glory' (1QH 3.27-34).

Various catastrophes like wars, famine, disease, deformed births, anomalies in nature, cosmic terror affecting both the heavenly bodies and the earth are also seen as the birth-pangs of the new era or as messianic woes (I Enoch 80.4-7; IV Ezra 5.4ff.; 6.13-16; II Bar.70.8), very much in line with the metaphorical language of the Old Testament (cf. e.g. Isa.13.8ff.; 66.8; Micah 4.9ff.). As birth-pangs, these cosmic phenomena are only the prelude to the imminent shift of the aeons and do not necessarily coincide with the final event itself.

The apocalyptic writers used this metaphorical language to instil courage into believers. In the midst of the catastrophic experiences of Jewish history, in the midst of the restrictions on the present, they wanted to show a glimmer of light: it will not be long, the end is in sight. This end will completely overthrow existing power politics. There is no need to despair because experiences in the present are so desperately terrifying. All the misery experienced at present is a symptom of the dawn of a coming age which is full of promise. The greater the wickedness of the present age, the greater the measure which God has determined, the nearer are the end and the new beginning.

IV

CONCLUSION

After this short analysis it seems to me that apocalyptic is very much in line with Old Testament, or more specifically prophetic eschatology. Both lines express one and the same faith in different situations. They are about faith in God who remains true to the covenant which he has made with his people. His grace lasts for ever.

In the age of prophecy one could still hope and trust that God's faithfulness to the covenant would be realized on this earth, in the history of the people. Later, after the exile, when the hoped-for new prosperity did not come about, when people felt treachery in their own ranks, when they were persecuted for their beliefs, they could hardly in all honesty continue to sustain this hope for restoration. In a quite hopeless political situation Israel's faith could only overcome its profoundest crisis and preserve its identity in faith if it believed in another phase of history, another world. If people had hoped in vain for the fulfilment of the covenant here on this earth, then Israel overcame the temptation to complete despair by arguing for belief in a

God who had as it were had committed himself, his word and his covenant to realizing this covenant in a completely different, transcendent way.

Here the apocalyptic writers are clearly inspired by religious ideas from Persia, where people had long been familiar with this dualism between the visible world which was evil in itself and an invisible world of sheer goodness which was already in existence. It is also easy to demonstrate Hellenistic influences. However, neither of these in any way vitiates the authenticity and the identity of Jewish faith, which seeks to preserve itself with the help of alien material.

Religious feeling is lived out within a particular culture. No individual culture can be exactly marked out from other cultural streams of the same period and on the same continent. Cultures penetrate one another. Alien influences also determine the identity of one's own culture, by the way in which they are integrated and assimilated, or by the way in which people dissociate themselves from them.

Early Judaism was confronted with new facts, with another world, with other cultures, and this compelled it to probe for deeper insight into its own faith. In this period, belief in creation and the covenant were enriched with new insights. Everything that happens takes its place and its meaning from this twofold perspective.

No creature is eternal. Nor is any people. Transitoriness and decay are part and parcel of creaturely existence. But God has made his people for happiness. If people did not find this happiness in history, on earth, they dared to believe in the inventive power of the faithfulness of God. They believed that on the basis of his creative omnipotence he could take a new initiative to give his people this promised happiness. If not now, then later; if not here, then elsewhere.

This belief in the omnipotence of the Creator who puts his omnipotence at the service of his faithfulness to the covenant led people to think in faith of a new aeon, a new earth and a new heaven, a paradise and an eternal life.

People arrived at this trust only by reflecting in faith on God's faithfulness to the covenant, taking account of the harsh historical facts which made this confidence quite incredible. In human beings as they are there is no grain of immortality, no iota of eternity. Only God is eternal. And so is his grace.

God lets his people share in his own eternal life. That has consequences for the history of this people and for the world in which it lives. On the basis of the most authentic biblical belief in creation one can assume that neither natural forces nor man are alone in governing history and the course of the world. God himself is the Lord of history, on which he continually brings his creative action to bear. He directs his whole creation towards the consummation that he wills for it, resolving matters with sovereign power.

The apocalyptists, who convey all this to us as a message, are also the first to think through Jewish belief in a universal and cosmic way. Furthermore, they succeed in presenting a view of unity in which there is scope for both an individual and a universal future.

This is really expressed in apocalyptic literature. This literature stresses the transitory character of humanity, history and the cosmos and therefore puts questions to God. More than anywhere else attention is paid here to human impotence, those who are shattered by history, cripples, failures, the dead. God's deliverance and faithfulness to the covenant are particularly associated with this kind of people, with these situations, with these conditions. The questions of Job are taken up again here, as are the problems raised by Koheleth, but this happens from a situation of extreme distress which allows of no more illusions and from the desperate situation of a whole people of believers. Apocalyptic represents the victory of the faith of Israel over extreme fear and dismay.

Of course this believing trust is expressed in concepts, symbols and images peculiar to its time. The conceptions which express what is hoped for are evidently part of their time and culture. That emerges clearly from the cosmological conceptions used, which apocalyptic shares with the Old Testament and almost all the world of antiquity. These are the ideas of people who have no notion of abstraction but think everything through in quite specific, material, corporeal terms.

Apocalyptists are not philosophers. They do not think in general categories. They are more impressionists. Consequently we find no doctrine in apocalyptic, far less agreement on any doctrine. Nothing in these conceptions is therefore binding and obligatory as such. They are different attempts to lend credibility to a belief in the future for people of this world, living in this history, taking account of the facts and the real possibilities, including the transitoriness of the cosmos as creation and the ultimate failure of those who make history.

I have dealt with all this in quite some detail because I am convinced that we can only understand the New Testament when we read it against this apocalyptic background. For the most part apocalyptic determines the climate of faith at the time of the preaching of

Jesus and in the period when the New Testament books were written.

I have deliberately devoted a great deal of attention to the different conceptions of one and the same apocalyptic faith which cannot be put over a common denominator. This has perhaps made it clear that not one of these conceptions may be regarded as binding on our faith. This insight is enormously important. For we shall find a number of these conceptions again in the New Testament. From there they made their way into church tradition and its doctrinal statements, into theology, spirituality and popular belief. But did that as a result give them a binding character? Did that make them compulsory teaching?

C. New Testament Insights

The New Testament books were written in the period of Jewish apocalyptic. Therefore the influence of apocalyptic ideas can without question be traced in the New Testament. Attempts to minimalize this influence or even to seek to ignore it can only be made on the basis of prejudiced dogmatic views or an irrational antipathy to apocalyptic, nurtured by misunderstanding. An unprejudiced reading of the New Testament immediately makes it clear that these works follow the line of contemporary apocalyptic.

We find three elements of apocalyptic expectation in the New Testament: confidence in being alive at the dawn of the end-time, belief in the resurrection of the dead, and the universal and cosmic dimensions of human hope. These three aspects are elements in our investigations of New Testament eschatology.

I

THE DAWN OF THE END-TIME

Almost all the New Testament authors believe that the end of the world is near, and that there will soon be a new world, a new aeon, a new heaven and a new earth. In this context Jesus usually speaks of the kingdom of God. In itself this is not a typical apocalyptic concept. It is the rule of God over his people, over all creation. This rule is announced and expected as an intervention by God in history which can be perceived in human experiences of happiness as liberation, life, joy, redemption and peace. However, in the proclamation of Jesus the concept also has an apocalyptic colouring in that the kingdom marks the end of the existing world and introduces a completely new age. Rudolf Bultmann claims – I believe rightly – that the intervention of God as ruler is 'an eschatological concept. It means the regime of God which will destroy the present course of the world, wipe out the contra-divine, Satanic power under which the present world groans – and thereby, terminating all pain and sorrow, bring in salvation for the people of God which awaits the fulfilment of the prophets' promises. The coming of God's reign is a miraculous event, which will be brought about by God alone without the help of men.'[1]

1. 'The time is fulfilled, and the kingdom of God is at hand' (Mark 1.15)

Mark sums up the proclamation and appearance of Jesus in programmatic fashion when he makes Jesus say: 'The time is fulfilled and the kingdom of God is at hand; repent, and believe in the gospel' (1.15). The real content of this message relates to the kingdom of God. As we shall see later, Jesus has something to do with it.[2] The question now is whether this kingdom of God as Jesus presents it also has an apocalyptic content. Is the statement that the time is fulfilled and the kingdom at hand also to be understood literally? In other words, does Jesus think that the end of the world will follow very soon?

Some commentators have given a positive answer to this question, referring to the so-called sayings about the end, i.e. sayings of Jesus which seem to indicate that he expected an imminent end to the world (cf. Matt.10.23; Mark 9.1; 13.30). The sayings of Jesus about this generation as the last generation on the earth (cf. Matt.11.16; 12.41,45; 23.36; Mark 8.12; Luke 11.30; 17.25) seem to point in the same direction. Today people are more inclined to interpret such sayings as consolation or encouragement addressed to a disappointed community which has long been hopefully expecting the end of the world and is now told to be patient; it cannot be much longer, the end of the world will come at least in this generation. [3]

It is extremely difficult to establish precisely which words go back to the historical Jesus himself and which were attributed to him by the community. Any statement by Jesus which refers to an imminent event, whether this is the kingdom of heaven or the kingdom of God (Matt.10.7; Mark 1.15; 9.1; Luke 17.20; 21.31; 22.18) or the coming of the Son of man (Matt.10.23; 16.27f.; 25.31; Mark 8.38; 13.26; 14.62; Luke 18.8) or the day of the Son of man (Matt.25.13; Mark 13.32; Luke 17.24,26,30; 21.34f.) – any of these sayings has to be investigated by criteria which are hard to lay down and to use, if we are to establish whether a saying goes back to the historical Jesus or is an addition and an interpretation by the early Christian community.

Exegetes and theologians still have great difficulties over the problem of the expectation of an imminent end. There is considerable disagreement as to whether Jesus himself dismissed an imminent end to the world or envisaged an imminent coming of the Son of man[4] – a typical apocalyptic figure who is mentioned for the first time in Dan.7.13f. and plays a great part in I Enoch 37-71.[5] At all events it is clear that there are hesitations about attributing this apocalyptic expectation to Jesus himself. Not only are dogmatic theologians cautious because of their difficulty in assimilating the fact that Jesus might have been wrong into their theological systems,[6] but many exegetes try to preserve Jesus from any taint of apocalyptic. In my view this latter approach stems from an irresponsibly negative attitude to apocalyptic.

It can hardly be denied that almost all New Testament writings on this level display marked apocalyptic colouring. The claim of some exegetes that apocalyptic took on a new lease of life only as a result of the resurrection of Jesus and the expectation of his coming in glory or his parousia seems difficult to substantiate. I believe that the expectation of an imminent and final saving intervention by God in the apocalyptic sense determines the whole atmosphere of the proclamation and appearance of Jesus. In my view this is quite evident from the sending out of the disciples (Matt. 9.35-11.1; Mark 6.6-13; Luke 9.1-6; 10.1-20). Here Jesus commands them to proclaim in every town and city that the kingdom of God is at hand. They are to lose no time, not even by greeting anyone on the way (Luke 10.4). If they are not welcome, they are not to persist but quickly to move on (Matt.10.14); they must not even spend time making preparations for their journey (Matt.10.9f.) since they will not have gone through the cities of Israel before the coming of the Son of man (Matt.10.23). That Jesus is convinced that the proclamation of the kingdom of God is extremely urgent because it is so near follows from the strict demands which he makes on the men who want to follow him as disciples on his preaching journeys (e.g. Luke 9.57-62). These requirements are not absolute demands on those who want to inherit the kingdom of God, but conditions for following Jesus as the one who proclaims the imminent kingdom of God.

Jesus proclaims that the kingdom of God is now actually present in and with his person, because he drives out devils by the finger of God (Luke 11.20), and because his disciples can hear and see that in him the prophecy of Isaiah is now fulfilled, according to which the blind see and the lame walk, the lepers are cleansed and the deaf hear, the dead are raised up and the poor have the good news proclaimed to them (Luke 7.22). This does not alter the fact that he also expects the revelation of the kingdom of God 'with power' (Mark 9.1). So he can also make his disciples pray for the coming of this kingdom (Luke 11.2-4) and can promise them that if they ask for it persistently their prayers will be answered very soon (Luke 18.2-8). The tension involved in the claim that the kingdom of God has already come but has not yet been fully revealed is also expressed in the paradoxical situations which are expressed in the so-called parables of the kingdom (Matt.13.33; Mark 4.26-28, 30-32). Even now, in and through Jesus, the kingdom of God is present, but in its almost imperceptible beginnings, in signs. It is like the seed and the leaven. However, this present bears the sure promise of the coming of the second phase of this kingdom, its revelation in full glory and splendour, which can be compared with the full harvest.

That Jesus himself was already instrumental in bringing about the dawn of the kingdom of God could strengthen his conviction that the complete revelation of the kingdom would not be long in coming. For that very reason, he can bless the poor, those who hunger and those who weep (Luke 6.20f.), since with the coming of the kingdom soon everything will be different for the very people who are hearing him in Palestine. In the parable of the fig tree Jesus makes it clear that the signs which he does and through which he makes the kingdom of God dawn by his presence indicate that the revelation of this kingdom in power cannot be far off (Mark 13.28f.). Originally 'these things' which are to happen and to show that the end is near were not among the cosmic catastrophes mentioned in the present text but were among the mighty acts of Jesus as mentioned in Luke 7.22.[7]

There are those who like to stress that Jesus expressly affirmed that he himself did not know the day of judgment: 'But of that day and that hour no one knows, not even the angels in heaven, not the Son but only the Father' (Mark 13.32; cf. Matt.24.36). This day is in fact the day of judgment on the world, 'the day of the Son of man' (Mark 13.26; cf. Luke 17.24,26,30ff.). Great stress is laid on ignorance on the part of Jesus in order to demonstrate that Jesus had no connection with apocalyptic, which was all too definite about the end. This is to forget that despite all the detailed descriptions of the end of the world, many apocalyptic authors say that its date is unknown. 'This is a typical piece of apocalyptic doctrine which stresses that the expectation of an imminent end of the world is a necessary element in the attitude of believers; it does not interpret away this expectation, as does modern theological reflection. The theologoumenon of the unknown date occurs throughout apocalyptic literature between 200 BC and AD 100 and is a central feature. Moreover it is specifically connected with the expectation of an imminent end of the world.'[8]

It is quite possible that until shortly before his death Jesus supposed that the prophecy of the imminent coming of the kingdom of God would be fulfilled. According to Mark's version of the last supper, Jesus expressly connects his death with the coming kingdom of God: 'I shall not drink again of the fruit of the vine until that day when I drink it new in the kingdom of God' (14.25; cf. Luke 22.16,18). According to the revision of this text which we find in the version by Matthew, not only Jesus personally but also his disciples will experience this kingdom of God after his death: 'I tell you I shall not drink again of this fruit of the vine until that day when I drink it new with you in my Father's kingdom' (26.29).

I therefore think that we have good reason for supposing that Jesus himself expected an imminent end to the world.

However, to conclude from all this that Jesus was therefore wrong seems to me to be a basic misunderstanding of his preaching. Jesus nowhere taught an imminent end to the world as such. He does not take any teaching about the kingdom of God itself beyond the point of the arrival of this kingdom. Jesus proclaims the kingdom of God; in and through his proclamation and his activity, in and through his person, now, he allows God to rule, in an abundance of goodness, of righteousness, of grace and love. Jesus does not give any new teaching about the kingdom of God, nor present any theory about the kingdom of heaven; he himself puts into practice an existing view of the rule of God.

He allows God to rule in quite specific situations. He liberates men in the name and the power of God. Nothing and no one keeps him from that: neither law, nor sabbath, nor tradition. He has eyes and heart only for the injured man who lies between Jerusalem and Jericho (cf. Luke 10.10-37); this is how he brings in the kingdom of God.

It has to do only with Jesus: the liberating and redeeming rule of God in the presence of Jesus' proclamation and his practice.

Of course Jesus does this in the apocalyptic context of his time. It is natural that he should express himself in categories which clearly were customary in his contemporary cultural and religious environment. In these the categories of 'time' and 'future', understood in a normal linear sense, occupy a well-defined place. The fact that Jesus thinks and expresses himself in patterns, imagery, concepts and views of his own time does not mean in any way that he makes these *as such* the content of his proclamation. We must look for the special character of the proclamation of Jesus in what he himself says or causes to be expressed within existing models of thought. Jesus proclaims and brings a God whose love for humankind is unbounded. He shows God's absolute transcendence in all its clarity. God cannot be comprehended. Nothing can describe him. He transcends all conceptions and all expectations. He is always greater, more, further. For God, nothing is impossible (Luke 1.37).

Jesus proclaims and introduces God as the end, the consummation of all things, a new beginning for all that seemed utterly lost. For Jesus God is always future, for everyone in all circumstances.

It goes without saying that Jesus expressed all this and made it clear in apocalyptic imagery and metaphor. He is a man of his time, a human being like other human beings in all things, sin excepted. Possible error belongs among the possibilities of this real humanity. But as I have said, Jesus never made his own personal conviction on this level the content of his proclamation.

Those who want to object that as God Jesus clearly knew that the end of the world was not near, will probably suppose that his Godhead lies alongside, apart from or above his humanity. But that is not the case. Jesus was God as man. He is God in human form.

Perhaps we can only communicate this insight convincingly in a somewhat naive way by pointing out that if Jesus himself knew that the end of the world was still a long way off, he evidently did not trouble to dispel the illusions of his immediate disciples. We shall in fact see that his disciples firmly believed that the world would end soon, and that they connected this with the parousia of their Lord.

2. The coming of the Son of man

As I have said, there is considerable disagreement among exegetes over the question whether Jesus himself expected an imminent end to the world. However, there is a much greater consensus in affirming the fact that for a generation after Jesus' death and resurrection his disciples longingly looked for the coming of their Lord in glory and power.

Whether or not they are to be attributed to the historical Jesus, as the creation of the early Christian community the sayings about the end which I mentioned earlier clearly show that in these circles, despite an initial disappointment, there were hopes for the revelation of the final kingdom of God which would put an end to this world's history. Jesus' disciples expressly rooted this hope in the resurrection event and the glorification which Jesus experienced.

The synoptic tradition

Differing expectations of the coming of the Lord in glory and power are to be found in different strata of the tradition which we can distinguish in the Synoptic Gospels. Some see the basis of this expectation in a belief in the glorification of Jesus at his death; others see it in the resurrection of the historical Jesus; yet others in the expectation of the coming Son of man with whom Jesus is identified and who was to come at the end of time to pass judgment on this earth and on human history.

In the Q tradition[9] the Jesus who is exalted and glorified at his death is the Son of man who is to come soon. To begin with in this tradition, people seem to have been so preoccupied with the imminent end of the world that they no longer felt themselves to be part of this world. It was no longer worth bothering with. Here the apocalyptic mentality comes through very strongly.

Later, also within this Q tradition, future expectations were increasingly motivated by the past, by the experiences which people had had of the historical Jesus. That will have come about as a result of the stimulus provided by the Mark tradition. This tradition found a hearing because even within the Q tradition people had to deal with the problems caused by the continued delay of the coming of the Son of man.

There are allusions to this problem in the so-called parousia-parables: the parable of the burglar (Matt.24.43f.; Luke 12.39f.); the parable of the watchful householder (Matt.24.45-51; Luke 12.31-46); the parable of the ten talents (Matt.25.14-30; Luke 19.12-27); and the parable of the flood and the fire and brimstone (Luke 17.26-30). These parables are meant to help believers to react prop-

erly to the delay in the coming of the Lord. In this situation the right
attitude is watchfulness: the Lord can come at any time. Caution is
also necessary, so that people are not too easily led astray into premature identification.

Luke's own version of these parables seems at first sight to play
down the imminence of the parousia in comparison with the Q tradition.[10] However, one can argue that in Luke the hopeful expectation
of an imminent parousia is quite simply sublimated into a constant
readiness for this future. Constant readiness is a consistent conclusion drawn from the conviction that the Lord will come soon.

In Acts, too, Luke continues to expect an imminent coming of the
Lord. The account of the ascension has marked apocalyptic colouring, and the ascension itself is described with the familiar exaltation
model. Pious men are taken up to God not only as an immediate reward for their righteous life but also because God wants to keep
them near him so that he can send them out later on a particular commission (cf. Acts 3.19-21). The account itself seeks to demonstrate
that the disciples have become convinced that Jesus now lives with
the Father, that he will not come immediately, that the time of the
church has now dawned, a time in which the spirit of Jesus is actively
present. In his power the disciples must now bear witness in Jerusalem, throughout Judaea and Samaria, and to the ends of the earth.
However, this does not do away with the idea of the parousia. The
Jesus who has been taken away from the disciples and transported
into heaven, will come again in the same way as they have seen him
go to heaven (Acts 1.4-11). The horizontal parousia, i.e. the expectation of the coming of Jesus in the future, is here given a new, vertical dimension. The glorified Lord works in and through his Spirit in
the present. But this exalted figure is immediately seen as the one who
comes. Because he will return he is glorified. In his glorified state he
influences the present, and will give it a future which he himself will
finally implement when he comes. [11]

We clearly find the same argument in Acts 3.19-21 and in the mission sermons of both Peter (10.42) and Paul (17.31).

The expectation of the coming Son of Man also plays a central role
in the Marcan tradition. Mark makes a firm connection between the
earthly, above all the suffering, Jesus and the parousia (8.27-9.8;
10.32-40). He makes no mention of any activity of the glorified but
hidden Christ in the present. His hope lies in the past appearance of
the historical Jesus and in the confidence that this same Jesus will
soon return as Son of man, even in this generation: 'For whoever is

ashamed of me and of my words in this adulterous and sinful generation, of him will the Son of man also be ashamed, when he comes in
the glory of his Father with the holy angels. And he said to them:
"Truly, I say to you, there are some standing here who will not taste
death before they see the kingdom of God come with power" '
(8.38-9.1).

Paul's view

Before we investigate the special position of St John, we must first
investigate what the other New Testament writers say. We begin
with Paul.

Paul's eschatology is characterized by an intensive and tense expectation of an imminent parousia. To begin with, Paul is firmly convinced that he himself will live to experience the coming of the Lord
(I Thess.4.15-17). Union with the glorified Lord is the real content of
Paul's eschatological hope.[12] Paul describes this hope in I Thessalonians in an utterly apocalyptic scheme: the Lord will descend from
heaven, the dead will be raised, the living – among whom Paul includes himself – will be caught up into the air in a flash, on the clouds
along with the risen dead, to meet the Lord, and so they will be for
ever with the Lord.

The parousia is also called the day of the Lord. On this day the
salvation which is already given by the cross and resurrection of
Christ is fully and finally manifest (I Thess.5.1-11; Rom.13.11-14).
It is also a day of judgment (Rom.2.5ff., 16; I Cor. 3.13-15), which
as such, from the perspective of apocalyptic, must be understood as
a day which brings to an end a world and a history dominated by sin.
This day is the ultimate goal of all Christian striving and of the whole
of Christian existence (I Cor. 1.8; 5.5; II Cor.1.14; Phil.1.6,20;
2.16).

In true apocalyptic fashion, Paul refuses to speculate on the time
and the hour. It comes like a thief in the night (I Thess. 5.1f.). People
must be on their guard. At all events, the end cannot be far off. Paul
is convinced of this not only in his earliest writings; he has the same
expectations in I Cor.1.7-9. There Paul gives the expectation of an
imminent end to the world as the motive for a celibate life. The time
has become short (I Cor.7.29); hard times have dawned (7.26), in
other words, the apocalyptic birth pangs have already begun. Christians are not to add to this suffering by taking on the cares that married life brings. In the same letter, Paul also says explicitly: 'Lo! I tell

you a mystery. We shall not all sleep, but we shall all be changed, in a moment, in the twinkling of an eye, at the last trumpet. For the trumpet will sound, and the dead will be raised imperishable, and we shall be changed' (15.51f.). So here Paul is just as sure as in I Thessalonians of the coming of the Lord in his lifetime. He will be changed as a living man, for only when one is changed can one inherit the kingdom of God (15.54).

The whole of Paul's ethic is governed by this expectation of the parousia. Christians are not to be conformed to this world. It is not worth the trouble. Therefore: 'Let those who have wives live as though they had none, and those who rejoice as though they were not rejoicing, and those who buy as though they had no goods, and those who deal with the world as though they had no dealings with it. For the form of this world is passing away' (I Cor.7.29-31). Paul also says in this letter that all that happened to Israel is written as a warning for 'us upon whom the end of the ages has come' (10.11). The celebration of the eucharist is also seen here in the perspective of the parousia (11.26). Finally Paul sums up this theme in his prayer, expressed with longing: 'Marana tha, Come Lord Jesus' (16.23).

The same conviction is expressed in the letter to the Christians of Rome. 'Besides this you know what hour it is, how it is full time now for you to wake from sleep. For salvation is nearer to us now than when we first believed; the night is far gone, the day is at hand' (Rom.13.11f.). This text is particularly instructive. It is sufficient indication that Paul does not use any concept, including that of the parousia, in a timeless way. Here he introduces a longer period of time into his own expectation of the parousia. Salvation – a clear reference to the parousia – is now nearer than it was. Paul arrives at this insight not through the actual delay of the parousia but because of a different theological attitude towards the Jews. In I Thess.2.14-16 Paul has evidently given up hope of the conversion of the Jews. On the contrary: the measure of their sins is complete. The wrath of God has come upon them to the full (v.16). Paul later had other experiences as a missionary among the Gentiles, and he developed new insights, including some about the conversion of the Jews. According to Romans he now believes firmly in this (11.11-15, 25-27). However, it still needs time. So the parousia has been postponed. Nevertheless, also according to Romans, the delay will not be long.[13]

In Philippians Paul expresses himself in a rather more complicated way. After years of apostolic life and witness he is sitting in prison. He does not know what awaits him. At all events, he expects imminent death. If he dies, he will no longer experience the parousia in person. But that does not make any difference to the situation of the Christians in Philippi. They can certainly still experience this parousia. Paul is confident that 'he who began a good work in you will bring it to completion at the day of Jesus Christ' (1.6; cf. 2.16; 3.20f.; 4.4f.).

We also find this theme of an imminent parousia in the Pastorals (I Tim.6.15; II Tim.1.12,18; 3.1-6; 4.1,18; Titus 2.13). Timothy is given the commission: 'I charge you to keep the commandment unstained and free from reproach until the appearing of our Lord Jesus Christ' (I Tim.6.14). The community entrusted to Timothy lives 'in the last times' (I Tim.4.1; II Tim.3.1). Whereas the author keeps this hope alive in Timothy, he expects his own imminent death: 'For I am already at the point of being sacrificed and the time of my departure has come' (II Tim.4.6,8).

In these Pastoral Epistles (I Tim.4.1f.; II Tim.2.18; 3.1-5), as in other New Testament writings (II Thess.2.1-3; II Peter 2.1; II John 7), there are vigorous attacks on people who teach that the resurrection and even the parousia have already in fact taken place. This assertion is clearly to be attributed to the increasing influence of Gnosticism. Generally speaking, gnosticism can be described as a spiritual trend with philosophical and mythical features and a syncretistic colouring; it flourished above all in the Hellenistic world. In Gnosticism there was marked emphasis on a spiritual contact with God, on union with the deity, above all through a direct knowledge – gnosis – of God. As a result of this spiritual process of knowledge the Gnostics thought themselves superior to anything this-worldly, material and corporeal. For some Gnostics the material element was evidently so unimportant (or even intrinsically sinful) that the material world and the body could play no part in morality. Because the Gnostics felt that their knowledge put them well above all that was earthly and corporeal, they denied the resurrection of the body. They were already risen. The glorified, heavenly Christ had already descended into the human soul to free it from its earthly, material prison and therefore this soul itself had already ascended to the authentic level of the spirit, where time no longer had any influence.

To combat these Gnostics, there was great stress both on the physical resurrection and on the parousia, which was still to come.

Although Paul, too, asserts against the Gnostics that the parousia has not yet come, he expects it very soon, as we have already seen. He often speaks of signs announcing it. Some authors are fond of pointing to these to stress their theory that Paul never thought of an imminent parousia. Paul in fact speaks of 'the great apostasy' which is still to come (II Thess.2.3). However, he may well have understood the fact that believers are made to fall away by 'tribulation' (II Thess.1.6f.) as a sign that the end-time had dawned. At any rate he envisages punishment for the oppressors and a revival for those who are oppressed 'together with us' (II Thess. 1.7-10). We find the same thing in II Tim.3.1-10: hard times are ahead, as is only to be expected in this last, decisive period.

Another preliminary sign is 'the man of lawlessness, the son of perdition, the adversary'. He must first reveal himself (II Thess.2.3-12). Paul takes over this figure from the apocalyptic of his time. There, however, his appearance immediately precedes the final judgment (cf. Matt.24.10-12; Rev.16.9,12; I John 2.18,22; 4.3; II John 7).[14]

According to Paul, the parousia must also be preceded by a mass conversion of Gentiles and the conversion of all Israel (Rom.11.25-32; cf. Mark 13.10; Matt.24.14). Paul himself saw it as his vocation to bring the Gentiles to belief (Acts 9.15), and he can delight in his visible success (Rom.1.8; Col.1.6; II Tim.4.17). It is his conviction that this event must contribute to Israel's salvation. Here his conviction rests on God's faithfulness to his covenant. In other words, from what Paul can see from his own contribution, he can be confident that the parousia is imminent.[15]

Paul also speaks of woes which precede the parousia (I Thess.5.3; Rom.8.18-22; cf. Matt.24.8; Mark 13.8) and of hard times (II Thess.1.4-10; I Cor.7.26). He knows from bitter experience that these woes have begun, and he can easily interpret his personal experience of persecution, suffering and the threat of death as so many signs of the imminent day of retribution.

So I think that we have good reason to conclude that Paul firmly expects an imminent end to the world. We also find this conviction in some other New Testament writings which I shall now review briefly.

In Hebrews a community living in the second generation after Jesus continues to preach confidence in the imminent dawn of 'the day'. So we read: 'Encourage one another, and all the more when you see the day drawing near' (10.25; cf.10.35; 3.12-19; 6.6-12). Of course the Epistle to the Hebrews makes more use of the pattern of a transcendent eschatology, i.e. a contrast between earthly and heavenly, but the horizontal eschatology – present and future – is by no means lost sight of. It is even possible to argue that the spatial imagery in which the whole event of faith is expressed here is used in the service of a new awakening of early Christian expectation of an imminent parousia.[16]

So Hebrews, too, continues to expect definitive salvation within the foreseeable future. The author discusses this theme in order to encourage believers to be firm and to continue to trust despite despair, disappointment and discouragement.

That is also the case in other writings. Christians were evidently often the object of mockery because of their confident expectation of the parousia. The author of II Peter sees the delay in the parousia as a sign of God's patience. However, the Lord will not delay longer with his promise, though for him a day is like a thousand years and a thousand years are like a day (3.1-10; cf. I Peter 4.7; James 3.7f.; Jude 17f.).

The expectation of an imminent end to the world is the basic theme of Revelation, which has rightly been called 'the book of a martyr for martyrs and through them for all believers who are not yet martyrs'.[17] Here the end of the world is promised to a persecuted and tortured community to encourage it and to urge it to be confident: the end of oppression and the punishment of its persecutors is in sight. It will happen soon (1.1,3,7,8,9,19; 2.16; 3.3-5,11-20; 6.11,17; 10.6; 19.6f.; 22.6,7,12,20).

Christian hope and apocalyptic

This analysis leaves no doubt that the first Christians expected an imminent end to the world, in a literal sense of the word. They gave a christological reason for this expectation, as a result of the Christ event, above all his resurrection and glorification. The historical Jesus, the crucified one, risen and/or exalted and glorified, would return as Lord and Son of man. The real temporal dimension in this expectation can hardly be denied: the advent of the Son of man is expected in an imminent future. However personalistic this event may be, as a coming of the person of the Lord and an encounter with him, it is an event for which people long as something which has not yet taken place. The content of Christian salvation is the person of Jesus, but this salvation is given to human beings as they actually are: people who make history, people who live for the future, in a world in which time and space have a role which cannot be ignored.

There would, however, be painful consequences if we proclaimed the firm conviction that we find in all the New Testament writings about the imminence of the parousia as binding *doctrine*. The parousia which is expected here has yet to happen. My analysis was intended to show that this aspect of the parousia, namely its imminence in time, was in no way incidental or purely hypothetical. On the contrary, this apocalyptic conviction is the motive for a particular Christian attitude, an ethical attitude, a well-considered approach to the world. On the basis of the firm expectation that the end of this world was near, Christians preached submission rather than revolution, tranquil acceptance rather than bold intervention to improve the world. Steadfastness and patience, watchfulness and caution, renunciation and self-denial fill the apocalyptists' catalogue of virtues. Apocalyptists are more concerned for the salvation of their own group, calling for retribution and vengeance on their persecutors, than to seek to win over others by missionary efforts. From a historical perspective, an apocalyptic expectation was never a motive for becoming involved in action to improve the world; at most it was a reason for people to be converted and to keep themselves pure from the stains of this world for the purity of the world to come.[18] It cannot be denied that we find traces of such an attitude, determined by the apocalyptic expectation of an imminent end to the world, in several fragments of the New Testament. So in this respect we need not really go back to apocalyptic.

As apocalyptic influence on thought diminished within the New Testament and was gradually replaced by another approach, i.e. Hellenism, we can see the Christian hope expressed differently in theory and in practice. In Hellenism there is less interest in the horizontal course of history as the succession of present and future. Thinking is more dualistic, and there is stress on the opposition between earthly and heavenly, between spirit and body. We already found the influence of this view in particular texts of Paul and in Hebrews. There we saw the gradual breakthrough of a transcendent eschatology, i.e. of the expectation on the basis of what happened here on earth of a transcendent, heavenly, supernatural metamorphosis, glorification or consummation. Here there is less stress on the category of time; what we now have is a spiritual or even ontological phenomenon as a result of which existence itself automatically becomes different.

These two dimensions of eschatology, the horizontal and the vertical, are never exclusive, either in Jewish apocalyptic or in the New Testament writings which we have investigated so far. However, in what has emerged hitherto there has clearly been a stress on the horizontal expectation of the future. While I have indicated the danger inherent in an apocalyptic approach in which future expectation rules out any interest in a this-worldly future for a history which still waits for its end, the apocalyptic orientation of hope remains particularly important and meaningful for religion and anthropology. It allows us to hope beyond all limitations because of its confidence in a happy ending for human beings as they join together in making their history. This ending consists in a definitive encounter with the Lord, eternal life in the gift of his presence.

The vertical dimension of the Christian hope which we have seen appearing now and then emerges completely and fully in the Fourth Gospel. We must now investigate it briefly from that perspective.

3. Eternity here and now

In the Gospel of John we find statements about eschatology which at first sight seem so contradictory that they led Rudolf Bultmann to conclude that in its present form the Fourth Gospel is not a literary and theological unity.[19] Discussion on the question, which we need not go into here, is still continuing.[20] The fact is that in this Gospel we have texts which depict eschatology as actuality, as eternity here and now, and other texts which seem to correct this view and opt clearly for an eschatology which is still to come. The strongly actualizing tendency which, according to Bultmann, is intended to demythologize eschatology by removing all historical and spatial aspects is to be attributed to the evangelist; the re-historicizing tendency is to be attributed to another redactor and in Bultmann's view is later than the evangelist's version, though other exegetes believe it to be earlier.

John places very marked emphasis on the saving significance of Christ for life today. The evangelist reads this significance out of the event of the cross. The death of Jesus is the beginning of his glorification. John sees death and resurrection together in the image of the grain of wheat which dies in order to bear fruit (12.23f.). It is not that death and resurrection simply coincide, but that resurrection, or, as John prefers to say, glorification, is the invisible reverse side of the death of Jesus.

The judgment of the Son of man

Through the death of Jesus which, as will immediately become evident, is in fact his glorification, everything has become new for humanity. The old has passed away and everything becomes new. The former world is finished. Satan has been deposed as ruler of this world. That throws everything into confusion: 'Now is the judgment of this world, now shall the ruler of this world be cast out. And I, when I am lifted up from the earth, will draw all men to myself' (12.31f.).

All that sounds thoroughly apocalyptic. The old world, the earth below, the sphere in which evil spirits are in power, must give place to a world which is from above, to which Jesus is exalted and from which he will draw all men to himself. However, it will immediately become clear that only the apocalyptic imagery as such remains. On closer examination John seems to keep the spatial and the temporal aspects of the expectation of salvation apart.

Jesus is the Son of man who is to be lifted up so that all who believe in him may have eternal life (3.14-16). Jesus pronounces the final judgment. God 'has given him authority to execute judgment, because he is the Son of man' (5.27). This judgment takes place now. It depends on the attitude which people adopt towards Jesus. 'He who believes in the Son has eternal life; he who does not obey the Son shall not see life, but the wrath of God remains on him' (3.36). 'He who hears my word and believes him who sent me, has eternal life; he does not come into judgment but has passed from death to life' (5.24). Human beings live in a world on which God's wrath rests. Jesus comes to give them a chance to pass over into a new world, into God's own world, the world of eternal life. If people do not take this opportunity, if they refuse to accept the offer of Jesus in faith, then they condemn themselves.

Jesus himself is, quite simply, life (11.25; 14.16). He is the bread of life (6.33,35,48). Whoever eats the bread that is Jesus lives through him (6.57) and will not die (6.50). Whoever follows him has the light of life (8.12). The words that he speaks are life (6.63), they are words of eternal life (6.68). If a man obeys his word 'he will never see death' (8.51; cf. 11.26; 12.25).

So the relationship with Jesus is decisive for eternal life. As a result, eternal life is no longer a future for which one longingly hopes, but is realized here and now, in and through faith. In Jesus' conversation with Martha on the death of Lazarus, the present gift of eternal life is even expressed against the background of belief in eternal life as a future, eschatological event. Martha expresses her own faith: 'I know that he will rise in the resurrection on the last day,' but Jesus responds: 'I am the resurrection and the life' (11.24-25a). In this reply Jesus seeks to make clear that the resurrection becomes actuality, happens now, in and through him. The resurrection already happens now, says Jesus, and it is through me that it happens. He gives life to those who have died.

All this is about life in the truest sense of the word, a life which has significance, content, meaning; it is a life which really deserves the name, a life that is worth the trouble of living. It is a life in and with God. Over against this is a life which really cannot be called life because it is not life at all: it is existence without God, subjection to the ruler of this world whose father was a murderer from the beginning (cf. John 8.44). Such an existence without freedom, in complete subjection, an existence in which people are not in possession of themselves because they are possessed, ought really to be called death.

So life and death here are clearly put in a different sphere; they are thought of differently from that life and death which can be determined biologically. The real life into which one is taken through faith in Jesus is not destroyed by death: 'He who believes in me, though he die, yet shall he live, and whoever lives and believes in me shall never die' (11.25-26a).[21] Thus real or eternal life is given by Jesus now, already: 'Truly, truly, I say to you, the hour is coming, and now is, when the dead will hear the voice of the Son of God; and those who hear will live. For as the Father has life in himself, so too he has granted the Son also to have life in himself' (5.25f.).

Heaven is a person

On the basis of his view of Jesus, John sees eschatology as above all actual, present and realized in the present. Jesus is and gives eternal life. Anyone who enters into a personal relationshp with him through faith has eternal life, already, now. In Jesus God has given himself to men in a final way. This eschatological time of salvation therefore exists in the presence of Jesus. In his exaltation to the Father he has not left his work behind him but by that very exaltation has become identical with his work, i.e. with the giving of eternal life, for all times. Jesus, dead and glorified, is the new age. Therefore the eschatology of the Fourth Gospel has rightly been called personalistic. It is realized in and through the person of Jesus, and it consists in a present personal relationship to him through faith.[22]

This view of the eschaton in Jesus Christ through which believers already possess eternal life now does not in any way exclude a future perspective. The presence of salvation is indeed the basis of its permanent character. The future is included in the present. Present eschatology, as this is called, does not exclude its future consummation. The present already has a hold on the future. This future is already there, but it has not yet been brought to completion. Moreover in the Fourth Gospel – perhaps by the hand of a second author – there is clear mention of a future which is still to come, of the end of time.

A term is in fact used here to express this end of time which we do not find anywhere else, either in the New Testament or in Jewish apocalyptic: 'the last day'. Even if we suppose that in many passages this expression suggests the work of another hand (6.39f., 44, 54; 12.48), it is quite generally assumed that the evangelist himself uses this terminology in the conversation between Jesus and Martha when the latter says: 'I know that he will rise again in the resurrection at the last day' (11.24). When Jesus replies that he himself is the resurrection in the sense mentioned above, this does not exclude a future resurrection of the dead. It simply means that the resurrection event happens in, with and through Jesus, and that the future character of this event is also exclusively concerned with Jesus and with the significance which he now has in the present.

The parousia is also made present in the farewell discourses, but again not in such a way that all perspectives on the future are lost.

Apocalyptic language is clearly used here when it is said that there are many dwellings in the Father's house and that Jesus goes there to prepare a place for his disciples (14.2).[23]

Jesus' words, 'When I go and prepare a place for you I will come again and will take you to myself that where I am you may be also' (14.3) tempt us to think of the *parousia*, which is usually translated as the return of the Lord. But this translation is not completely accurate. As a secular Greek term, *parousia* means the visit of a ruling prince to one of his own cities. The prince did not come to ascend the throne or to intervene, but simply to be among his subjects.[24] The quite specific reference of the words of Jesus from the farewell discourses quoted here is therefore to the return of Jesus at his resurrection (cf. 14.18). In and through the resurrection event Jesus comes to his disciples to be present among them and therefore already to take them up into the power of his resurrection existence. Through faith in Jesus, the disciples are where Jesus himself is: in the house of the Father, at the place determined for them, with the glorified Christ in the presence of God. Therefore the disciples, too, can ask the Father personally on that day for everything, even without the intercession of Jesus as mediator. For they themselves are with the Father, who has accepted them in his love (16.23,26). Since the resurrection the disciples have been 'where Jesus is' (12.26; 17.24). Taken into communion with Jesus, they are now already with the Father.

All this still happens within the situation of faith, but it requires a full revelation of what embraces them and also that this full revelation which is already there in germ shall bring forth and bear fruit. The glory of the Father into which believers are taken up by faith has still to be made manifest. That is the significance of Jesus' prayer: 'Father, I desire that they also whom you have given me may be with me where I am, to behold my glory which thou hast given me in thy love for me before the foundation of the world' (17.24). The reference here is clearly to a future and final vision of the glory of Jesus, different from the glory which Jesus has already revealed in the faith of his disciples (cf. 2.11; 11.40). This is the final consummation of faith of which I John says: 'We are God's children now; it does not yet appear what we shall be, but we know that when he appears we shall be like him, for we shall see him as he is' (I John 3.2).

I therefore feel that Bultmann is right to conclude from this actualizing of the parousia and the perspective on the future which is inherent in it as a question and a promise that the consummation of faith takes place in the vision of the glory of Jesus at death: 'The community lives, and the believers live, from the future; and his faith has meaning so long as this future is not an illusionary dream or a *futurum aeternum*. Thus the petition is for the realization of the future ... Thus the petition can only be a request that the separation from him be a temporary one, that they should be united with him again after their worldly existence ... The only thing that is clear is that an existence for the believers with the Revealer beyond death is requested, and thus promised. Death has become insignificant for them (11.25f.); but not in the sense that they can ignore it because their earthly life is now complete and meaningful in itself; but because their life is not enclosed within the limits of temporal-historical existence.'[25]

The question how and when this consummation of faith in and through the vision of the glory of Christ will take place is never raised in the Fourth Gospel. It is only held out as a goal, as the object of hope and trust.

Individualistic salvation?

Thus in the Fourth Gospel we quite clearly have a strikingly different view of eschatology from the one which we have found in the other New Testament writings. We can hardly minimalize this difference by calling it another emphasis. It is a view with a fundamentally different orientation.

Some scholars use the term 'individualistic salvation' to describe this characteristic of salvation in the Gospel of John. Although we should not make this description too exclusive, it is beyond question that no other New Testament author is as interested as John in a personalistic view. As a result, his interest in the future of the world and of human history pales. He is not at all interested in the parousia as an eschatological event. Entry into the heavenly world to see the glory of Jesus now, already, in and through faith, takes over the function attributed elsewhere in the New Testament to the parousia and the final event, the general judgment which seems to bring the world and history to an end.

John is clearly no longer so directly influenced by apocalyptic thought-patterns, although these still seem to be current in his community, among other things in connection with hope of an imminent end to the world (cf. 21.22f.; I John 2.8). John expresses the Christian hope in categories, thought-patterns, conceptions and concepts from a culture which is increasingly determined by Hellenism, and specifically by Gnosticism. In this thought-world questions are raised about the meaning of human existence, the origin and goal of life. There is an anxious quest for a meaning in life and for personal fulfilment, fascination at the spiritual dimension of human existence. John translates and interprets the Christian hope in terms of this new time and culture, with its other interests, questions and problems. As a result he personalizes and individualizes this eschatology. In Jesus he sees the beginning and end of everything, the real significance of all existence, the content of all life, the goal of all striving. Jesus is the light that illuminates the life of man and the world. He is and reveals truth. Whoever believes in him is made free by this truth (8.32), and only through that achieves life worthy of the name. In this truth the believer discovers the love of the Father 'who gave his only Son, that

whoever believes in him should not perish but have eternal life'
(3.16).

II

STRONGER THAN DEATH

So far we have been considering the expectation of an imminent and
final saving intervention by God, in and through the glorified Son of
man, on behalf of the believing community. This expectation was
coloured through and through by apocalyptic. In the Fourth Gospel
there is more emphasis on the fact that the end-time is realized now,
already, in and through a relationship with the glorified Christ in
faith. In this way we get a view of the hope of the Christian communities as such. They hoped for an imminent end to the world.
There was also room within this collective hope for an individual
hope of life after death. It is this aspect of Christian hope in the New
Testament communities which I now want to illuminate.

1. Life after death

In the New Testament, resurrection from the dead is clearly a matter
of faith. After the resurrection of Jesus this faith is grounded above
all in the resurrection event which happened in Jesus himself. That
means that it is extremely difficult in our investigation to determine
with certainty whether the remarks about a resurrection of the dead
made by Jesus go back to him or whether they were attributed to him
later on the basis of the Easter experience of the disciples. We saw
earlier that the expectation of a resurrection of the dead was current
in apocalyptic as an essential element of belief in an imminent restoration at the end of time. In view of what we have discovered so far
we may assume *a priori* that Jesus shared this expectation. So I do
not feel that we need to investigate what are authentic sayings of Jesus in this context, as distinct from statements attributed to him by
the early community.

A God of the living

We find a particularly important testimony in what in all probability is an authentic saying of Jesus handed down to us by Mark (12.18-27).[26] The Sadducees, a group from the prosperous upper class and the highest priestly class which was very conservative in religion and theology, refused to affirm belief in the resurrection because this belief only emerged in early Judaism and nowhere appeared in the written law. However, these Sadducees were not condemned or regarded as heretics by official Judaism because of this 'unbelief'. They even had a majority in the Sanhedrin, the supreme authority among the Jews. The president of this Sanhedrin was a high priest, and he was always a Sadducee.

In the conversation which Mark reproduces, some Sadducees seek to mock belief in the resurrection by referring to the obligations of levirate or kinship marriage: whose wife in heaven will the woman be who had married seven brothers one after the other? There are two parts to Jesus' answer. He replies to the specific question of the nature of the resurrection by referring to a conception which we have already met in apocalyptic: 'For when they rise from the dead, they neither marry nor are given in marriage, but are like angels in heaven' (Mark 12.25; cf. II Enoch 51.4; II Bar.51.10). By this Jesus means that resurrection existence is not the same as life here and now, which is maintained by procreation. That those who are raised are like angels in heaven also means that no mortal can imagine such a life. No idea of it can match human projections; it is fully determined by the sovereign omnipotence of God.

Jesus then goes into the fact of the resurrection. He produces an argument from scripture for this. The book of Moses says that as God of Abraham, Isaac and Jacob God is not a God of the dead but of the living (12.26f.). It is not out of the question that here Jesus is referring to the current view within apocalyptic according to which the patriarchs, as the prototypes of all the righteous, are now alive with God (cf. IV Macc.5.37; 7.19; 13.17; 18.23; Ass.Mos.1.15; 10.14). As an argument against the opponents of resurrection belief that would not be very convincing, because they reject apocalyptic outright. However, it is important that here Jesus refers to the fact that God is God as a basis for belief in the resurrection. In denying the resurrection of the dead the Pharisees show that they simply have no idea who God is. He is not a God of the dead but of the living. Jesus' experience of God makes him sure of resurrection. If God makes a covenant with man, if God gives himself to man, his action cannot be undone by anyone or anything, not even by death. In the covenant God gives himself as God, i.e. as the eternal one. The ultimate ground for the certainty of resurrection therefore lies in belief in God's faithfulness to his promise, to his covenant, to himself. This free faithfulness to the covenant will not be broken even by death.

The beyond as retribution

Matthew and Luke make Jesus repeatedly speak of a life after death: 'Do not lay up for yourselves treasures on earth, where moth and rust consume, and where thieves break in and steal, but lay up for yourselves treasures in heaven, where neither moth nor rust consumes and where thieves do not break in and steal' (Matt.6.19f.). Luke gives this saying a special colouring by making amassing treasure in heaven dependent on a social attitude, the giving of alms: 'Sell your possessions, and give alms; provide yourself with purses that do not grow old, with a treasure in the heavens that does not fail, where no thief approaches and no moth destroys' (12.33; cf. 12.16-21). Here there is clearly an allusion to retribution after death, and therefore to a life after death.

We find another, perhaps authentic saying of Jesus that refers to a beyond in Matthew: 'Enter by the narrow gate! For the gate is wide and the way is easy, that leads to destruction, and those who enter by it are many. For the gate is narrow and the way is hard, that leads to life, and those who find it are few' (Matt.7.13f.). By his own revision of the saying Luke leaves no doubt that destruction and life are used here in their early Jewish sense as terms which have a clearly apocalyptic meaning. He writes: 'And someone said to him, "Lord, will those who are saved be few?" And he said to them, "Strive to enter by the narrow door; for many, I tell you, will seek to enter and will not be able. When once the householder has risen up and shut the door, you will begin to stand outside and to knock at the door, saying, 'Lord open to us!' He will answer you, 'I know not whence you come' " ' (13.23-25). The door is doubtless meant to be the door of heaven which is common in apocalyptic literature. This door gives access to the room, or rooms, in which Abraham, Isaac and Jacob, along with all the prophets, are already present (cf. Luke 13.28f.; Matt.8.11f.).

It is striking that here Jesus gives no direct reply to the question seeking information as to whether or not there are many who will be saved. Jesus gives no further information. He has not come to satisfy curiosity. He comes with a summons, with an appeal. Here he addresses an urgent appeal to everyone personally to make the utmost effort to achieve salvation. Jesus addresses everyone personally; he does not speak with anyone about the fate of others, but about his or her own future.

Rather different sayings of Jesus talk about a reward or punishment after death and thus presuppose a resurrection. So, 'There is no one who has left house or brothers or sisters or mother or father or children or lands, for my sake and for the gospel, who will not receive a hundredfold now in this time, houses and brothers and sisters and mothers and children and lands, with persecutions, and in the age to come eternal life' (Mark 10.29f.; cf. Matt.19.27-29. For a heavenly reward see e.g. Matt.5.12; 13.43; 25.31ff.; Mark 10.21,40; Luke 10.20; 12.8; 14.14; 22.29f.; eternal punishment is mentioned *inter alia* in Matt.11.23f.; 13.41f., 49f.; 25.31ff.).

Sayings of Jesus from the Q tradition similarly speak of life after death. 'Do not fear those who kill the body but cannot kill the soul, rather fear him who can destroy both soul and body in hell' (Matt.10.28). At first glance here we seem to have a Greek, dualistic view of human beings, as comprising an immortal soul and a mortal body. However, on closer inspection this is not the case. The first clause in fact reckons with the possibility of also killing the soul, just as one can kill a body. According to the Greek doctrine of the immortality of the soul this is of course nonsense. The Greek word *psyche* is translated soul here, but clearly means something other than a part of a human being. Rather, it is a synonym for authentic, true life. No human being can destroy this life. However, that cannot be said of earthly life, which is here translated by the word body. In that case the meaning of the saying of Jesus is that of course life, true life, worthy of this name, is put at risk by the attitude which one adopts towards him.[27] Perhaps in order to avoid any misunderstanding, Luke gives another version of the same saying: 'Do not fear those who kill the body, and after that have no more that they can do . . . Fear him who, after he has killed, has power to cast into hell' (12.4f.).

It is quite possible that the parable of the foolish and the wise virgins (Matt.25.1-12) has an eschatological point. Because of the implicit christological relevance of this parable the bridegroom to come may be a symbol for the returning Christ who comes to judge. Here again there is mention of knocking on the door which, as I said above, is perhaps the door of heaven. The parable of the talents

(Matt.25.14,30; Luke 19.12-27) can also be given an eschatological interpretation in the same way.

In the parable of the rich man who wants to build bigger barns to store his harvest, Luke illustrates the catastrophe of a sudden death: 'But God said to him, "Fool! This night your soul is required of you; and the things your have prepared, whose will they be?" So is he who lays up treasure for himself, and is not rich toward God' (12.16-21). Laying up treasure for oneself gets in the way of careful and open attention to others. One is rich before God only if one shares with others, if one gives one's treasures to the poor. If one is rich before God, one need not fear even sudden death, for one can still enjoy credit with God even beyond death.

In the parable of the unjust steward who is praised for his concern (Luke 16.1-9) we can also find an allusion to individual death and life after death, in which the believer 'is received into eternal habitations' (v.9).

In the pericope about Lazarus and the rich man (Luke 16.19-31) it is said that immediately after his death Lazarus is carried by angels into Abraham's bosom, i.e. that he is given a place of honour at Abraham's right hand. We hear that the rich man, immediately after his death, goes straight to the underworld where he has to suffer acute torment. Here life after death is clearly envisaged in bodily terms, as was also the case in apocalyptic.[28] It is hard to determine whether what we are to think of here is a physical resurrection in the later and usual sense of the word or a shadowy existence in Sheol, envisaged in physical terms, though already with a distinction between righteous and sinners. At all events, the parable is about the whole man. The same goes for the saying that Jesus addresses on the cross to one of the criminals crucified with him. When the robber asks, 'Jesus, remember me when you come with your kingly power', Jesus replies, 'Truly, I say to you, today you will be with me in paradise' (Luke 23.42f.). Here Jesus' kingdom is identified with paradise. We saw in apocalyptic that this concept is synonymous with the final kingdom, or heaven.[29] Jesus promises that he will receive this criminal, today, in heaven. Jesus welcomes him, when he himself is glorified by the Father at his death. This saying here undeniably has an individual eschatological significance, though its content is clearly more markedly christological.[30]

All the texts that I have mentioned briefly here give us good reason for claiming that Jesus himself expected life after death for the individual, and thus had an individual eschatology. His disciples clearly shared this conviction, but connected this individual eschatology directly with the resurrection and glorification of Jesus. One might say that they saw death to some degree as parousia, as the coming of the glorified Christ to welcome his disciples to where he is, with the Father, in paradise.[31]

In Acts we find a clear instance of an individualized eschatology. Stephen, on being stoned, as it were experiences the parousia immediately before his death: 'Full of the Holy Spirit, he gazed into heaven and saw the glory of God, and Jesus standing at the right hand of God; and he said, "Behold I see the heavens opened, and the Son of man standing at the right hand of God . . . " And as they were stoning Stephen, he prayed, "Lord Jesus, receive my spirit"' (Acts 7.55f., 59). The whole context, the open heaven, the Son of man standing at the right hand of God, exalted, to receive his martyr in honour, suggests an immediate resurrection after death. This is a conception which we have already encountered often, e.g. in II Maccabees and in apocalyptic.

The life after death which keeps being mentioned is envisaged as a new mode of existence for the human being as a whole; there is no question of the ongoing survival of an immortal soul. Where there is already some reflection on this mode of existence, which seldom seems to be the case, this happens in terms of the monistic view of man (man as an indivisible unity), as found in the Old Testament and the great apocalyptic tradition. After their death human beings will display the physical characteristics which they had during their earthly existence (cf. Matt.5.29f.).

Belief in a future world is taken for granted in all these writings. It is expressed, without any prior reflection, in conceptions which are peculiar to the time. These conceptions themselves are nowhere presented as doctrine, but serve as the means of expressing an experience of God or of Christ. The power, the kingdom of God and his anointed, does not end with death but extends beyond the limits of death.

The resurrection of martyrs

There is no need to say any more about the Gospel of John in this connection. I have already commented on the way in which eschatology is related to the present and made personal in the Fourth Gospel.

We find some texts in Revelation which are very important for our theme. In fact they seem to speak of an immediate resurrection of martyrs, who stand in worship before the throne of God. In Revelation the fact that they are completely in God's hands is a pledge and a foretaste of the goal towards which the suffering, martyr community is going. In the salvation already given to the martyrs the author already sees the realization of the salvation which they bring to the community now under persecution. All this is described particularly clearly in the vision which follows the breaking of the fifth seal: 'I saw under the altar the souls of those who had been slain for the word of God and for the witness they had borne; they cried out with a loud voice, "O sovereign Lord, holy and true, how long before thou wilt judge and avenge our blood on those who dwell upon the earth?" Then they were each given a white robe and told to rest a little longer, until the number of their fellow servants and their brethren should be complete, who were to be killed as they themselves had been' (6.9-11). The death of the martyrs is here compared with the sacrifice of animals. The blood of these sacrificial animals was poured out at the foot of the altar in Jerusalem. The blood of the martyrs is poured out at the foot of the altar in heaven. In Jewish thought, blood is the seat of life. So martyrs live in heaven. They pray for the end of the oppressors to be hastened so as to bring an end to the suffering of the martyrs on earth, and similarly to crown them for their martyrdom. The heavenly intercession is a theme which we also find elsewhere (cf. I Enoch 47.1; 97.3,5; 99.3; Luke 18.7). According to this vision, the heavenly martyrs receive a glorified body, which is here symbolized by a white garment.[32] In another vision, of the great multitude which no one can number (7.9-17), the author seeks to disclose the meaning of this suffering to be expected before the dawn of the great persecution of the community. He does this by recalling the image of heavenly worship and the happiness which the martyrs enjoy with God. These martyrs have themselves 'come from great tribulation' (v.14), but now they lead a new heavenly and bodily existence – again the image of white raiment (v.13) – praising and serving at the throne of God.

There is also explicit mention of a resurrection of two witnesses in the mysterious chapter 11.1-14. These are usually thought to be Enoch and Elijah, who, as we saw earlier, according to tradition did not die but were caught up alive. However in 11.5 there is mention of a penal fire and of the closing of heaven, and an express allusion to the miraculous power of Elijah (cf. also II Sam.22.9; I Kings 17.1; II Kings 1.10,14). There is also mention of turning water to blood and

of the visitation of the earth with all kinds of plagues. This automatically reminds us of Moses (cf. Ex.7.17-20; I Sam.4.8). The two witnesses here could therefore quite well be Elijah and Moses.[33] It is said
of them that they will be killed for their witness, but that after three
and a half days the breath of life will go into them from God and they
will stand on their feet. A voice from heaven will say to them:
' "Come up hither!" And in the sight of their foes they went up to
heaven in a cloud' (v.12). Then follows an earthquake, in which a
tenth of the city collapses. The survivors on earth are terrified and
offer God worship.

Thus here there is explicit mention of a resurrection and a glorification before the general resurrection. Although this resurrection of
the two witnesses who died as martyrs is not confirmed as such and
in itself, but is thought of functionally, namely as a divine legitimation of their testimony towards their persecutors, one thing emerges
from this account: the idea of a resurrection after death and before
the general resurrection was a conception current at that time.

We find another particularly clear statement about this resurrection life immediately after death: 'Blessed are the dead who die in the
Lord henceforth. "Blessed indeed," says the Spirit, that they may rest
from their labours, for their deeds follow them!' (14.13). This text
also seems to suggest the resurrection of the whole person. From now
on the dead live in blessedness with God in the human form they had
on earth; their deeds accompany them.

The vision of the thousand-year kingdom (20.1-10) must also be
interpreted in this perspective. This particularly difficult text seems
to express the expectation of a special, future resurrection of Christian martyrs before the general resurrection of the dead. It is envisaged above all for those who fell victim to the final persecution
through the beast. There is no mention here of an earthly messianic
kingdom to precede the definitive heavenly glorification, as is sometimes claimed by those who wrongly see this text as a parallel to IV
Ezra 7.28ff., where there is mention of the resurrection of the Messiah along with all who were with him during the four-hundred-year
period.[34] The scene with the thrones in v.4 takes place in heaven and
is an anticipation of the final judgment in favour of the martyrs. Consequently this context also presupposes their resurrection as an
anticipation of the heavenly resurrection. According to the view of
history in the Apocalypse, the rule of these glorified martyrs with
Christ takes place after the return of Christ to earth from heaven.
The rule of the crucified and risen one takes place in heaven (ch.1).

Chapter 20 must be interpreted in the light of the view of history in the book of Revelation. The context speaks of an imminent time in which every form of evil on earth will finally be dealt with (vv.1f.), and then people will continue to live on earth (v.3). These people will still be affected by the suffering which goes with the end-time itself, whereas the martyrs are no longer exposed to it (vv.7-10). According to Rev.6.9-11, too, new life is given in heaven and the martyrs rule from heaven. The first resurrection (20.5) can thus be regarded as a heavenly event, as is also the case in II Macc.7. In 20.5 we have one of those extremely rare texts in which the heavenly glorification of the martyrs after their death is expressly called a resurrection.

In the next section I want to discuss in more detail the resurrection from the dead as seen by Paul.

2. Resurrection from death

For ever with the Lord

The first text which we need to investigate is I Thess. 4.13-5.11. We already know its specific context. Paul is encouraging Christians who are anxious about the fate of their dead who died before the parousia. They are not to be sorrowful like men who have no hope. Indeed part of their faith is that Jesus died and rose again and that God will similarly bring those who fell asleep in Christ to join him in life. The latter presupposes a resurrection but means more than a transportation to heaven. The risen will be glorified with Christ.

In the death and resurrection of Jesus God has manifested himself as Lord of an absolute future. He is involved even in the being-without-a-future which is the fate of the dead. So the conviction that believers who have died will share in eschatological salvation follows from faith in the saving will of God as this was revealed in the Christ event. The glorified Lord will himself descend from heaven. First the dead who fell asleep in Christ will rise, and then those who are still alive will be transported with the risen dead to meet the Lord. And in this way they will be for ever with the Lord.

Here a profound conviction of faith is expressed against an apocalyptic scenario. Dead and living together will experience the parousia. This was the problem with which Paul was concerned. Neither the resurrection nor the parousia are questioned in Thessalonica; all the anxiety is about fellow believers who have already fallen asleep in the meantime. Here we seem to have a community in which the community spirit was felt so strongly that there was also a desire to experience the parousia as a community. If the dead have no part in the parousia, and if the living do not find their dead in the Lord, then the meaning of the parousia itself becomes obscure to them. The parousia is only meaningful if all Christians, dead and alive, see one another again, if they are again united as a community in which they can be always one in Christ.

Paul wants to set the fears of this community completely at rest. Whether alive or already dead, all Christians will live in union with Christ. In this trust and faith Christians can console, encourage and support one another.

It emerges clearly from the text that neither the Christians of Thessalonica nor Paul himself had any conception of an intermediate stage in which the *souls* of believers already came to appear before God. As we saw earlier, at this time people had such a strong expectation of an imminent parousia that they had no thought of an intermediate period. They were only interested in the coming parousia, in the fact that all believers would be for ever with Christ. Therefore the dead first had to arise in order to be transported with the survivors to another world, to heaven, whence the Lord would come to meet them and take them to himself there.

The resurrection body

Paul goes in detail into the problem of the resurrection in the two letters to the Christians of Corinth. He has learned that in this Greek city there are Christians who deny the resurrection. It is usually assumed that these were believers who were strongly influenced by gnosticism and thought that the resurrection had already taken place, as a purely spiritual event. But they could also have been Christians who accepted the immortality of the soul from Greek anthropology but simply did not know what to make of an additional resurrection of the body.[35] In fact these remarkable Greeks had themselves baptized for the dead (I Cor.15.29). Probably they did this in place of those who had died unbaptized, in the hope that this vicarious event might do something for the dead. So they believed in a life after death, but as the ongoing existence of the immortal soul.

Be this as it may, Paul, who as a Jew thinks of a human being as a unity, is concerned only that Christians should believe that human beings rise as human beings. Because he thinks in this way, because

he sees human beings living an undivided life in the body, he also imagines their resurrection as an event which concerns those who have
lived a bodily life and died a physical death. For Paul – unlike the
Greeks – the body means the whole person, not just a part (and that
the less important part) of man. Body is a common Semitic term for
man or person. This significance can clearly be seen in the eucharistic
words of Jesus. When Jesus says 'This is my body', it is as if he were
to say, 'This is what I am, this is my person.' No one ever thinks that
Jesus here was talking of part of his existence, of one aspect of his
humanity, namely his body, separated from his soul.

This Jewish picture of humanity helps us to understand why Paul
attaches so much importance to the resurrection of the body: he simply means the resurrection of the human being. Unlike the Greeks,
Paul simply cannot imagine existence without a body. When he
wants to speak of a situation of salvation after death he must think
of this in bodily terms, since nothing else would make any sense to
him. For him resurrection is something which happens to a human
being who lives in the body and has died in the body, or it is nothing
at all.

In stressing the bodily resurrection Paul also wants to safeguard
the identity between the person who lives in history and the person
who rises. The same person is involved, who lives a bodily life in history, who has died and rises again. In reflecting on this identity, Paul
must nevertheless already have come under the influence of Greek
thought. It is not that he assumes the existence of an immortal soul
or that he completely spiritualizes the body, but at all events he no
longer seeks to base the identity between the dead and risen person
on the material identity of the body, as happened in apocalyptic literature. Paul therefore seeks to clarify his views in a series of antitheses between the bodily existence of our present experience and the
bodily existence of the risen person.

First of all he says that there are different forms in one and the
same existence: 'And what you sow is not the body which is to be,
but a bare kernel, perhaps of wheat or of some other grain. But God
gives it a body as he has chosen, and to each kind of seed a body . . .
What is sown is perishable, what is raised is imperishable. It is sown
in dishonour, it is raised in glory' (I Cor.15.37f., 42f.). Thus there are
discontinuity and continuity in the bodily sense: the grain of wheat
itself later exists in a completely different form. This continuity is
given and guaranteed by the Creator God who is also the cause of the
discontinuity: he gives the grain of corn, which he makes capable of

taking on various appearances. So, too, he gives the dead person another mode of existence: during his earthly existence the person was transitory, small and weak; now God makes the same person exist in untransitoriness, in glory and power.

Then comes a second antithesis: 'It is sown a physical body, it is raised a spiritual body. If there is a physical body, there is also a spiritual body. Thus it is written: The first man Adam became a living being; the last Adam became a life-giving spirit . . . The first man was from the earth, a man of dust; the second man is from heaven. As was the man of dust, so are those who are of the dust; and as is the man of heaven, so are those who are of heaven. Just as we have borne the image of the man of dust, we shall also bear the image of the man of heaven' (15.44-49).

However, things get a bit complicated. Paul begins from the text: 'Then the Lord God formed man of the dust from the ground, and breathed into his nostrils the breath of life; and man became a living being' (Gen.2.7). In this way a physical body arose out of two elements: the dust of the earth and the divine breath of life or *pneuma*. That is the first man Adam. The second Adam, Christ, is here identified by Paul with the divine breath of life, the *pneuma*. We are created in the image of man from dust which was brought to life. At the resurrection we shall be created anew after the image of the second Adam, the man who gives life. In other words, we shall not rise with a body which is taken from the dust of the earth but with a heavenly body which is itself living, spiritual, supernatural. We shall become the image of the glorified Christ.

In this case can one still speak of continuity? Paul replies in a third antithesis: 'Flesh and blood cannot inherit the kingdom of God, nor does the perishable inherit the imperishable . . . For this perishable nature must put on the imperishable, and this mortal nature must put on immortality. When the perishable puts on the imperishable, and the mortal puts on immortality, then shall come to pass the saying that is written: "Death is swallowed up in victory" ' (15.50-54). In addition to the contrast between an earthly and a supra-earthly body in origin – one is made of the stuff of the earth and the other is from heaven – there is now a difference in their nature. The earthly body cannot become heavenly immediately. It must first change. Even if people are still alive at the parousia, it is impossible to move simply from earthly to heavenly life. Earthly, bodily existence must first be changed (15.51). Flesh and blood cannot inherit the kingdom of God. Our transitory existence must be clothed with the bodily existence of the untransitory, heavenly, immortal man, that is, with the existence of the glorified Christ. The second Adam becomes the source of untransitoriness and immortality. Or, as it is said elsewhere: 'And we all, with unveiled face, beholding the glory of the Lord, are being changed into his likeness, from one degree of glory to another; for this comes from the Lord who is the Spirit' (II Cor.3.18), or also: 'But our commonwealth is in heaven, and from it we await a Saviour, the Lord Jesus Christ, the Lord, as saviour, who will change our lowly body to be like his glorious body, by the power which enables him even to subdue all things to himself' (Phil.3.20f.).

In content, these antitheses do not add very much, but they can remove a number of misunderstandings. At all events they make it clear that resurrection has nothing to do with the reanimation of a body, with biological factors, with flesh and blood. So it is not really Paul, with his grandiose stress on the resurrection of the body, who makes this faith so difficult for us. That only becomes the case if the term 'body' denotes a part of a human being. In that case the resurrection of this individual part must be understood as reanimation, or, as it was later put, as the reunion of soul and body. Of course we shall have to return to this problem again.

I would like also to point out briefly that Paul connects belief in the resurrection of the dead with belief in God: he feels called on to reprimand the Corinthians because, 'Some have no knowledge of God' (15.34). It sounds like the echo of a saying of Jesus that we have already heard addressed to the Sadducees who denied the resurrection: 'You are wrong: you know neither the scriptures nor the power of God . . . God is not God of the dead but of the living; you are quite wrong' (Mark 12.24,27).

Paul feels compelled to return to the problem in the second letter to the Christians of Corinth. In a vivid text in which the body is sometimes called a tent, sometimes a dwelling and then again a garment, we read: 'For we know that if the earthly tent we live in is destroyed, we have a building from God, a house not made with hands, eternal in the heavens. Here indeed we groan, and long to put on our heavenly dwelling, so that by putting it on we may not be found naked. For while we are still in this tent we sigh with anxiety; not that we would be further clothed, so that what is mortal may be swallowed up by life. He who has prepared us for this very thing is God, who has given us the Spirit as a guarantee. So we are always of good courage; we know that while we are at home in the body we are away from the Lord, for we walk by faith, not by sight. We are of good courage, and we would rather be away from the body and at home with the Lord. So whether we are at home or away, we make it our aim to please him. For we must all appear before the judgment seat of Christ, so that each one may receive good or evil, according to what he has done in the body' (5.1-10).

Interpretation of this difficult text remains much disputed. It is enough for our purpose to note that Paul again expresses his hope in a physical resurrection in glory. This prospect gives him strength to withstand the difficulties of this time (4.16-18). Precisely as a result of the difficulties which he experiences in this earthly life in the body, he longs all the more ardently for another, heavenly existence. Paul does not sigh and feel burdened – as do the Gnostics – because he exists in the body; he laments the fact that this mode of existence simply represents a transitory stage with all the difficulties and dangers associated with it.[36] He longs to come home.

Evidently Paul is afraid of a mode of existence outside the body, which is what is perhaps referred to here under the imagery of being naked and unclothed. The Greek conception of an immortal soul which exists without a body, a conception with which he surely became acquainted in the meanwhile, terrifies him. He wants to pass over straightaway from one physical mode of existence to the other. Paul remains faithful to his view in I Corinthians: this transition does not happen immediately. First the earthly, physical mode of existence must be changed. Whether this transformation takes place at death or at the parousia does not seem to be something which bothers Paul. Here he is more concerned with the certainty of the hoped-for transformation than with the time at which it takes place. However, in view of the specific context I believe that Paul expects this transformation at death, when 'we are away from the body and at home with the Lord' (v.8).

Here the glorified resurrection body is called the work of God, 'a house not made with hands, eternal in the heavens' (v.1). Here too Paul continues to think along the lines of his first letter to the Christians of Corinth. At death we shall be clothed with the glorified body of Christ so as to be the image of the second Adam. We find the same idea here again. If we remember the words of Jesus about the temple of his body 'which is not made with human hands' (Mark 14.58; cf. John 2.20f.; Heb.8.11), then I think we may take up a convincing interpretation of 'this dwelling which comes from God' which sees it directly as the person of the glorified Christ.[37] In fact Paul affirms that we now already have this eternal dwelling in heaven, the Risen

Christ. It is the risen Christ who allows us to share in his personal glorified physical mode of existence, and in this way the mortal is swallowed up by life (4.1). Mortal existence is clothed with the immortal raiment of the glorified body of Christ.

Finally I would like to draw attention briefly to the fact that Paul makes this hoped-for glorification at death expressly dependent on life here and now: 'For we must all appear before the judgment seat of Christ, so that each one may receive good or evil, according to what he has done in the body' (v.10). Paul does not resolve upon a flight from this history but looks for a crowning, a glorification of his existence in this history.

Resurrection in dying

I have argued that it is already possible to read a resurrection at death, on leaving our earthly dwelling, out of II Corinthians. This seems to me to be even more clearly the case in the letter to the Christians in Philippi. Here Paul expects an imminent death. He even longs for it. On the other hand he knows that he cannot be of any further use through his apostolic activity. In the end he does not know what to choose. 'It is my eager expectation and hope that I shall not be at all ashamed, but that with full courage now as always Christ will be honoured in my body, whether by life or by death. For to me to live is Christ, and to die is gain. If it is to be life in the flesh, that means fruitful labour for me. Yet which I shall choose I cannot tell. I am hard pressed between the two. My desire is to depart and be with Christ, for that is far better. But to remain in the flesh is more necessary on your account' (1.20-24).

For Paul death means gain because through it he finally comes to be with Christ, without any hindrance. Death does not free him from a bodily existence which is a burden, or is evil, as such, but from an existence which is characterized by suffering and torment, from an existence which is still constantly threatened, from a world full of injustice and lies. Through death he comes safe home to another world. Communion with Christ, which is truly experienced in and through this faith and the sacraments, is only experienced finally, in the most intensive way, at death.

Here personal death is seen as an individual experience of the parousia. Now Christ no longer comes to the world, but at their death men and women go to Christ. As in the letters to the Christians of Corinth, here too death is seen as a transformation of the earthly mode of existence: 'But our commonwealth is in heaven, and from it we await a saviour, the Lord Jesus Christ. who will change our lowly body to be like his glorious body, by the power which enables him even to subject all things to himself' (3.20f.). Here, too, as in II Cor.5, it is said that believing Christians now already have their homeland in heaven, i.e. in the glorified existence of the Lord.

Paul expects at his death what the Christians of Philippi may possibly experience as the coming of the redeemer from heaven, i.e. at the general parousia. His body will be newly created, made identical to the glorified body of Christ. So he will finally be with Christ. Here Paul refers explicitly to the omnipotence of the risen Christ, through which he is even capable of recreating the dead.

Thus this letter speaks quite plainly of being with Christ after death, even before the general resurrection at the parousia. If we take into account both Paul's unchanged anthropology and also the specific context of this work, not least the polemic with the Gnostics who believe that they have already attained the resurrection, this final and supremely intensive communion with Christ is quite clearly thought of as a new glorified physical mode of existence. Human beings change at death. They are made to resemble the glorified Christ, taken up in the Lord and to the Lord. Thus they achieve their real destiny: life in an unveiled, final communion with Christ. This destiny is our home, heaven.

I think that I have demonstrated conclusively how Paul believes that this final goal is reached at the death of the individual believer. In my view exegetes and theologians go too far when they cite Paul here as evidence for the existence of an intermediate state, i.e a period between the death of the individual and the final general resurrection. So we cannot use Paul to speak of a provisional blessedness, far less of a glory in which only the human soul will share.[38]

Paul never thinks in terms of an intermediate period, even in the letter to the Philippians. Even there he supposes the parousia to be very near (3.20), along with a general resurrection of the dead (3.11). The christocentricity, the stress on being one with Christ, has become so all-prevailing that Paul really thinks everything else unimportant as long as communion with Christ is realized to the full. So he simply allows two models of expectation to stand side by side as they are: the earlier one, which hopes for a general parousia in the apocalyptic sense, and the later one, with a more personal orientation on a communion with Christ in living and dying.

It remains for us now to make a necessarily short investigation of New Testament ideas about the future of this world.

III

THE PURPOSE OF THE COSMOS

The New Testament closely resembles the Old Testament and indeed apocalyptic in being interested only in God's saving action with mankind. Now this saving action is wholly concentrated on the Christ event.

The Old Testament saw creation from the beginning as a saving event for humanity and in humanity. In creation the God of the covenant reveals his omnipotence in the service of his saving and liberating love for humankind. The New Testament shares this creation faith. In a later reflection on the universal significance of Christ, Christ too is involved in the event of creation.[39] 'From him and through him and to him are all things' (Rom.11.36): 'There is one Lord, Jesus Christ, through whom are all things and for whom we exist' (I Cor.8.6; cf. Heb.1.2). 'Without him was not anything made that was made' (John 1.3): 'He is the image of the invisible God, the first-born of all creation; for in him all things were created, in heaven and on earth, visible and invisible, whether thrones or dominations or principalities or authorities – all things were created through him and for him. He is before all things, and in him all things hold together' (Col.1.15-17).

As a result of this orientation of the creation on Christ the New Testament is necessarily interested in the cosmic consequences of the event of redemption that is realized in and through Christ. But that happens only in so far as this redemption, like the event of creation, is concerned with humanity, or humanity-in-its-creation. What we have already discovered in the Old Testament and apocalyptic, we rediscover in the New Testament writings: God involves his whole creation in his redemptive activity. The whole reality of creation is at the service of God, to realize his saving action in mankind. Jesus, and more particularly the glorified Christ, now has the same power over creation at his disposal. He has a 'power which enables him to subject all things' (Phil.3.21).

The New Testament has the same ideas about 'all things', the universe, as the Old Testament and almost all the world of antiquity. These hopelessly mistaken conceptions are therefore in no way binding. It is worth while noting that the New Testament authors themselves do not reflect further on current ideas which they take over as they are without even recognizing the contradictions in them. Thus, for example, it is said that both the heaven and the earth are created by God, yet this heaven created by God is also called God's throne and his abode (Rev.4.2ff.). Although it is the dwelling of the immortal God, this heaven will pass away just as the earth will pass away (Matt.5.18; Mark 13.31; II Peter 3.7). It is also said of Christ who has ascended to heaven and who is expected to return from there (I Thess. 1.10; Phil.3.20) that he 'has ascended high above all heavens' (Eph.4.9f.), as though heaven was not God's real abode. Above all, Revelation has countless instances of the way in which different and contradictory cosmological conceptions can be combined without any problem in one and the same writing.

The New Testament authors use the cosmological imagery current in their time – there was nothing else that they could do. However, that is not the real content of their proclamation; it is the conceptuality with which they seek to express a binding message. This message must then be heard on each occasion in a specific context. Of course, in principle it is by no means impossible that the New Testament could also make a binding statement about the effect of the Christ event on the cosmos; however, that seems to me to lie so far outside the sphere of interest of the whole of biblical thought that we can say *a priori* that the cosmos is discussed only in connection with humanity-in-the-cosmos, with whom God is always concerned in creation and redemption.

We are now going to look at a number of texts in which creation or the cosmos is described in terms of the saving activity of Christ; it goes without saying that this is exclusively from an eschatological perspective.

1. Natural catastrophes on the day of judgment

I have already discussed at some length the New Testament expectation of an imminent end to the world, which is to be introduced by

the arrival of the glorified Christ, the parousia. Along the lines of the
Old Testament expectation of the day of Yahweh, and above all as
this conception was interpreted in an increasingly more literal way
in apocalyptic literature, in the New Testament the day of the Son of
man is sometimes also imagined as a time of judgment and condemnation in which cosmic catastrophes play a major role.

This is the case in the so-called Marcan apocalypse (13.24-32; cf.
Matt.24.29-31; Luke 21.25-27). In this eschatological discourse
there is mention of terrors in which the sun will become dark, the
moon will give no light and the stars will fall from heaven.[40] This
picture recalls the primal chaos dominated by darkness (Gen.1.2).
The return to this situation here becomes the universal sign of the
end of the world and at the same time of the coming of the Son of
man (v.26). It is more than probable that Mark regards this as a real
historical event,[41] though he does not think this through consistently. In fact, despite the fact that the stars fall for heaven, the earth
remains intact; mankind is little affected, as the elect are gathered
from the four winds, from the end of earth to the end of heaven
(v.27). At all events, this clear inconsistency allows us to interpret
this account as being in figurative language – all the more so since in
the meantime we have come to know that our planet is not as large
as all that and cannot accommodate very many stars! – even if the
author himself perhaps took this event literally.

It is interesting to note that here Mark does not connect these catastrophes with the punishment of sinners (though that is perhaps the
case in the parallel texts of Matthew and Luke) but regards them exclusively as signs accompanying the appearance of the Son of man
'to gather his elect' (v.27). The primal chaos evoked by the general
darkness precedes the new creation of a final situation of salvation.[42]

In Hebrews, too, natural catastrophes are connected with the eschatological judgment. The author wants to motivate a community
of the second and third generation, in which the zeal of faith threatens to diminish, to return to active belief. He does this by referring to
the final judgment. God once revealed himself on Sinai with tangible
signs, but Israel did not accept this revelation and therefore did not
escape God's condemnation (Heb.12.18-21,25, with an allusion to
Ex.19.12-18; Deut.9.9ff.). If the community of the new covenant
which no longer has 'what may be touched, a blazing fire' (12.18),
i.e. earthly things which can be perceived by the senses, but the heavenly reality itself, 'Mount Zion and the city of the living God, the
heavenly Jerusalem' (vv.22-24), refuses to hearken to the one who

speaks from heaven, then salvation is no longer conceivable when God again shakes the earth as he did at the theophany on Sinai. For 'his voice then shook the earth; but now he has promised, "Yet once more I will shake not only the earth but also the heaven." This phrase, "Yet once more ", indicates the removal of what is shaken, as of what has been made, in order that what cannot be shaken may remain. Therefore let us be grateful for receiving a kingdom that cannot be shaken' (12.26-28).

In the first divine revelation only the earth shook; at the last the heaven will also shake, i.e. everything that is created and transitory, all that has been made (v.27). These created things vanish.[43] The author stresses this so strongly in order to bring out the heavenly that remains. And now believers have access to the heavenly (12.22-24). They now have a kingdom that does not fall. Therefore, too, they have every reason for thanking God and worshipping him as he wants: in reverential fear (v.28). In all this the author wants to urge his community to direct their gaze in trust to this abiding, final future. This future must now be taken account of in the present. People can be sure of it. The future comes from the same unshakeable heaven from which that voice rang out which believers have heard and accepted. The credibility of the promised heaven lies in its origin: it is not made by human hands but is heavenly. On the other hand, human beings themselves have control over this future. What they do in the present has implications for the future. Now people must listen to the one who speaks from heaven. If they do not do that, they will have no share in the heavenly and will disappear with all that is created.

Of course, it is clear that the author of this letter is writing in a dualistic thought-pattern which sees both a vertical tension between the earthly and the heavenly and a horizontal tension between the present time and the eternal future. However, this dualism is never represented as a real opposition, for the heavenly affects the earthly, and the eternal future has already begun in the present. Here the categories of time and space have become dimensions of our reality: 'To speak about heaven means to speak about that wider sphere in which earth and man can develop. Spatial designations like depth (root), height (vision), breadth (radius of action) and length (perspective) do not threaten earthly humanity but express coordinates within which human beings best function.'[44]

The shaking of earth and heaven, the vanishing of all creation at the final judgment, is evoked in Hebrews to lead believers again to active trust and steadfastness, to sharpen their perception afresh, away from the transitory and towards that which cannot be made to shift. We may not read a real doctrine of the end of the world out of these texts.

Of course we encounter these cosmic catastrophes again in the Book of Revelation, specifically in 6.12-17. Here there is a description of the great day of wrath, the wrath both of the one who sits upon the throne and the wrath of the lamb (vv.16f.). This is clearly the day of the last judgment (cf. 14.10,19; 19.15). In the description of this day of wrath the same imagery is used as in the prophetic threat of the day of Yahweh which will strike terror in his enemies. So this is pictorial language. All mountains and islands are moved from their place (v.14), but people can still hide in caves and clefts in the hills (v.15), and they can call to the mountains and rocks to fall on them and hide them from the countenance of the one who sits on the throne (v.16). In a later vision in which the seventh seal is broken (8.1-12) the whole cosmos still seems to be intact, for only now is a third of it destroyed; whereas in 6.13 one could already read that the stars of heaven fell on the earth, in 12.4 we discover that a third of the stars of heaven are extinguished and thrown on the earth. So here we have specifically apocalyptic terminology. We have imagery depicting the wrath of God by which he will prepare an end for the hostile powers who threaten his faithful and will transform the situation to their advantage. So here there is no trace of a doctrine of final catastrophes, but a recollection of the final judgment to come, in which the enemies of the community of God are to be destroyed. In this way the author of Revelation wants to encourage his persecuted and tormented community and to urge them on to persistence and faithfulness.

2. The passing away of heaven and earth

There is mention not only of natural catastrophes at the end of time but also of a passing away of heaven and earth.

Thus we read in the Synoptic Gospels: 'Heaven and earth will pass away, but my words will not pass away' (Mark 13.31; cf. Matt.24.35; Luke 21.33), and, 'Till heaven and earth pass away, not an iota, not a dot, will pass away from the law until all is accomplished' (Matt.5.18; cf. Luke 16.17). In these statements the accent beyond question lies on the abiding and permanent validity of the words of Jesus about the law. It seems to me quite acceptable that an apocalyptic conception of the real passing away of heaven and earth should form the background to these statements, but the statements clearly do not present a doctrine to this effect, any more than it is an Old Testament doctrine that the sun and moon are eternal (Ps.89.36-38) or that all the heavenly bodies are founded for ever (Ps.148.1-6), since in yet other places we are told that earth and heaven may pass away (Ps.102. 26-28). All these and similar statements are simply concerned to express the permanence and eternity of God.

In I Cor.7.31b we find: 'The form of this world is passing away'. This remark fits perfectly into Paul's apocalyptic views which I mentioned earlier. Because of the imminence of the parousia which is to bring an end to this world there is no point in conforming to this world.

The constancy of the Lord alone is also made clear in Hebrews by a reference to the transitoriness of heaven and earth: 'Thou, Lord, didst found the earth in the beginning, and the heavens are the work of thy hands; they will perish, but thou remainest; they will all grow old like a garment, like a mantle thou wilt roll them up, and they will be changed. But thou are the same, and thy years will never end' (1.10-12).

As in the pericope about the shaking of the earth and the tottering of all creation (12.26-28) which I have already mentioned, here the author also wants to stress the eternity of the Lord (cf. 1.8; 7.3,8,16f.,21,23-25,28). The changeableness and transitory nature of all creation are the background here. From his first chapter onwards the author wants to keep his community intent on what is really at stake, the authentic, the reliable, the eternal. Here there is no explicit doctrine of an end of the world, any more than there is in Ps.102.26-28, which is quoted. The sole concern is with the one who is eternal; in the psalm this is the creator, and here it is Christ the Lord.

A similar text brings us to quite a different climate. I John 2.17: 'The world passes away, and the lust of it.' Here there is mention of the world, not simply of the cosmos as the created world but of the specific historical world which is hostile to God. Here the world is the centre and field of force of all the evil desires which alienate people from God and their true destiny. Hence the admonition: 'Do not love the world or the things in the world' (2.15). For this world is passing away in the sense that it is deceptive. It does not claim to be absolute, necessary, definitive. Forget that: only God and doing his will abide for eternity (v.17b). Thus the author is not talking about the end of the world in the literal sense of this word but of a right relationship to this world: do not require of this world what it cannot give although it promises it: reliability, absoluteness, eternity.

Things are much more complex in II Peter 3. This chapter is about the parousia. There are people who mock Christians for their expectation of an imminent parousia. Here the author says that this very behaviour is a feature of the end-time (3.3). These mockers do not take into account the fact that God has already once dealt with the sinful world by the flood (vv.5f.). Soon God will again intervene in judgment and condemnation, with much more cosmic consequences than was the case with the flood: 'Then the heavens will pass away with a loud noise, and the elements will be dissolved with fire, and the earth and the works that are upon it will be burnt up' (v.10). Or also: 'On that day the heavens will be kindled and dissolved, and the elements will melt with the heat' (v.12).

Because the author is here arguing with mockers, he takes the opportunity of depicting the day of judgment (v.7), the day of the Lord (v.10), the day of God (v.12) in as terrifying a way as possible; it is a radical annihilation of everything tainted by sin. In other words, the cosmic catastrophes mentioned here serve as metaphors of judgment, that is, as images which are more of an indication of the cruel character of the condemnation of sinners than a literal account of what will really happen. Here the author does not give an account of the end of the world, but encourages humiliated and disturbed Christians, while calling on the mockers to reflect and repent.

In fact the author does not stop at this scene of condemnation. At the same time he allows the promise 'of new heavens and a new earth in which righteousness dwells' to shine through (v.13). The end is positive. There is a final rule of God over the righteous.

3. A new heaven and a new earth

In Revelation we find once again the two themes of II Peter 3. There is mention of a passing away of earth and heaven (20.11) and of a new heaven and a new earth (21.1ff).

The great visions of Revelation give a view of a radically different situation from that in which believers now find themselves. At the end of time a general judgment will take place. The appearance of the judge here will be so awe-inspiring that earth and heaven will flee

before his face. Their place will be found no more (20.11). This is
clearly an image in which the majesty of the judge of the world is
depicted as intensively as possible. One cannot take the flight of earth
and heaven literally; otherwise, where could the throne of the judge
be put, the fiery sea into which death and the underworld are
thrown? The author is solely concerned to make clear that each person will be judged according to his deeds and that for the faithful
there will be an end to all misery, even to death and the kingdom of
the dead, the underworld (20.14).

Then the final situation of salvation is described as a new heaven
and a new earth, as the new Jerusalem. God takes up his abode
among men. Here we get the same description of this new heaven and
new earth as in II Peter 3.13: 'Where righteousness dwells'. The vision of Revelation points to the realization of the prophecy of
Isa.65.11-22: whereas Isaiah spoke of a historical recreation of
heaven and earth around the earthly Jerusalem as a centre, here John
speaks in apocalyptic terms. An already pre-existing heavenly Jerusalem descends (21.2; cf. I Enoch 53.6; 90.28ff.; IV Ezra 7.26; 8.52;
10.27ff.; 13.26). To this the existing earth and heaven must first give
place (20.11; 21.1).

Here John uses the imagery of apocalyptic. In it attempts are made
to express the inexpressible; often, as happens here, in poetic descriptions aimed at a reality which breaks apart any language and any
conceptuality and any imagery as being much too narrow. Chapters
21 and 22 must be read one after the other as a whole.[45]

As I have already said repeatedly, apocalyptic is concerned to encourage tormented people: everything will soon be quite different;
hang on, for all will be made new. How, the apocalyptists did not
know. However, hope can no longer be directed towards an event
within the world and within history.

So we cannot say that Revelation proclaims a doctrine about a
general judgment, about the end of history, the passing away of
heaven and earth. Anyone who claims this does not take into account
the purpose and the language of apocalyptic. The author wants simply to encourage a tortured community and to exhort it to stand
firm: soon they themselves will rule and will no longer be oppressed
and persecuted: 'They will rule for all eternity' (22.5; cf. 20.4).

From the texts that we have so far analysed in this chapter we
could hardly conclude that the New Testament presents a binding
doctrine about the passing away of heaven and earth. However, we
have constantly come up against the apocalyptic background which

envisages the disappearance of this age and the coming of a new one. Of course we cannot bind ourselves by apocalyptic conceptions, but we can accept the explicit meaning of these conceptions, namely that the final consummation of human hope, like its beginning and its abiding realization, comes expressly from God. That is indicated by the phrase 'from heaven'. Because human salvation comes from God, is God himself, it cannot be bound to this earth and remain limited to our history. All that is on earth and in our history is transitory and passes away. However, in and through Christ God has given us an eternal country. In the heavenly glorified Christ God gives us himself as future.

Now this future concerns human beings as human beings. That was expressed strongly in what we saw in connection with the resurrection of the body. Human beings live in the world. Even as believers, they realize themselves within this world. God as future intervenes in our human history. Here he motivates and moves our freedom. The future which is God himself has already begun here and now. Our future is decided in the present. We have heard like a refrain: 'We must all appear before the judgment seat of Christ, so that each one may receive good or evil, according to what he has done in the body' (II Cor.5.10); 'He who does the will of God abides for ever' (I John 2.17); 'Their deeds follow them' (Rev.14.13). People are brought before God to be judged as people, with their actions, that is, with the piece of history which they themselves have made, with the world which to a considerable degree they have determined by their actions. In this sense the cosmos, as the human world, and human history as such, is included in the destiny of mankind. I believe that we can read this with unmistakable words in the New Testament also. I would like to quote three texts in this connection.

The first is well known: 'I consider that the sufferings of this present time are not worth comparing with the glory that is to be revealed to us. For the creation waits with eager longing for the revealing of the sons of God; for the creation was subjected to futility, not of its own will but by the will of him who subjected it in hope; because the creation itself will be set free from its bondage to decay and obtain the glorious liberty of the children of God. We know that the whole creation has been groaning in travail until now; and not only the creation, but we ourselves, who have the first fruits of the spirit, groan inwardly as we wait for adoption as sons, the redemption of our bodies' (Rom.8.19-23).

In this text the term creation means all the phenomena of nature

and history in so far as they are created and form the spoilt world of
fallen men. Creation is thus the broken world of sinful mankind, including mankind itself as sinful creatures. It is said here that this creation is insufficient in itself and that it is driven by an ardent longing
to be able to see 'the revealing of the sons of God'.

In this powerful text, in which Paul reflects on suffering that still
constantly torments Christians – despite the fact that they are
already redeemed, – he talks about the suffering and the future of
creation. Paul wants to encourage these Christians in their suffering.
This present state counts for nothing in comparison with the glory
the revelation of which is to be expected. And this revelation cannot
be long in coming. Here Paul points to the suffering of creation. In so
doing he alludes to a contemporary interpretation of Gen.3.17f.
which attributes the wretched situation, the transitoriness and
nothingness of creation, to a curse which it incurred because of the
sin of Adam.[46] But this curse is not final. If the whole creation is involved in the sin of mankind, it will also participate in the complete
liberation of mankind. The revelation of the glory and the glorious
freedom of the children of God will also mean liberation for the
whole of creation. The glory of the children of God will stream over
it. In fact, creation does not await their redemption directly for itself,
far less of itself; it will be the glory of the children of God which
shines on them or into which it is taken up, in which it participates.

As I have said, Paul is concerned to encourage Christians in their
suffering and tribulation. Therefore he points to the suffering of creation which – again in a very contemporary, but also in an Old Testament way (cf. Isa.43.1; 66.7ff.) – he interprets as the birth-pangs of
a new, messianic period: from a Christian perspective, the parousia.
The more these pains intensify, the nearer comes the hour of redemption. From this perspective Christians may look for meaning in their
suffering. Christ himself entered into glory at the climax of his suffering, through death. Now believers have a share in this suffering,
so that they may soon also have a share in his glory (8.17), and the
suffering is nothing compared to the glorification which is to be expected (v.18). That is in fact the point, the essence, the basic purpose
of Paul's argument in this text.[47] At the same time he also quite deliberately says something here about the future of the human world,
which is evidently still unredeemed. It is quite natural that he should
say nothing about cosmology, but it is equally evident that the world
as creation and as the world of mankind is of great interest to him.
Just as creation is involved through God in human sin, so it is simi-

larly brought by God to share in the glory of the children of God. That is the hope which lives in it from God.[48] Paul does not say anything about how this will happen.

However, the text does remind believers of their responsibility for creation. They must be aware that this creation waits on them to bring about its liberation. So Christians must work to share in the redemption of creation, to give it its authentic form, its real nature, in and through which it shows itself, *qua* creature, to be neither absolute nor divine.

A second text relevant to our problem is the Christ hymn in Col.1.15-20. It is generally assumed that the text as we now have it is a revision of an earlier version which was perhaps of Hellenistic Christian origin. Here the author of Colossians corrects a more triumphalist christology.[49] The earlier texts spoke only of the pre-eminence of Christ in creation and redemption. Here Christ is mentioned as head of the body. The body is the cosmos. The final redactor extends this pre-eminence to the body which is the church (v.18), and he stresses above all that Christ's prime role in reconciliation and the making of peace follows from the shedding of his blood on the cross (v.20). The author of the letter thus gives full expression to the historical dimension of redemption, which had been neglected by the author of the original version of the hymn. Creation is seen in the light of redemption. Creation comes to itself, to completion, to unity and peace, through the intervention of God in the reconciling Christ event. Christ glorified, the 'first to rise from the dead' (v.18), is 'in all things the first', the one who unites the universe with its creator. The author of Colossians took over this hymn, which he corrected in some ways, because he found his own thinking, utterly inspired by Paul, in it. I therefore think that we can conclude that this hymn clearly bears witness that the crucified and glorified Christ brings the creation as a whole to its destiny. It expresses the eternal value of the creation as the world of men. Christians who sang this hymn in their liturgy are reminded that as a community, as a church, they now already have Christ as their head and that in him and through him they have already been brought peace and redemption, all as a fore-taste. They have to put this into practice in the world, to show it, not triumphalistically but by following the way of Christ, who has brought this peace and reconciliation through his blood, poured out for and on behalf of others.

Finally the third text: 'When all things are subjected to him, then the Son himself will also be subjected to him who put all things under him, that God may be everything to everyone' (I Cor.15.28). That does not happen until the last enemy, death, has been overcome (cf.15.26). In other words, as long as death rules or is a reality, the revelation of the meaning of history is not yet complete. The real goal and final meaning of everything is union in God, in and through the glorified Christ. That is the future of man and his world. This future is already given and has begun in the risen Lord. The power of his resurrection (cf. Phil.3.10) is at work through his Spirit in our history. So we cannot say that our history is gradually evolving towards its future. The future comes from God, from 'heaven', to our existence in the present, in the world. We believe that our present history is moved by its future: the glorified Christ. He is therefore constantly involved in directing our human history towards himself. The power of our resurrection, his Spirit, is Christ himself, who has already come to us and in whom we already experience his parousia in faith. Through the same power in which he comes to us, to live in us, he takes us to himself so that we may live completely in him.

The future of man and the world does not therefore fall within our history nor does it take place within this creation. Our future and the future of the history that we make on this earth is the glorified Christ himself. In other words, the future of our history and our world, our history-making existence in the world, does not lie in its prolongation. Yet the future of our history and our world is always also a matter of concern. For all the discontinuity which needs to be stressed if we are not to be led astray into nonsensical imaginings, continuity is guaranteed through the creating and redeeming God who will reveal himself and give himself to our experience as the total meaning of all things, when he himself is all in all. I shall return to the way in which we might conceive of this in the last, systematic, part of this book.

PART THREE

Vision of the End

An unshakeable conviction
that you will be renewed and newly created
when they say of you 'fallen asleep'.

Ida Gerhardt

I

THINKING OF THE FUTURE

We have come to the end of a tiring voyage of discovery. We have now arrived at heights from which we have a view of the broad panorama of biblical expectations of the future, difficult though they are to chart. They differ so much that it is impossible to make them point in any one direction. We must respect this feature. We can hardly divert them from the channel they have dug for themselves through the landscape of time, religion, society and culture which is their background. Now, however, we can go on to talk with some knowledge about the hope embodied in the various future expectations of people who describe their own life story in the Bible.

On our journey we also found the material with which we can lay the biblical foundations for a Christian hope. Knowledge of what we have discovered in the second part of this book is an indispensable prelude to showing that the content of this third section does not consist of unproved assertions but is built on a broad and solid biblical basis.

Thus we can already elucidate the meaning of eschatology from scripture. The term itself is a recent one and is used for the first time in the seventeenth century. It can be derived from a saying of Jesus Sirach: 'In all you do, remember the end of your life, and then you will never sin' (Sir.7.36). 'End of life' is a rendering of the Greek *ta eschata* and was translated into Latin by the term *novissima*. Eschatology is really a commitment to trust in God in situations in which human beings are confronted with their own definitive helplessness, with their radical limitations in every respect. Eschatology speaks of God in the light of human death, in the light of questions about the end of a history which has been made by transitory human beings, in the light of ideas about the end of a world which is also thought to have a beginning, a world which need not exist and therefore will not necessarily continue to exist.

However, for people to talk about *God* in the context of these experiences of utter limitation becomes a meaningful possibility only on the basis of the kind of experience of God which people actually have within these limitations. I have to stress as firmly as possible that the subject-matter of eschatology contains answers which will only satisfy the questions of a *believer*. It would be wrong to make the mistake in the realm of eschatology that has all too often been made in the theology of creation. There people have often looked for answers to scientific questions about the beginning of the world, of the universe, of mankind. Questions have been asked about the time and manner of the origin of reality. For answers to this kind of question one must go to scientists. The Bible is not a book which gives neutral information about existence. It offers insights into existence. Scripture gives an answer to existential questions, i.e. to questions which arise from profound human experiences, in the light of which people feel called to seek redemption rather than a solution. Nor does the Bible disclose any meaning; it simply shows us a way forward.

So eschatology does not give any answers to scientific questions about the end of man, history and the cosmos, to questions which often amount to no more than curiosity about the time and nature of the end of all things. Eschatology does not give an answer to scientific questions about the end of all things any more than creation gives a scientifically based explanation of the origin of all things. Here, too, we must be careful that we do not misinterpret revelation and faith as explanatory knowledge to be used where human reason gives out. Revelation is not offered as scientific information from a supernatural divine source; but it gives unexpected insights into human experience – even into what people already know themselves - and it shows above all an outcome for all human situations. People cannot adopt a neutral attitude to the insights given by revelation; revelation stands their existence on its head. Their life changes completely. Faith consists in living differently, sharing a different life.

Eschatology, then, does not give us any new information about the future of mankind or the future of our history and our world. It only says that mankind is approached by God from the future, always, in all circumstances, even when we come up against our limits. At the same time, it indicates that human beings have to take account of this future here, today. Life today changes as a result of this eschatological perspective on the future. However, eschatology as a discipline must investigate how we can responsibly, as human beings endowed with reason, integrate the perspective on the future offered by revelation into our existence. Thus it is clear that faith comes first and only then, in and through theology, a scientific reflection on this faith. Faith is autonomous, and as such does not long for anything else. Theology looks for scientific insights by which one can more readily give the assent of faith in life and through life, as questioning and reflecting human beings.

1. Earthly and heavenly future

From our investigations in Part Two it became particularly clear that a view of God in this eschatological perspective is strongly dependent on human experiences of the helplessness and the limitations which I have just mentioned. Only by faith is God discovered as a future beyond death, when people can no longer find traces of a God of righteousness within the limits of a life which ends in injustice. God is only envisaged in faith outside human history when people can no longer see any future within history. God is only experienced as future for the world on the basis of a conviction of the indissoluble unity of man and the world. As a result it is impossible to think of God as a future for humanity without at the same time seeing him as a future for the world of mankind.

From the whole of the account in Part Two it emerged that this view of God as future is strongly conditioned by the general religious and cultural climate in which one looks at God. People always encounter God as their God, as the answer to their questions, as an appeal to their possibilities. Thus the picture human beings have of themselves also to a large degree determines the picture they have of God. This extremely important insight allows us without any anxiety to stress the relativity of the conceptions, the patterns of expectation, the images and symbols in which the various biblical conceptions of God-as-future are expressed. Perhaps we may replace them by others which in the light of our own time and culture seem better capable of focussing on God-as-future.

Believers only discover God-as-future with any clarity in the Christ event, or more accurately in the resurrection and glorification of the crucified Jesus of Nazareth. In the resurrection and glorification of his Son God has revealed that he really is as this Jesus proclaimed and brought him, namely the absolute future for all human beings in all situations. Jesus brought God as future. God endorsed this proclamation and life-style of Jesus by giving Jesus himself a future in a situation in which a human being is cut off from any future by death. The crucified one lives. He is glorified. The glorified and crucified one continues to bring God as future by the working of his Spirit.

As a result we know from the past, in the present, what our future holds. It is the God whom we heard and saw at work in Jesus as the source and content of salvation or completely human happiness for all, the God who now brings us to this faith in and through his Spirit, by whom we dare in confidence to live in trust as followers of this Jesus, who always remains our future. At the same time this means that any statement about our future must be tested by the historical Jesus-event and the working of his Spirit in history and the present. We cannot and may not think of our future other than as the consummation and crowning of what has already begun in and through Jesus and continues in the power of his spirit.

However, while the past and the present lead to a certain definition of the content of our Christian expectation of the future, we must still let the future be the future. That means that the special nature of life in the future is not yet experienced by any mortal. Or, to put it in John's words: 'We are God's children now; it does not yet appear what we shall be' (I John 3.2). The future as such remains the object of expectation and confident hope. 'We await our blessed hope, the appearing of the glory of our great God and saviour Jesus Christ' (Titus 1.13; cf. I Cor.1.7). This future is a communion with Christ of the kind that no one can experience in the present: 'We know that when he appears we shall be like him, for we shall see him as he is' (I John 3.2). John immediately argues that such an expectation of the future governs life in the present: 'And everyone who thus hopes in him purifies himself as he is pure' (3.3).

Eternity in time

What we expect and hope, then, has already begun and is already taking place to the degree that people share in the mystery of Christ, i.e. to the degree that they live as followers of Jesus of Nazareth. That people can and do this is not an achievement of their own but takes place through the active presence of the glorified Lord, God himself, in their life: 'If a man loves me, he will keep my word, and my Father will love him, and we will come to him and make our home with him' (John 14.23). Thus the parousia or the coming of Christ-with-power is a constant event. Christ comes to live in men, now (cf. Gal.2.20). We should clarify this aspect of Christ's coming more, if only because it would help more people to pray certain texts in the eucharist with integrity. I have in mind texts like 'ready to greet him when he comes again' (Eucharistic Prayer III), 'looking forward to his coming in glory' (IV), and so on. Texts like this presuppose an expectation which is not alive. On the contrary, the vast majority of churchgoers would reject such texts instantly if they realized that they were really praying about waiting for the end of the world. 'Looking forward to his coming in glory' can and should correspond to a real attitude on the part of all believers. Believers may look to the end of the world full of confidence, but very few of them are very expectant that it will come! So simply because of the absolute integrity which we need in prayer, we should put more stress on the present coming of the glorified Christ in and through his spirit. In fact Christ does not return as an individual but in and through his Spirit in a community of persons. His coming takes place where his Spirit can work to the full in people, for he himself has become Spirit (II Cor.3.17). We pray in hopeful expectation for this coming of the Lord in our life, in our history, to renew the face of the earth.

So we must direct all our attention to the coming of the Lord in the present, not only for the sake of the authenticity of our own prayer but above all to have our attitude constantly determined and renewed by this coming. The Lord is not at our disposal. We do not have him. He himself wants us to be fully at his disposal at his coming. He seeks to be Lord for us and over us. In us he means to establish his kingdom on earth. In order to give our world and our history the form of his kingdom, he seeks control over us, to take us into his service.

This aspect of the Christian hope for the future, its inner-worldly power which renews all things, has recently been rediscovered and applied to specific situations at the level of the church, society and politics. Christian hope cannot in fact be narrowed down to an individualism of salvation in which this salvation is seen as coming from God in a purely supernatural way, or in a transcendent and heavenly way. Already in the Old Testament people knew that God wanted to be our God here on earth, to bring happiness to people as they live, as whole people. God did not just put people on earth as a test, in order later to transport them to heaven as a reward. He created the earth for human beings, and he himself makes history on this earth with and through them.'The heavens are the Lord's heavens, but the earth he has given to the children of men'(Ps.115.16).

I shall not spend longer on this aspect of Christian eschatology, but not because I think it to be less important or less relevant. On the contrary, the specific realization of this particular aspect of the Christian hope is the only way in which Christians and their churches can proclaim the other aspect of the same eschatological hope in a credible way, not in theory, but in praxis, by offering others an experience in which they can share. The reason why I do not go into this in more detail here is simply that I feel that the mass of literature on the question relieves me of the need to: it provides thorough information, well-argued insights and urgent tasks to perform. There is plenty there for us to get on with!

I would, though, like to make one brief point. Those who do not look for the coming of Jesus in their life here and now, i.e. those who do not allow Jesus to be Lord over their existence because they do not seek to follow him at all in their way of life, can hardly honestly hope to see him at his coming at the end of time. In other words, hope in the Lord for what comes after this life becomes quite incredible and false unless he is already expected now as the ever welcoming Spirit who comes to direct life and to make people disciples of Jesus. For in the end we all know what the Lord will say and do at his coming at the end of time. 'When the Son of man comes in his glory, and all the angels with him, then he will sit on his glorious throne. Before him will be gathered all the nations, and he will separate them from one another . . . Then the King will say to those on his right hand: Come, O blessed of my Father, inherit the kingdom prepared for you from the foundations of the world; for I was hungry and you gave me food . . . Truly, I say to you, as you did it to one of the least of these my brethren, you did it to me. Then he will say to those at his left hand, Depart from me, you cursed, into the eternal fire prepared for the devil and his angels; for I was hungry and you gave me no food . . . Truly, I say to you, as you did it not to one of the least of these, you did it not to me' (Matt.25.31-45).

2. From earth to heaven

In what follows I shall restrict myself deliberately. I shall speak only of the transcendent aspect of Christian eschatology. In so doing I shall follow the main lines of the thought of believers within the tradition, in order to make responsible use of the insights of faith which have been gained here from a time-conditioned context.

People gradually came to be less interested in the universal aspect of eschatology, in the parousia as such, universal judgment, the end of the world and of history, for two reasons. First, the parousia, which was generally thought to be imminent during the early days of the Christian church, in the form of the coming of the glorified Lord at the end of the world, failed to materialize. And secondly, the church was experienced as the community to which the glorified Lord had already come in his Spirit. Stress was laid on eschatology realized in the present. This was helped on by the development of the practice of the sacraments and theology. As a result, interest was directed towards the active presence of the Lord and his Spirit here and now. Still, to begin with, expectation of an imminent end to the world continued to govern views about the Christian life-style. The Lord made present in and through the sacraments was seen more as the source of a spiritual union with him than as an active force for following him, driven by his Spirit, to renew the face of the earth. Many factors played a part here. This is not the place to go into them in detail. Be this as it may, the whole climate in which Christians lived oriented them on a markedly individualized eschatology. There was reflection on the future of the individual after death.

As the young churches were founded and developed within a cultural context which was determined above all by Hellenism, it was natural that Hellenistic philosophies should also exercise influence on Christian proclamation and life-style. Cultures do not simply exist side by side without affecting one another. They interpenetrate one another mutually. As far as our problem is concerned, the Hellenistic view of man – if one can speak of a single view accepted in Hellenism, which was by no means clearly the case – was to play a major role in the proclamation of Christian belief in the resurrection and rational reflection on it. I have already discussed this on a number of occasions. We found the earliest traces of this influence from Hellenistic thought in the books of Koheleth and Wisdom. We saw Paul in particular struggling with this problem in his letters to the Christians of Corinth.

The first thing that forced itself on Christians in a Hellenistic world was reflection on the relationship between their own belief in the resurrection and the assumption of an immortal soul as this was taught in certain Hellenistic groups and movements. It is all too evident that the influence of this teaching was enormously great. Even now, most Catholic Christians think that the doctrine of an immortal soul is part of the binding doctrine of faith, indeed that it is even a dogma. At all events, the communication from the Congregation for the Doctrine of Faith which I have already mentioned has done nothing to correct this false conception; quite the contrary.

In the following chapters I shall try to investigate how Christians who affirmed the resurrection of the body as a datum of faith reacted to a doctrine which spoke of an immortal soul.

II

RESURRECTION AND IMMORTALITY

1. Dualism: body and soul

Semitic thought saw human beings predominantly as indivisible unities. It imagined them as it saw them, as bodies. Anachronistically, one could call this Semitic view of the human being monistic. In Hellenism we have a dualistic picture of humanity. A distinction was made there between soul and body. The origin of this distinction within the one human being is said to go back to the Orphic mystery religions of Thrace. It was taken up by Pythagoreanism (Pythagoras lived about 580-500 BC), which taught that the soul lives in a human being as in a prison or tomb and must seek to free itself from this prison by asceticism or catharsis. This distinction was later to be expressed in a more ethical and religious sense. Perhaps one might say that at that time the human being was already thought of as *homo faber*, determined by his or her actions and an indissoluble unity with them and their consequences. Good deeds are rewarded and evil deeds are punished. Human beings cannot escape this unity with their actions, even through death. Reward or retribution retain their significance beyond death. That has to be so, simply for justice to be done. We can still hear a clear echo of the ethical origin of belief in immortality in Plato (428-348 BC): 'If death were a separation from everything, it would be a godsend for the wicked, when they died, to be separated at once from the body and from their own wickedness along with the soul' (*Phaedo* 107c). When the body dies, 'something' of the human being survives death, for justice to be done.

From that point the argument was taken one stage further. The element which can withstand death, which seems to be eternal, the soul, is more important than what disappears with death, the body. In this view corporeal soon becomes synonymous with inferior, transitory; it is also a source of misleading appearance and alienation. What is more valuable, authentic, important, genuine, true, is the soul. Therefore the moral task confronting human beings is obvious. They must detach themselves from the transitory, changing and deceptive world of the body in order to bring everything under the control and hegemony of the soul by virtue of its capacities of knowledge and insight. One cannot yet speak of a dualism in the real sense of the word; this is more a polarity within unity.[1]

Plato above all developed this ethical dualism further and gave it a philosophical basis.[2] Through particular expressions which we find above all in the dialogues *Phaedo* and *Phaedrus*, Plato himself directly stimulated the ontological dualism of his own school and of later Neoplatonism (c. AD 200-527). Plotinus (AD 204-270), the main representative of this philosophical trend, brought the dualistic interpretation of Plato's doctrine of living to a climax both in his metaphysics and in his epistemology and ethics. Body and soul are now seen as two separate entities each completely independent of the other. In essence, by nature, they are quite different. The soul is spiritual and pre-existent, i.e. it exists before the body; it is of divine origin and essentially immortal. The body is material, of less value and transitory. The soul is a prisoner in the body and is only freed from it at death, when it is again able to live in its own environment which is purely spiritual, eternal and divine.

This doctrine continually met with a sceptical reception, even in the Greek world. Marguerite Yourcenar gives an apt illustration of this scepticism when she makes the Emperor Hadrian complain on the occasion of the death of Antinous: 'Our philosophers care little for such niceties . . . Only the soul was important, they said, arrogantly positing as a fact the immortality of that vague entity which we have never seen function in the absence of the body, and the existence of which they had not yet taken the trouble to prove. I was not so certain: since the smile, the expression of the eyes, the voice, those imponderable realities, had ceased to be, then why not the soul, too? Was it necessarily more immaterial than the body's heat?'[3]

Be this as it may, the early church was to take over the twin concepts of soul and body. It was compelled to do so by the Gnosticism which arose in its own ranks. We have already seen that Gnosticism was a movement in which people denied that bodily, specifically historical existence had any religious and moral significance, and attributed meaning only to the soul. Understandably, at this point advantage was taken of Hellenistic dualism. In these circles the resurrection of the body was consistently rejected as unimportant. People had already risen spiritually.

Christians vigorously attacked this crude denial of their heritage on the basis of Jewish creation faith, which attached positive significance to the material world, and the character of Christianity, which was grounded in the saving act of God in the man Jesus Christ, in the word made flesh, culminating in the physical resurrection of Jesus from the dead. Against the Gnostics, they stressed the significance of the resurrection of the body, at the same time acknowledging the value of existence in the body, in specific history played out here on earth. In order to avoid any Gnostic spiritualizing of the resurrection the earlier expression 'resurrection of the body' was increasingly replaced by the formula 'resurrection of the flesh', this flesh in which we live now.

If there was to be a philosophical and theological basis for this belief in the bodily resurrection and it was to be defended against the Gnostics, different arguments could be adduced: the omnipotence of the creator (Clement of Rome, Justin, Tertullian, Cyril of Jerusalem); the course of nature (Clement of Rome, Tertullian); the intention of the Creator for his creature (Athenagoras, Gregory of Nyssa); the link between resurrection and ethics (Cyril of Jerusalem).[4] The intention of these church fathers and theologians is always to stress the value and the significance of the individual who lives a particular bodily life. Like the whole of the material world, the human body is a creation of God and as such is good, called to achieve its destiny with God. None of this good creation is lost, but at the end of time achieves a good consummation at the resurrection of all flesh.

However, this anti-Gnostic stress on the resurrection could not prevent the early church from soon integrating the Hellenistic conception of an immortal soul into its eschatological hope. On the one hand we can rediscover here something of an Old Testament interpretation of humanity as the image and likeness of God (Wisdom 2.23), while on the other it was seen as an excellent possibility of thinking meaningfully about the communion with Christ which according to Paul one enters immediately after death. It now began to be supposed that the immortal soul appears before the judgment seat of God immediately after death. It survives in the underworld for an intermediary period, awaiting the universal judgment and the resurrection of bodies. To begin with, an exception was made for the martyrs, as for the patriarchs and prophets. These were all said to have been admitted to final communion with Christ immediately after death, not in any provisional way. It is not inconceivable that the early church simply took over this conviction, which we have already encountered in early Judaism, apocalyptic and certain New Testament writings, without reflecting further on the problem of the resurrection of the body. There are good reasons for assuming that here people really believed in a physical resurrection that had already taken place.[5]

It was only when people felt themselves compelled by the Gnostic position to put the bodily resurrection at the end of time, because they could no longer interpret the resurrection as a purely spiritual process, i.e. in the Gnostic sense, that they also saw the 'consummation' of the martyrs as something that merely affected their souls. That is already quite clearly the case with Cyprian. In his view, the souls of all the righteous, without any distinction, after death immediately enter the heavenly glorified community of Christ. Only the resurrection of the body is needed to make their blessedness complete.

In this last stage we can see how despite all the anti-Gnostic stress on the resurrection of the body, the Hellenistic view of human fulfilment in a purely spiritual blessedness, immediately upon death, still persists. Here the resurrection of the body is not of course denied, but it is suppressed in the specific experience of Christian hope by the longing for the soul to enjoy the blessed vision of God after death. This is particularly clear in the theology of St Augustine (354-430), who was inspired by Neoplatonism.[6]

This produces a problem in later theology: what is the significance of the resurrection of the body at the end of time if one accepts that the soul enjoys the blessed vision of God directly after death? And how can one give any explanation of an identity between the long-decayed body and the glorified resurrection body that is expected?

2. Man as indissolubly one

In early scholasticism (a certain scholarly method of teaching theology, beginning in the tenth century), despite all the influence of Neoplatonism people continued to insist strongly on the unity of the human being. The soul is part of a human being, not man or woman in themselves. That implies that the human being really dies at death and that the survival of the soul with God cannot yet be thought of as complete blessedness.

It was Thomas Aquinas (1225-1274) above all who, during the golden century of scholasticism, again thought of man as an indissoluble unity. In this he was indebted to the anthropology of the Greek philosopher Aristotle (384-322 BC), though he developed on his thinking in a very original way.

According to Thomas a human being does not consist, as in Neoplatonism, of two individual substances which could survive independently of each other. Being human simply consists in the living unity of body and soul. Authentic existence, the very being of the soul itself, is its existence in the body. Bodily life is the life of the soul itself which can only exist in and through the body, by which the soul expresses itself and realizes itself in the world of time and space. Neither soul nor body has an independent existence. Human beings cannot be taken apart like the two parts of a box. The essential nature of humanity is to be a composite of soul and body. Soul and body are both designations of the whole person from two different aspects.

Therefore death represents the end of the whole person, the destruction not only of the body but also of the soul, insofar as this necessarily realizes itself in a body. The body, which is no longer sustained by the soul, falls apart into its material components, and the soul, which is spiritual, continues to exist, not as human but as something human which is permanently in search of the body. It exists in separation from the body, in an unnatural state (*In IV Sent.* d.43, q.1, sol.3, ad 2; I, q.29, a.1, ad 5; *De Pot.*, q.9, a.2, ad 14; *ScG* IV, 79).

Despite this unnatural state of the disembodied soul, Thomas still affirms what seems already to be a universally accepted doctrine, that of the blessed vision of God by the disembodied soul. Thus he writes: 'As to perfect blessedness which consists in the vision of God, there are some who affirm that it is impossible for the soul to attain this without a body . . . That is clearly false . . . It is evident that the souls of the saints, who have a disembodied existence, walk by sight in the vision of God's essence, which is true happiness . . . Because complete human happiness consists in looking on the nature of God, this complete happiness does not depend on the body. Therefore the soul can be happy without the body. It must be realized that something can belong to the perfection of a thing in two ways. First, as constituting its nature; thus soul is part of man's perfection . . . Secondly, as required for its full development; thus good looks and swift wit are part of his perfection. Although the body does not belong in the first way to the perfection of human happiness, it does so in the second way' (I II, q.4, a.5). In other words, in St Thomas' view the blessedness of the soul is already complete before the resurrection of the body.[7] He is generally of the opinion that the resurrection of the body *intensively* increases the blessedness of the soul (*In IV Sent.*, d.49, q.1 a.4, sol.1; q.4, a.5, sol.2, ad 1; *De pot.*, q.5, a.10). The quality of the enjoyment of blessedness is improved and strengthened, but only in an incidental way. In fact it does not need to be real. Later Thomas also assumed an *extensive* increase in blessedness at the resurrection of the body. But if we note that the reflection 'on taking the body again the happiness does not grow intensively but extensively' follows the detailed account which I have quoted in which Thomas affirms the complete blessedness of the disembodied soul (I-II, q.4, a.5, ad 5), then we may take this extensive increase to be only an accidental happening.

It seems to me clear that here Thomas is making concessions to the prevalent view in which belief in an eternal future for man had already been expressed: the blessed vision of God by the soul immediately after death, and the resurrection of the body at the end of time. The philosopher Thomas must have found it desperately difficult to attribute perfect blessedness to the disembodied soul. In his anthropology the body is really not subsidiary to the soul.

In his philosophical anthropology, Thomas has quite an easy solution to the problem of the identity between the dead body and the resurrection body. Before him, various theologians had regarded the resurrection either as the raising of the dead body or simply as a new creation. Thomas sees another way out. He had defined the soul as *forma corporis*; i.e. the soul forms, determines, makes the body what it is. Only through the soul is a piece of matter *my* body. Corporeality can only be understood in terms of the soul. As form, as a totality, the body receives its significance, its special character and its meaning from the soul, which expresses itself and constitutes itself in it. So if the soul gives matter a particular form, makes it a human form, this body is naturally the body of this particular soul. Through the soul anyone can speak of his body and the body of the other. Furthermore, the material of which the body consists changes during the evolution of life itself. When one is seventy the body no longer consists of identically and numerically the same particles as those in which one could delight as a child. However, the body remains one and the same person who, throughout this whole process of material change, can always talk of *his* body. This identity of the body is guaranteed by the soul, despite any material difference.

Our body is more than the whole of our organs. It derives its unity not from the parts of which it is composed but from within, from its own inwardness, from what Thomas calls soul. The soul experiences its body. The body does not experience the soul.

Thus in the light of his anthropology Thomas can demonstrate the identity of the dead body and the resurrection body. If a disembodied soul (which is very difficult to conceive of in the light of Thomas' own anthropology) expresses itself anew and realizes itself in matter, then this matter becomes the body of this particular soul. The soul simply cannot accept any other body than its body, since only the soul gives the body identity. Only through the soul can one speak of my body, of its body.

So all this follows from Thomas' view that the soul is the *forma corporis*. That cannot be interpreted in dualistic terms. As such soul and body depend on each other. They do not exist outside this togetherness; they are not two substances but co-principles of the one human reality. Therefore Thomas also affirms a tendency, an impetus in the separated soul towards the body. This is a correct anthropological approach which, as has been said, he does not maintain consistently because of what he supposes to be a binding rule of faith.

Thus Thomas does not maintain a numerical unity between the dead body and the body which rises, as does Bonaventura.[8] He defends a formal unity on the basis of the soul which guarantees the identity of the body. Yet even on this level he hesitates to maintain this consistently. Under the pressure of a strong tradition he also affirms a numerical identity (*In IV Sent.* d.44, q.1, a.1, sol.1 and 3; *ScG* IV, 84). He even affirms that at the end of time the angels will gather together all the material particles of the dead bodies (*in IV Sent.* d.43 q.1, a.2. sol.3).[8]

3. Doctrinal statements for orientation

We have seen how there gradually developed within the Christian tradition an eschatology with a twofold aspect, in two phases. The resurrection of the body is always affirmed quite explicitly. As soon as a Hellenistic dualism was taken over into Christian terminology, this resurrection was transferred as an event to part of man, to his body, and put at the end of time. The spiritual soul survives death.

To begin with, people imagined this survival of the soul as a provisional existence in an underworld; however, after the time of Cyprian there was an increasing conviction that the souls of the
righteous delighted in the blessed vision of God immediately after
their death. Theologians took great pains to support this view with
various rational arguments, and it was gradually so universally
accepted and taught everywhere that it could be identified with the
proclamation of faith.

We find this development in the statements of the church's teaching office. First of all we must note that we may not identify statements of the teaching office directly with the teaching of the church.
The church as a community in Christ, as the body of Christ, is inspired and directed as a whole by the spirit. John writes of all believers without distinction: 'The anointing (what he means is being
permeated by the Spirit) which you received from him abides in you
and you have no need that anyone should teach you; his anointing
teaches you about everything, and is true, and is no lie' (I John 2.27).
Paul puts it no less clearly: 'For by one Spirit we were all baptized
into one body – Jews or Greeks, slaves or free – and all were made to
drink of one Spirit' (I Cor.12.13). It is the Spirit of truth (John
14.17), which teaches us by constantly reminding us of what Jesus
taught (John 14.26). Within this community, which is directly governed by the Spirit of Christ, the teaching office has its own irreplace-
able role. No individual Catholic Christian can dispute this in
principle. There can be some real difficulties as a result of the way in
which this teaching office functions, the way in which it is exercised
in practice. Be this as it may, it is important that the teaching office
should not simply be identified directly with the church.

The real purpose of statements by the teaching office must always
be interpreted and understood. To take them literally is fundamentalism. Doctrinal statements by the church must be seen in the specific context of their origin. Why did the teaching office define this
particular principle at a particular time? What led it to do this? What
was the real occasion? What historical background must we take
into account here? What did people want to guarantee and what to
condemn?

Furthermore, we must be clear from the start that the teaching office of the church cannot make any binding pronouncements on a
scientific or philosophical anthropology as such. With the help of a
valid anthropology it can certainly seek to express or guarantee
truths of revelation. Thus it can also judge that other anthropologi-

cal approaches cannot be reconciled with certain truths of faith. But the teaching office does not teach any anthropology; it simply uses existing anthropological views to express a truth of revelation in them. The doctrine that is taken over in this way can be connected so closely with facts of revelation that it almost appears as a necessary guarantee for the reality of faith itself. In this connection such a doctrine is called a Catholic truth in the tradition, but it is not simply a truth of revelation as such. At most one can say that for the moment it is impossible to see how one can express the truth of revelation other than in this teaching taken over from elsewhere.

On the basis of these considerations we shall now look briefly at the statements by the teaching authority of the church on the problem in which we are interested. It is immediately striking that in them there are repeated references to the concepts soul and body, which came into being in philosophy, but always with the sole intent of expressing the redemption and final salvation of human beings in their actual lives.

First, we shall look at some statements which stress the unity of soul and body particularly strongly, under the pressure of various trends of thought which make it difficult or impossible to accept final salvation from God for man living in history, as a unity and a totality.

Thus the teaching office attacks views which think too highly of the human soul, as though it were of divine origin and nature, and views which disparage the body as though it were intrinsically sinful and thus neither fitted nor destined ever to have a part in eternal salvation, whether now or in the future. We already find such statements stressing the unity of soul and body in 400 at the Council of Toledo, at 543 at a synod of Constantinople, and again in 561 at a synod in Braga in Portugal.

Other doctrinal statements say that man has only one soul and that this is individual. These are definitions which are clearly directed against the doctrine that all souls or spirits participate in a single spirit. In the view of the teaching office this diminished the significance of the individual which consists in his distinctiveness and his inalienable responsibility. This position was adopted for the first time at the Eighth Ecumenical Council of Constantinople in 869-71 (D 336). Later, in 1311-1312, at the Council of Vienne, the same doctrine, the salvation of the individual in his or her indivisible unity and totality, was expressed in terms which had been taken over from this Thomistic anthropology; the soul is in fact described as the *forma corporis* (D 481). This formula was adopted in order to combat a view widespread at that time to the effect that human beings had a number of souls, spiritual and sensual. That was grist to the mills of the Albigensians and Waldesians, who saw spirit and matter, good and evil as two independent foundations of reality and rejected everything connected with the body as evil in itself; this also included the sensual soul.

The Fifth Lateran Council of 1512-1517 again adopted the formula of Vienne. That also happened for a specific reason, as a result of the doctrine that all men participate externally in an independent immortal spirit. According to this doctrine the individual dies completely, but the spirit in which he shared during his existence, albeit externally, i.e. without possessing it, continues to live on. This is a persistent view which seems to find a response even now, though in a different form. Against this the Council stated that the soul is individual and has an individual body (D 738). There is a formal denial at this Council that there is a single impersonal soul which as such is immortal and in which all human beings participate externally. By contrast the Council teaches that the soul makes the individual what he or she is and that as such it is completely dependent on God, being called by God to personal eternal life. Thus here there is a formal definition of the resurrection of the individual which is made in order to guarantee this datum of faith, the immortality of the individual soul.[9]

A second series of doctrinal statements defines the same human unity, but I shall only mention them briefly here because they insist on the identity of the body which is alive now and the hoped-for resurrection body.

The so-called *Faith of Damasus*, the authorship and date of origin of which are unknown, states that at the end of time, purified by the death and the blood of Christ, we shall be raised by him in the flesh in which we now live (D 16). The teaching of the Eleventh Council of Toledo (675) was: 'We confess: after the pattern of our head (Jesus Christ), the resurrection of the flesh will happen to all the dead. Now we do not believe that we shall be raised in an airy body or in some other body, as many wrongly suppose, but in this body in which we live, move and have our being' (D 287). This rather crude statement is simply meant to teach that those who now live in the body will rise in the form which they now have. The background to this declaration is determined by anxiety over any form of Gnosticism, a heresy which we have already met, and docetism, a doctrine in which the body of Jesus is said to be mere illusion, so that the physical resurrection of Jesus need not be taken seriously and in no way can be regarded as a model for the resurrection of bodies at the end of time.

In 1053, Leo IX again expressed this as follows: 'I believe in the true resurrection of the flesh which I now bear' (D 347), and in 1208 this was repeated by Innocent III: 'With our heart we believe and with our mouth we confess the resurrection of the flesh that we bear and no other flesh' (D 427). Both statements express one and the same concern: they refer to the positive significance of the body and existence in the body against those who despise all that is bodily as such or reject it as being intrinsically evil. The Fourth Lateran Coucil of 1215 attacked the Albigensians with the same formula (D 429), which was reiterated by the Second Council of Lyons (D 464).

The disembodied soul

Finally in this context there are some statements which seem to define the survival of the soul after the death of the body.

In the thirteenth century it is generally assumed that the souls of the righteous are taken up into heaven immediately after the death of the body, and that there they look on the Being of God. Pope John XXII (died 1334) had his doubts about this. He referred to the authority of Augustine and Bernard of Clairvaux and insisted that the saints remained 'under the altar' (Rev.6.9ff.), i.e. in a provisional intermediary state, where they waited for the end of time. Only at the end of the world did they reach their heavenly goal and the blessed vision of God.[10] On his death bed this much disputed and contentious Avignon pope more or less revoked his teachings. His successor, Benedict XII, quickly put an end to the confusion that had arisen by declaring in the constitution *Benedictus Deus* of 1336 that the souls of all the saints and those who have been purified will look on the Being of God even before becoming reunited with their body and before the universal judgment, without the mediation of any creature (D 530). This pope also taught that the pains of hell also torment those who die in mortal sin directly after their death. According to the same apostolic constitution, any intermediary period can be considered only as a period of purification with the general judgment and the reunion of souls with their bodies still in the future. But heaven and hell begin for everyone after death.

I hope that this brief account has shown sufficiently clearly what is the real intent of these various statements by the teaching office of the church. It is always the same, to guarantee the belief that God calls specific human beings, in their individuality and their totality, to eternal communion with him. Because various perspectives were controlled by anthropologies which did not allow the datum of faith to be expressed properly, the church's teaching office decided on an anthropology which did.

Since then it has been generally accepted in Catholic theology that death consists in a separation of soul and body. Only the body dies, which seems natural in view of its material character. The soul survives, and as its nature is spiritual, this is what might be expected. But that creates further problems. If the soul is by nature immortal, how far is eternal life then a gift of grace? That is a problem which, as we shall see in a moment, is the subject of special attention above all in Protestant theology.

This conception of soul and body, according to which the disembodied soul enjoys the vision of God directly after the death of the body, deals a fatal blow to belief in the resurrection of the body. This resurrection is not denied by any Catholic theologian, but one can hardly fail to note that the article of faith becomes secondary as a result, an appendix, a luxury. The soul already delights in the blessed vision of God, and that is the essential content of what is understood by the term heaven. The soul, which is always regarded as the most important part of man, is already completely happy. To hope for an even more intensive happiness through the resurrection of the body seems to indicate an inability to be satisfied, which is hardly appropriate for the Christian.

Piety and popular devotion have never really come to terms with this theological position. No one who has a personal veneration for a particular saint could ever believe for a moment that this saint was not absolutely happy and still longed for the resurrection of his body. Moreover, saints tend to appear in popular piety as human beings. Believers normally have no difficuty in imagining them as glorified people in heaven. They are not thought of as souls.

In contemporary Catholic theology there is a marked trend which takes account of this. Before we consider it, I would like briefly to investigate thinking on these problems in the Protestant churches.

4. Voices from the Reformation

Contemporary Catholic thought meets up in a welcome way with the broad stream of contemporary Protestant thought on this problem.

Since Karl Barth and dialectical theology, Protestant thinkers have almost all referred to the unbridgeable qualitative gap which exists between the mortal creature and the immortal God, between time and eternity. According to Barth the life of man can only be described as meaninglessness, corruption, nothingness. Such an existence is already a standing-in-death. Sin is death, the end of the human being as a human being. Living in sin is not life. Therefore resurrection does not mean an event at the end of time, but is something which takes place where and when God graciously does away with the infinite distinction which exists between him and sinful creatures. Resurrection means that man is taken by God to an infinite remove from his existence, in order to live in God's eternity. People are dead. God is the only one who can raise them to new life. God removes human beings from their existence in sin, their non-life. The real relationship between God and man cannot be better expressed than by the term 'raise up'. That is the real meaning of Barth's famous remark: 'The resurrection of the dead is a paraphrase of the word God'.[11]

What can be said generally of human beings in their relationship to God is demonstrated in their actual death. Death represents the final end of a human being. Only the free, resurrecting power of God can save people from this abyss. According to Barth, talk of the immortality of the soul is an expression of and a claim to human self-righteousness. Human beings can only believe and trust in God's radically unmerited, gracious resurrection from the dead.

We can find this antithetical thought, in which there is a denial of the immortality of the soul but an affirmation in faith of the resurrection of the body, in a great many Protestant theologians.[12] What Barth says, namely that at death 'man is only the spent soul of a spent body, and he cannot live at all unless the God who let him live and then die gives him new life',[13] is affirmed and taught by a majority of Protestant theologians.

But if we die completely at death and there is only hope of a resurrection from the dead, what happens between death and resurrection?

Some theologians argue for a resurrection at death.[14] Every dead person is taken out of time into God's eternity. That is the view of Ernst Jüngel, who with Barth says of the permanent relationship of God to the creature in death that this relationship also includes the end of a human being: 'The end must be distinguished theologically from a break. Nothing follows a break . . . God follows the end. On the other side of something that has ended stands not nothing, but the very God who was at the beginning.'[15] Barth himself was content with Paul's saying that the dead are 'in Christ' (I Thess.4.13). 'As the "firstfruits of them that slept " (I Cor.15.20), Christ robbed death of its sting and brought life and immutability to light.'[16] In his abiding relationship to the creator, which is what makes him a person, the dead person is hidden with God.[17] Jürgen Moltmann says that if we look on love as participation in the innermost love of God, we can 'be certain that through the pains of dying human beings enter the joy of this love which they have experienced here to a small degree. They need not think of purgatorial fire or sleeping in the tomb, but can believe with Paul that through death they will be directly united with this Jesus Christ through whom they have experienced love here.'[18]

Other Protestant theologians assume a real intermediate period between death and resurrection and see death as a kind of sleep.[19] For yet others, being dead is a radical not-being, a sinking into nothingness.[20]

Thus in general one can say that the Christians of the Reformation argue for the resurrection of the dead and are allergic to the immortality of the soul, which seems to them to suggest the autonomy of the creature. Interpretation of the resurrection differs, as we see, extending from a resurrection at death, through a waking from sleep, to a completely new creation.

5. A contemporary voice

For the sake of completeness – and again as a step towards further investigation – I must also mention briefly the special contribution to these problems made by contemporary Anglo-Saxon process theology.[21] I cannot go in detail here into this particularly illuminating method of theological work, which opens up unsuspected perspectives on God and faith as such.

I shall, though, quote Charles Hartshorne, rightly said to be the most original representative of process philosophy, in his own words. In his view human immortality consists in the fact that after our death our life continues for ever in God's remembrance. 'Our adequate immortality can only be God's omniscience of us. He to whom all hearts are open remains evermore open to any heart that has ever been apparent to him. What we once were to him, less than that we never can be, for otherwise he himself as knowing us would lose something of his own reality.Hence if we can never be less than we have been to God, we can in reality never be less than we have been . . . Death cannot mean the destruction, or even the fading, of the book of one's life; it can mean only the fixing of its concluding page. Death writes "The End" upon the last page, but nothing further happens to the book, by way of either addition or subtraction.'[22] It seems that here Hartshorne thinks that man is preserved as subject in God's memory.[23] For Hartshorne this is the only form of immortality which can be affirmed meaningfully: our capacity to have new experiences is not unlimited. With our death the book of our life is closed but not destroyed. What more can one wish than a gentle and understanding reader who assesses us properly, and for ever?

This view of immortality as life in the memory of God is reminiscent of what was said in earlier centuries about the external participation of the individual in an eternal and immortal spirit. The Spanish writer Miguel de Unamuno had already made a similar comment before process theology: 'If there is a Universal and Supreme Consciousness, I am an idea in it; and is it possible for any idea in this Supreme Consciousness to be completely blotted out? After I have died, God will go on remembering me, and to be remembered by God, to have my consciousness sustained by the Supreme Consciousness, is not that, perhaps, to be?'[24]

I do not believe that such an account of things corresponds closely enough to eternal life as it is promised in the risen and crucified Jesus. Immortality as conceived by Hartshorne is not the life of the subject, with his or her own awareness, relationships and personal activity. At death the human being is simply fixed and nailed to his or her past, included in a gallery of wax figures.

III

MODELS FROM MODERN THOUGHT

1. The anthropological approach

We have followed the development of thought from eschatological beliefs to mediaeval theology as it were in seven-league boots. One particular anthropology played a dominant role in it. The few pages which I have been able to devote to contemporary Protestant thought are enough to suggest that here this anthropology is almost exhausted. That may have come about as a result of a typically Protestant attitude which is extremely reluctant to see any trace of autonomy in human beings, of the kind which might perhaps be expressed in the idea of an immortal soul; the influence of modern anthropologies can also be seen here.

Of course, reflection on the human condition has not ceased since the Middle Ages; on the contrary, its development has been accelerated. I cannot hope to describe this whole development here, even in broad outline. That would call for another large book.[1]

I shall, though, begin my discussion of anthropology from certain contemporary achievements in this field. It is essential that we should incorporate these insights into our talk of eschatology. It is inconceivable that a teaching office should oblige us to continue to adopt a mediaeval view of man at the very point at which thought is advancing so fast that we can hardly keep up with it.

Generally speaking, a human being is seen nowadays as an indivisible unity. However, there are a number of dimensions to this unity. On the one hand, human beings recognize in themselves biological features which they can also see in the lives of plants and animals, and which they can also find in physical and chemical constants. On the other hand, the human being has a self-awareness, an experience of being himself or herself, as a result of which he or she cannot identify directly with their biological structure. This is not something that they have; it is something that they are. The human being in some way transcends the fact that he or she simply exists in bodily form.

Here I am deliberately following an anthropological line, albeit not the only one that can be taken today – which rejects both monism and dualism. In other words, human beings cannot say that they are purely and simply material; nor, however, can they be explained in purely spiritual terms. Moreover, human beings are not made up of two independent parts. In essence, the spirit is not radically different from whatever is bodily.

We affirm a distinction between spirit and matter, between soul and body, but within the one, indivisible person. Spirit and matter must be seen as two co-principles which can be themselves, and realize themselves, only in their joint existence, in which they form the one indivisible reality which is the human being.

However, it is clear that here we have two metaphysical principles, principles which together make up man. The term spirit or soul, called *psyche* on the basis of its Greek origin, is not the same in this context as what is meant by the same word in psychology. In a metaphysical context, i.e. in a discussion of what makes human beings what they are, the spirit or the soul is the formal principle of everything, whether conscious or unconscious, somatic or psychical. It is of course essential to understand this distinction between *psyche* in the psychological sense and spirit or soul as an essential human principle. The latter case is concerned with what makes a human being human, and this does not coincide with psychological human potentialities. I do not stress this distinction so much in order to avoid a monism which might seem to make resurrection faith quite unthinkable as because I cannot see how monism can do justice to the phenomenon of our human reality.

Matter as such is experienced, recognized and described by the spirit as being something different from the spirit. The spirit itself depends on this matter for its existence, in order to realize or express itself in it. When I say that the soul expresses itself in the body, I mean far more than that the soul uses the body for its outward expression. Were that the case, I would in fact be implying a marked dualism, in which an independent soul could or could not manifest itself with complete freedom. By 'express' I mean the self-realization of the soul in and through the body. In other words, the soul does not exist outside this self-expression in and through corporeality. 'We do not express what was already impressed on us.'[2]

So however much the spirit is directed towards the body in order to be itself, the body is no less dependent on the soul to realize itself as body. Corporeality can in fact only be understood in terms of the soul, for the body as such receives its significance and its meaning from the soul. As I said earlier, the body does not derive its unity from the organs of which it is composed, but from within, from the soul. This soul also shows its power of giving unity to bodily existence in space and time, in extension, in composition, in divisibility. The soul can accept and integrate all this in its own terms.

The body makes it possible for the soul to realize itself in its relationship to itself, to other people, to the cosmos, to God. Thus, for example, the eye as a physical organ enables me to see the world around me from my perspective, on the basis of my situation in space and time.

Thus through his or her spiritual and bodily mode of existence a human being is essentially related to the world, to the whole universe. Consequently human beings are also essentially historical; they are that piece of history that they make in common with others. Spiritual and corporeal people fulfil themselves exclusively within a network of mutual relationships to the cosmos which surrounds them and gives them form as a universe of people, animals, plants and things. We might say that as beings consisting of spirit and body men and women to some extent themselves make up the universe. They are not and do not possess part of the universe, but they are this universe in so far as it is concentrated in their persons; they are partially the universe. They are the ones who speak of this universe as such, who perceive it, explore it, accept it, live their life and realize themselves in it.

Thus present-day anthropology stresses the unity and indivisibility of human beings, though it also affirms the polarity of soul and body within them. Reflecting in faith on eschatology, some theologians[3] seek to evaluate this anthropological view and want to remove the last remnants of a Hellenistic dualism from it. They do this above all because of the conceptual difficulties arising from this dualism, and in order to stress again the fundamental significance and supreme importance of the resurrection of the body, and to give reasons before the forum of human reason with its search for insight.[4]

It should have emerged from my detailed account of the biblical evidence and my short summary of the church's tradition that we need to proclaim in faith from different starting points and different aspects that the final determination of men and women as they are lies with God and is offered to them as a gift from God. And an attempt is made to express precisely this datum of faith in various forms, symbols, concepts and images, whether the imagery is that of resurrection, glorification, eternal life, immortality of the soul, the blessed vision of God, the resurrection of the dead or the resurrection of the flesh.

In the language and expression of the proclamation of this central truth of faith, those concepts and modes of description are used which are available and seem most appropriate for formulating this truth of faith and protecting it against any distortion. Faith does not create any anthropology of its own. The tradition of the church and the statements made by the teaching office do not proclaim any binding scientific view of man. If the teaching office makes pronouncements which presuppose or contain a particular anthropology, this is only because that view of humanity proves to be useful for expressing Christian faith in a particular framework of historical thought, whereas another anthropology, within the same framework of thought, seems to be completely inappropriate.

Traditional thinking about the final future of humanity within a dualistic anthropology makes it particularly difficult for modern men and women, who live and think spontaneously on the basis of a different anthropology, to confess a faith which is already too firmly rooted in antiquated patterns of thought. Dualism, even in a weak form, creates more problems than it solves. It is the reason why in particular circles the resurrection of the body, or perhaps the flesh, has been taken literally, as the opening of graves and the resuscitation of bodies, as the reunion of soul and body, as reincarnation at the end of time. People might well have imagined all this in centuries long past, when there was no idea of either the antiquity or the enormous extension of humanity. Today it is quite nonsensical. In addition, as I have already pointed out, the doctrine of the immediate vision of God by the disembodied soul made the resurrection of the body quite superfluous as a separate event involving this material element. At all events, the doctrine of a blessedness of the soul made a marked contribution in historical terms towards regarding bodily existence as intrinsically insignificant, if not contemptible. At the same time, this stress on the blessedness of the soul was the reason for the individualizing and privatizing of the life of faith in an imaginary world of pure inwardness or ethereal supernaturalness.

So in the light of modern anthropology we may look for a new formulation and account of the real truth of faith: the final determination of human beings as they are and in their lives, lies in and with God, and it is God himself who brings man to this goal.

Nowhere, ever, does God concern himself only with souls; he is always, everywhere, concerned with human beings. He has created these human beings as an indissoluble union of soul and body. They are and become themselves not as solitary individuals who live segregated lives of their own, in their own inwardness, in a purely spiritual, impregnable citadel, but in and through mutual relationships with others. As I have already said, it is existence as a body that makes it possible for the soul to communicate with others. It is the soul which makes the body 'human', which through relationships realized in the body humanizes the relationship to the whole universe with all that it contains. Whatever emerges in the form of human relationships – other people, the cosmos, the time and space in which they take form, the material things they use, the life of animals and plants which plays their part – all this is humanized by the person who lives a spiritual and bodily existence. Everything is taken up into humanity, from which it also takes its name and receives its real significance. The human being realizes himself or herself as a human being in a network of relationships, and in all the phases of its existence is woven into the whole which God has created and which he gives to mankind to humanize.

I therefore believe that we can say that this specific human being who makes a piece of history and is partly governed by this history, who humanizes matter by giving it form and meaning from within, is at death brought by God to his or her goal. Human beings are glorified by God as human beings. God does not fulfil disembodied souls, but human beings. God fulfils his own creatures as he created them. Therefore a human being never comes to God alone, but along with everyone and everything that has made him or her this person, through which he or she has become this person. At their death, human beings also bring before God their fellows through whom they live and who live through them. At their death they bring something of human history before God in order to allow it to be crowned by him. Their human work, their environment, that part of nature which they have made into culture – everything through which and with which, from which and for which they live – comes to a final goal at death.

We express this in the confession: 'I believe in the resurrection of the body'. The concept of resurrection is not, of course, to be taken literally. If we were to do that we would presuppose that a dead person sleeps, lies there, and gets up when he or she is aroused. A dead person does not sleep and therefore cannot be woken, even by a trumpet blown by an angel. So he or she cannot rise in the literal sense of this word. A human being is changed at death, and does not return to the life that he or she experienced before this death; this way of living is not taken up again and prolonged throughout eternity. There is another way of life. That is made clear to us in the New Testament. When Lazarus, or the son of the widow of Nain, or the young daughter of Jairus, are raised from the dead, they all return to the life which they knew before their death. Then they died again. The risen Jesus did not resume the way of life that he had before Good Friday. That is expressed in all the accounts of the resurrection appearances, in which it is noted that Jesus was not recognized immediately. But it is the same Jesus, the crucified one, who lives his risen life in another way. This, too, is expressed in all the accounts of his appearances, when it is said that Jesus was recognized afterwards. We also heard Paul stressing emphatically that human beings must be changed in order to be accepted into final communion with the glorified Christ.

2. Dying is resurrection

Those who conclude from what I have said that human beings *qua* human beings are brought to fulfilment in and with God at their death have understood me rightly. However, I would stress that they are *brought* to their fulfilment, not that they *come* to their fulfilment. This fulfilment is a gift of grace and not the result of a natural development. Of course we can only speak meaningfully of a resurrection in death if we realize that resurrection has nothing to do with corpses. Corpses do not come to life again at the resurrection. Resurrection is not a resuscitation. People were led to hold such a view by a dualistic view of humanity. I have rejected this, not because I have an aversion to anything that comes from tradition and is not supported literally by the Bible but because I have taken over the insights of contemporary anthropology and consequently want to avoid any form of dualism. Therefore I want to use the term body to express the human being in his or her totality. That the Bible also does this, as we saw, is no reason for preferring this terminology to that of the church's tradition. But if scripture does this, at least we can comfortably follow suit. When scripture speaks of the body, it means what today we might call the person (that should be clear from the second part of this book). Everything that I said there about being human finds an echo in this concept. Human beings are persons in their openness, in relationships, in communication. When the Bible speaks of body, what it means is our concept of person – certainly not part of being human. When Jesus says at the last supper 'This is my body', he does not mean it is part of himself, what he is in the purely corporeal aspect of his humanity; he is saying to all who are with him, 'This is what I am for you', and they immediately understand what he means. So by bodily resurrection I mean resurrection or glorification of the person, of the human being *qua* human being – for the analysis of biblical data showed that we may use these terms as synonyms. So we are no longer talking of a disembodied soul which after the death of the body is admitted to the blessed vision of God, but of a human being who at death is glorified by God in every respect of his or her humanity. The fact that we cannot imagine this event lies in the nature of the event itself. It does not take place within our history, on our earth, and is therefore not the object of human perception. Paul already insisted on the complete otherness of the risen body as compared with the historical body (I Cor.15.35-54). As we saw in our analysis of this text, Paul could only express this otherness in hints, by dissociating everything connected with historical existence as such from resurrection existence. Is resurrection existence then unimaginable in the light of this existence; is it conceivable at all?

In raising this question I do not presuppose that resurrection existence could ever appear as evidence, as a compelling conclusion from a correct argument. It is a datum of faith, something that we affirm because God promises us this existence in and through the resurrection of Jesus. Argument and reflection come after the assent of faith. As I said above, we look for arguments to enable us to offer and acheive this assent of faith more readily.

3. Arguments for immortality

As resurrection faith used to be conceived of universally in the context of a dualistic anthropology, in the tradition we come up against arguments which assume the immortality of the soul. The basic presupposition here is always that a spiritual nature implies intransitoriness. This spiritual nature of the soul is defended from very different perspectives.

A first trend is indebted to Plato. In his view, the soul is spiritual because it enables human beings to know unchangeable, eternal ideas. Whereas we never arrive at permanent knowledge through our sense organs, but on the contrary are led astray by this sense perception, through a spiritual capacity we can recognize the unchangeable and permanent truth. Now since only like can know like, the soul which brings us the knowledge of eternal truth participates in the eternity of this truth. So because the soul knows unchanging truths and lives in contact with absoluteness, permanence and eternity, it is itself immortal.

Others see the awareness of time as a transcending of time and therefore as eternity. The fact that people can know time in its three dimensions of past, present and future indicates that human beings stand outside and above this time. Despite everything, human beings see time, which is experienced as a succession of moments, one of which must inexorably disappear to make possible the one that follows, as a unity. This happens in and through a spiritual process in which human beings themselves transcend time and in this way experience eternity.[5]

The arguments based on what is called the natural longing for immortality are of a different kind. It is said that this longing is given with human nature and therefore cannot remain unfulfilled. In mediaeval theology this *desiderium naturale* played a major role.

Yet others see the experience of love as a foretaste of immortality. In love human beings transcend themselves in every sphere of their existence, even in the sphere of the experience of time and transitoriness that goes with it. Love fights against time, in which the loved one inevitably decays. Love wills and experiences eternity.

Another argument in the Dutch-speaking world, which has been put forward convincingly by D. de Petter,[6] arises out of the experience of the absurdity of death. 'The essential element in the experience of the death of our fellow human beings is the perhaps unexpressed but nevertheless evident insight into the absurdity, the impossibility of death *in so far as it affects not only organic life but also the person of our fellow man*, as is misleadingly suggested by the cessation of any further contact with the persons of the dead. The reason for this insight, which we vaguely sense, is the absolute disproportion between the organic event of death and the possibility that the end of the person in our fellow human beings may be connected with it.'[7]

Kant's postulate of eternity comes from a different philosophical climate. He says that he cannot prove the existence of an immortal soul. However, it is presupposed by the practical reason, by the moral task that every person has to fulfil. The moral will ultimately coincides with the moral law itself. As people cannot achieve this complete equality of form here on earth, according to Kant they must postulate that there is an eternity in which moral development can attain the perfection desired. Kant goes on to say that there must be a convergence between morality and happiness. However, this is far from being always the case within our history. Hence again the postulate of eternity, in which morality and happiness coincide completely.[8]

Certain arguments brought together here to make the immortality of the soul acceptable to human reason in search of insight recur in a slightly different form as arguments for the resurrection of the human person in the way I have described, i.e. as something that happens to the whole person at death. I shall go into some of these arguments in more detail.

4. Arguments for resurrection

Many contemporary Catholic theologians try to make resurrection at death in the sense mentioned above understandable or comprehensible, following in the footsteps of the great master Karl Rahner.[9]

The all-cosmic man

Rahner's starting point is that through its essential connection with its own body, the soul is also at the same time bound up with the totality in which the body participates or shares. This totality is the unity of the material world. The soul participates in this totality by virtue of its own corporeality. In this sense one can say that human beings in their corporeality possess the totality of the universe in a partial way. They are therefore not part of the universe; the universe itself is concentrated in their persons. While at death the soul loses its individual body, it retains its relationship to the whole in which the individual body participated. At death the soul does not become acosmic but all-cosmic. In death, human beings have closer and more intensive contact with the basis of the unity of things. The soul can communicate better with everything, with the whole, through the loss of its limited individual corporeality.[10]

I personally have great difficulties with this view. How can one explain the fact that the relationship with the cosmos as a whole remains the same and even becomes more intensive when the medium through which this relationship is realized, i.e. the individual body, dies? However, my main objection is that here death takes on a positive significance. We cannot accept this as either human beings or as Christians. We know from the Synoptic Gospels how Jesus of Nazareth regarded his own death. The Fourth Gospel certainly gives quite a different version, but I attempted to show earlier how we have to understand this.[11] I stand, rather, in a particular line of tradition which, while not so marked in the Old Testament, was worked out particularly strongly by Paul, and sees death as a consequence of sin (which Rahner himself stresses in his various remarks about death). However we are to understand the connection between sin and death, at all events it indicates that even from a purely Christian perspective death in itself is simply a non-thing, is purely negative. Death is the visible form of sin and the sum of evil as radical annihilation. Paul does not weaken his own theology of death in any way when he says that for himself dying is a gain.[12]

A number of theologians follow Rahner. Ladislaus Boros does this in language and thought categories which are strongly influenced by Teilhard de Chardin.[13] The world as it evolves is characterized by two movements which go in opposite directions. The first movement consists in a transcendence of self, in a move from less to more, from below upwards. The second move is that of entropy, loss of energy, misuse, collapse. We also find these two contradictory but indissolubly connected movements of evolution in human life. Just as the evolving world gradually becomes smaller, exhausts itself and uses itself up in order to make possible the phenomenon of humanity, so the individuals use themselves, their own energy, to become persons. To the degree that individuals involve themselves and incorporate themselves in the world in order to control it and humanize it – to the degree that they extend and transcend themselves in love – they grow as persons. Human beings are persons the more they go out and beyond themselves in and through the movement and the experience of love. However, diametrically opposed to this is the movement of entropy in humanity; the misuse of energy, loss, collapse, growing old, dying. But because these two movements, those of gain in humanity and personhood and loss of vitality and energy, are closely connected, one can confidently conclude that if at death human beings suffer a complete loss of energy, at the same time they become totally personal, one with everything and everyone.[14]

Individual and person

In the Dutch-speaking world I know of no one who has sought more to make the positive significance of dying acceptable than L.Bakker.[15] In a clear, rich and particularly valuable analysis he shows how the human being develops from being an individual into being a person. The fact that the human being is an individual underlines his or her limitations, shortcomings and separateness. In the process of becoming a person, a man or woman seeks to break out of the limits of individuality by forming relationships, by communication, openness and self-disclosure. Those who are in love want to be completely one with each other. That desired unity can never come about in this life. The limits of individuality cannot be fully and finally broken through and transcended. Even in the deepest and most intimate love the 'I' always remains 'I' and the 'other' always remains 'other'. The 'we' people dream about is never completely achieved. This radical crossing of boundaries towards the other in order to realize the greatest possible personal communion in love only becomes possible with the loss of all forms of individuality in death and through death. Total life is impossible without the experience of total death in dying.

It is clear that Bakker's thought moves in the direction of Rahner's, but his perspective is more psychological and ethical. The sayings from the New Testament which he cites repeatedly as so many variants of the claim 'Whoever loses his life will gain it', are adequate illustration of his approach. That is also beyond doubt a valuable view of dying. Bakker sees dying as a deliberate process that has various stages, and he contrasts it with dying as a fate which people experience.

However, it is not in fact the case that mere passing away falls short of dying in the sense intended by the author, but that being dead ends dying as a conscious process. The subject who accepts death in dying no longer exists. Moreover, not every passing away can become a dying. Here I am not just thinking of a sudden and unforeseen death, death through natural catastrophes, violence and war; dying as the author sees it presupposes psychological, moral and religious possibilities which very many people simply cannot summon up. They simply cannot make their passing away into a dying. My objection is therefore not only that this particularly able theologian sees death too positively as dying, but that he remains on a merely psychological and ethical level, and does not pay sufficient attention to death as a fact.

Bakker himself says that being an individual is also necessary to arrive at a personal union in love. But this positive characteristic of being an individual cannot do away with the negative side. In my view, he sees being an individual in too negative terms. I in fact believe that particularly in a loving relationship in which those involved strive for the greatest possible self-surrender and self-transcendence, the individual is the constitutive element in an extremely positive sense. Love goes out to the unique, the original, the only, to everything that makes the person loved this person and not any other. And is that not his or her individuality? Knowledge looks for universality, while love looks for the unique. You do not love someone because there are so many of the kind around but because he or she is unique. Moreover, it is precisely because of the fact that the other *qua* other is an individual, that love becomes a call to self-transcendence. The loving acceptance of the other in his or her individual limitations is the greatest challenge to self-transcendence. Dostoievsky gave consummate expression to what I mean here. He makes an elder tell the story of a doctor: ' "I love humanity," he said, "but I can't help being surprised at myself; the more I love humanity in general, the less I love men in particular, I mean, separately, as separate individuals. In my dreams," he said, "I am often very passionately determined to serve humanity, and I might quite likely have sacrificed my life for my fellow creatures, if for some reason it had been suddenly demanded of me, and yet I'm quite incapable of living with anyone in one room for two days together, and I know that from experience. As soon as anyone comes close to me, his personality begins to oppress my vanity and restrict my freedom. I'm capable of hating the best men in twenty-four hours: one because he sits too long over his dinner, another because he has a cold in the head and keeps on blowing his nose. I become an enemy of the people the moment they come close to me. But, on the other hand, it invariably happened that the more I hated men individually, the more ardent became my love for humanity at large." ' [16]

It just is not the case that love extends to individuality, that this individuality is a challenge to self-transcendence in love. I believe that love is the relationship which makes individuality possible. In love one not only affirms the other *qua* other, as not oneself, but also grants the other his or her otherness and confirms him or her in it. Only in love does the individuality of the other really become evident, for only in and through love does the individual become himself or herself *qua* other. So love does not stifle any individuality but creates and gives individuality, and does so precisely by the self-transcendence of love.

I am not saying in any way that Bakker would deny this, but I find little or nothing of this positive aspect of individuality in his account of the relationship between individual and person. It is remarkable, but certainly since Friedrich Schleiermacher (1763-1834), in a particular tradition it has been good form to burden the individual as such with all the sins of Israel.[17] I am convinced that this goes against everything we know of love. Love has everything, but everything, to do with the individual as individual. Otherwise, we must follow W.F.Hermans in asserting: 'There were people in abundance, soon more than the world could feed. In individual terms it did not happen like that. When A failed, B succeeded. Healthy, fine crops did not always grow from the seed corn that a farmer scattered on his land. All in all, just enough came or survived. In the Bible one can read here and there that we are blades of grass.'[18] Love does not want the end of the individual *qua* other; it seeks the furtherance of the individual. In love one does not want to become fused with the other but to preserve his or her otherness.

Spiritual surplus

Although I find L.Bakker's assessment of dying worth noting, I feel much more sympathetic towards the account by E.Schillebeeckx. He rightly stresses the cruel earnestness of death. 'The incomprehensible character of death consists precisely in the fact that in this death the person – and here it makes no difference whether the death is premature or not – comes completely to grief in his or her own sphere. Dying is not just impotence in the biological sphere, but, on this basis, at the same time formally and existentially a failure: the person can no longer fulfil his or her humanizing task; alienation has them completely in its grasp. So death dehumanizes not only the body but also the person.'[19] 'If death is nonsense in and of itself, an element of meaning in it can come only from the meaning-ful God. That does not explain death in any way whatever, but there is the certainty of *faith* that despite everything, the absurdity of particular situations in life . . . is not the last word, that one can talk about life. There is a "nevertheless" in the promise of God in and through Jesus, whom the believer can confess as Christ.'[20]

If Schillebeeckx puts so much stress on the devastating event of death, how can he make comprehensible the resurrection faith which he confesses with conviction? 'Anyone who now accepts in faith that God is also future for the dead, so that they live, is confronted with the question: Is death, despite its absurdity, complete annihilation, a reduction to nothing? . . . In that case the question arises whether death means the same thing as being reduced to nothing in the radical sense.'[21] To this question he replies: 'Being human may be radically annihilated, but there is a surplus which is not reduced to nothing. It now follows its own, purely material nature, first still as a piece of biological corporeality (living organs) and finally as a multiplicity of chemical materials which never disappear but are incorporated into the great totality of nature . . . It emerges from the fate of the body that at least in respect of the material element, that part of man which was humanized, there is no question of annihilation . . . Moreover experience, the only basis of all meaningful talk, gives no indication for postulating that the annihilation which in fact affects the human element of the person affects what can be called the "surplus" of the human being as person. Here thinking is at its extreme limits, but to deny what has been said earlier would imply that we attribute less consistency to the personhood of man (during his life) than to his humn corporeality . . . Of course, I too do not know what a dehumanized dead person might be: it is impossible to express this in positive terms. However, it is all the more evident *a priori* that there must also be a surplus of human beings as persons, because we really do consist of an element which is not nature, the principle of personhood itself.'[22]

So just as there is a material surplus, according to Schillebeeckx, *a fortiori* there is also a spiritual surplus. However, he does not want to see this as a variant of the immortal soul or as a move which makes it possible for us to be able to accept the resurrection. Of course the fact, based on experience, that an anti-creative act of annihilation cannot be postulated takes on a particular function within resurrection faith. The concept of a spiritual surplus offers the believer only the possibility of thinking through faith in the resurrection more meaningfully than on the assumption of complete annihilation. Here, at any rate, the insight of faith into the unity of creation and covenant finds better recognition than in the assertion of a total annihilation which would postulate a radical new creation at the resurrection.

I personally do not feel very happy with this concept of a spiritual surplus. It is so desperately difficult to conceive of without again positing an immortal soul. Schillebeeckx certainly does not want to do this. But how else is one to think of this spiritual surplus?

Experience of absurdity

I now want to attempt to make even belief in the resurrection plausible. We cannot see and interpret death as other than radical annihilation. Being dead means being no longer there. It is the absolute end. That is what makes death so cruel and the sum of all misery, the greatest of evils. It is possible to speak of good dying, but there is no such thing as a good death. The person is simply no longer there.

Revelation says that God fulfils human destiny even beyond death. We believe in a God 'who gives life to the dead and calls into being the things that do not exist' (Rom.4.17). But no one can prove that. The ordinary person rightly says, with utter scepticism: 'No one has ever come back.' At most we can attempt to make clear that this faith is not completely unreasonable. Arguments may well differ; the important thing is that they may help people to believe that human destiny is finally in God's hands. Plato put it like this: 'On these questions one must achieve one of two things: either learn or find out how things are; or, if that's impossible, then adopt the best and least refutable of human doctrines, embarking on it as a kind of raft, and risking the dangers of the voyage through life, unless one could travel more safely and with less risk, on a securer conveyance afforded by some divine doctrine' (*Phaedo* 85c-d).

We have received this divine revelation in and through the revelation of Jesus. The crucified one lives. But the question remains: how, as thinking people, can we make this faith in this divine revelation acceptable to our own tentative search and to others? So it is a question of thinking *within* faith. I have presented different attempts to make plausible the hypotheses of immortality and resurrection. If anyone is reassured by them I shall be particularly delighted; but none of these arguments have satisfied me.

I find the most convincing argument for believing in an eternal life, as responding to a Word to which we listen, in the human protest against death, in the refusal to accept death, in the experience of the absurdity of death. Thus far I find myself on the same wavelength as my teachers de Petter and Schillebeeckx. In protest against death it emerges that we somehow, in whatever way, know, realize, that death is not part of being human. This negative experience is possible only if it is matched by or coincides with a positive experience. We know that we are finite only if we know what infinity is. This knowledge is intuitive; that means that we cannot express it conceptually, it is not the result of a direct perception. But it exists as a fundamental awareness. Outside this knowledge of infinity there is no basis for, no sense in, talking about finitude. We recognize sickness as such only if we know what health means. A limit can be experienced as a limit only when we know in whatever way that something lies outside, above, alongside this limit. I think that we can detect this intuitive knowledge that death is not part of humanity, is not human, is unacceptable, from the universal protest against death as overwhelming annihilation.

I do not think that in using this argument I can be accused of idealism in the philosophical sense. Idealists claim that human thought must somehow be matched in reality. We can conceive of immortality and eternity, so they must exist. By contrast, my view is that we come to believe in eternity through experience. The concept of eternity itself is preceded by an experience. This experience is not a thought-construction but can be found in the experience of negativity. In fact, eternity is the result less of positive experience – although I do not exclude this completely; quite the contrary – than of resistance against finitude, against transitoriness, against death. Death is generally experienced as negativity. No thinking person can find death normal. It is impossible to find death as normal as the breaking of a dropped glass, the fading of a flower, the end of a career. The distinction between the acceptance of the sad fact that someone we love is growing old and passively suffering a distressing process of decay and the acceptance of the fact that this person is simply no longer there is not one of degree; it is infinite and qualitative. We can accept the former, but we fight against the latter with every fibre of our being. In experiencing this difference we have some inkling of eternity. Becoming old is part of life, of being human, but death is not. A person can come to terms with growing old, becoming sick and even dying. But death overwhelms us. Death is a brutal and total force to which we are handed over without protection. We simply cannot accept death because we somehow recognize that death is violent and therefore unnatural. We may speak of a happy release, of a death which takes pity on a person, of death as liberation, but we do so only in situations in which death and its devastating power have already made a devastating incursion into life. In such instances we are aware of resisting before death finally comes, fighting against moral wretchedness, against impotence, sickness, pain, and collapse, but this is and remains a protest against death as a superior power, as violence.

So in the experience of finitude as finitude we see something of an intuitive, i.e. a direct, awareness of infinity. This awareness expresses itself in protest. It would be very narrow-minded for us to see protest only in negative terms. Protest is an action against something for a positive cause. In our case it comes about through a positive concern to protect life against any possible form of annihilation.

If we no longer protest against death but learn to accept it obediently as part of humanity, then we clearly lose something of this humanity. The perspective from which we express the judgment that death is part of humanity clearly narrows our view. We simply cease to see what is happening around us. Our gaze does not embrace everything. We do not meet the terrified look of the dying person, looking desperately for our aid in helplessness and loneliness. We can only claim that death is the normal end of life when we turn away from the completely defenceless person who dies alone, leave people alone, abandon them to the violence of death. If we take pain away from people we deprive them of their capacity to love. Does not the contemporary attempt to accept death as something normal betray humanity more than the protest against death? Is the acceptance of death really more rational than resistance against death?

As I have said, the normal and general human protest against death, which is not unique to Christianity or to a particular culture, reveals an intuitive knowledge of eternal life. This is not just a thought but a longing, a wish, a petition, a request, an awareness, knowledge that cannot be articulated further. We can speak meaningfully of finitude only because we are intuitively aware of infinity, not as a thought construction but as experience, something that we feel. This is the only possible justification and explanation of our protest against the finitude of life, and it seems to me more reasonable and human than the acceptance of death as an inescapable fact.

This awareness of infinity or eternity is alive in human beings as totalities. It is there in the man or woman taken as a whole. It is no mere intellectual insight, nor the result of a spiritual process, nor inward experience, but a deep awareness that governs human beings in all their complexity, in all their capacities, in their very being. In other words human beings *are* deliberate protest against finitude.

But what is the origin of this awareness, this intuitive knowledge? In former days people would have said that it comes from the soul, from the spiritual element of our existence. I do not want to reject this answer out of hand provided that we do not see the soul as an independent reality and do not give the spiritual element a separate existence alongside the corporeal element. For we experience finitude with and in the body, and this gives us an awareness of infinity. It is not just my soul or my spirit which protests against death; my whole being is one great protest against it. I therefore believe that we can say that the intuitive knowledge of infinity, an awareness by which all human capacities are influenced and shaped, is given with humanity itself.

5. God: origin and destiny

The creative redeemer

As believers, may we not seek to clarify all this from the creaturely insight that we participate in God's existence? Our existence is a participation in God's existence. We can also say that God himself exists in us or even that God is, quite simply, our existence, provided that we add that God lives fully in us freely and as a gift, as something given. In other words, God's innermost existence, the existence that he lives out in us, is not exhausted by us, nor does it simply coincide with our existence. We are God as gift. To use Schillebeeckx's words: 'The creature – world, history, man – is the presence of and the area in which God is "*qua* gift"; God himself is the presence of and the area in which God is "in the nature of the case", in and through his absolutely free being-as-God itself.'[23]

In other words, because God lives in us, because we live, move and have our being in him, we have an awareness of infinity. If God himself lives totally in us without coinciding with us – for despite all God's immanence, i.e. despite all God's being and going, in and with and alongside us, he remains transcendent, he goes beyond us – our existence is already a participation in the being of God himself. In this context we should not regard God's existence as something separate, outside and above us, however much he transcends us. God lives out his own existence as a gift to us. The giver himself lives in his gift; he *is* his gift, without simply coinciding with it.

May we not, then, say that God lives out his infinity in us and that as a result we strive with all our power against our finitude? If we participate through our very existence in the being of God – thanks to the God who gives himself – we participate in his eternity and cannot end our future.

Here I clearly part company with the view of J. Pohier.[24] He is my brother in theology, as intelligent as he is devoted to the truth, and he rightly says that *qua* creature the creature is limited, finite, transitory, mortal. By definition, a creature is not God. So we must negate all that we say of God when we are talking of creatures. God alone is eternal; human beings are mortal precisely because they are creatures. Pohier himself comments that this view brings him close to the most traditional theology, which also spoke of Adam's immortality as a supernatural gift, though the classical theologians also intimated that immortality is not part of human nature, even of the spiritual soul.

According to Pohier's theology of creation, God puts man completely outside himself, as it were alongside himself. There can hardly be any question here of God's immanence in the creature. That is confirmed by Pohier's view of the Shekinah, God's coming in a sphere that remains open. As a result, there is again particular stress on God's absolute transcendence. In my view, however, this also makes God's existence separate. That must logically result in the quite unacceptable view that God and his creation amount to more than God alone.

As Pohier himself rightly observes, the concept of creation is meaningful and understandable only within the language of faith. Creation is not in fact a basic explanation of the origin of reality but an interpretation of reality in faith. That is quite true, and we shall return to the point. But creation is inconceivable apart from the participation of the creature in the creator. Participation is something quite different from emanation; it is a kind of out-flowing of God beyond himself. Participation presupposes an independent subject, which participates actively in the existence of God. At the same time, in the context of belief in creation, the term signifies that God himself brings into being this autonomous subject as such, as being free, independent and different from him. This happens not only at the beginning of this existence, but throughout the process in which this existence realizes itself.

So in the creature there is more than a dependent relationship with the creator. The creator himself lives – in the action of giving – in the creature. So there exists in the creature a mutual relationship which is willed and constituted by the creator himself. In the creature it is the creator himself who, by virtue of his participation, also responds, reacts to the creator as he is in himself, where he exists as absolute, boundless, unlimited. In fact we are of God's people; in him we live and move and have our being (cf. Acts 17.28). It follows from this that the finitude of our future is unacceptable, and that our longing for eternal life is not megalomania, as Pohier might suggest. God who lives in us goes with us (Ex.34.9), on the way to life, to eternity.

But does that not mean that we are immortal by nature? It would be impossible here to go into the complex problems which this view raises because of the way in which the accepted terminology with its coupling of nature and grace, nature and supernature, used to function in earlier theology. There creation and redemption were sometimes so interwoven that one got the impression that both interpretations of faith could not go back to one and the same God. In my view, the difference between creation and redemption is only a logical one, purely a theoretical question. For believers, nothing exists by nature or of itself. All is gift in everything and everyone. All is grace.

That is precisely what the term creation means as an interpretation in faith of existing reality. God gives himself freely to the creature. He himself grants the creature its independence, originality, freedom and understanding, its emotional life and all that is involved in being a creature. Only the believer recognizes reality as God's active presence. In and through faith one consciously experiences existence in dependence, in relationship to the creator, in gratitude and worship. If faith is refused, this relationship to God is no longer experienced and it makes no sense at all to speak of creation.

This approach should also demonstrate that only a believer can say that the mutual relationship of creature and creator remains even when someone dies. But the believer in fact affirms that on the basis of his creation faith. Creator and creature are not scientific terms, but terms of faith.

The creator who redeems

The history of revelation tells us how this belief in creation and redemption came about. The Bible is full of stories by and about people who saw a redemptive creator at work in special events in their own lives, in their own world. There are stories steeped in faith, but there are also stories which sadly speak of unbelief. We constantly move from one to the other. Again and again we see one and the same God at work, taking new initiatives in order to free people from the short-sightedness of their unbelieving life. These divine initiatives culminate in the Christ event. In the proclamation and life-style of

Jesus of Nazareth, God himself does everything possible to move men to affirm him as their creator, as the one who awakens their freedom, their own creativity, their trust and their longing. In Jesus God wanted to lead people to absolute trust in him, to a conscious existence in gratitude, in the experience of dependence which dares to trust in grace alone. In Jesus God wanted to free people from their unbelief, as a result of which they refused to accept that he lived in them no matter what, declining to accept their existence as coming from him, as unmerited grace. From a biblical perspective this unbelief is sin.

The man Jesus is sent by God to make clear to people that God is with them, always and in all situations, as a source of the future, of newness, of life, provided that they recognize this active presence in faith and confess it or make room for it. In the death of Jesus God seeks to convince humankind that he himself goes with the dying to death and that as a result death cannot be the final end. The crucified Jesus lives.

So in my view the death and resurrection of Jesus make possible belief in human resurrection. In this sense the resurrection of the crucified Jesus is the foundation of our resurrection. Without this resurrection of Jesus we could not give any content to this concept of faith, nor could we even have faith in the resurrection. Only in Jesus do we see the God who gives himself to us in the Son, dying with us. Only in the resurrection of the God who died with us in Jesus do we see the resurrection as a gift of God offered to all. The spirit of the one who raised Jesus from the dead lives in all of us.

So the resurrection of Jesus is the foundation of our belief in the resurrection. Through this faith we are saved. Through faith we rise. Anyone who believes in him has eternal life. Now, already, the explosive force of the resurrection of Jesus lives in us, to the degree to which, driven by his spirit, we oppose any form of annihilation.

Creation and redemption are the work of one and the same God in three persons. If we then assert that the creator himself lives fully in the creature and that the creator brings his creation – which is himself as gift – to fulfilment, we see all this as believers, who know of the Jesus event and are moved and driven by the Spirit. Through God, who has expressed himself and given himself to us in his Son, through the Spirit who shows us the Father and the Son, we live freed from the short-sightedness of unbelief and have come to the light, the truth and life.

This belief in creation and redemption together is not evident from nature, by itself. If we are left to ourselves, outside the perspective of creation, death can only be seen as total annihilation, as the ultimate. Only faith goes further, faith in the resurrection which, by reflecting in faith, we can show to be belief in a creator who preserves his creation, comes to terms with his creatures, liberates and redeems them even beyond death. The creator has made this belief possible for us in and through the resurrection of the crucified Jesus and the gift of the Spirit.

That the creator who redeems brings us to our destiny beyond death because with us he transcends boundaries, because our limitations do not exist for the one who lives in us, means more than a response of the transcendent God towards us which does not correspond to anything in the creature. In its independence the creature is God-in-us. In the creature God himself responds as the one who is immanent in us, in the relationship of the God who transcends us — for all his immanence.

So as Schillebeeckx rightly says, seen from the perspective of faith, death is not an act of 'annihilation against the creation'.[25] It is impossible to speak in faith of death as a total death, as an annihilation. That is the one thing that would make resurrection faith utterly inconceivable. The resurrection must take place in the person who died. There must be someone who rises, who is raised, who is created anew by a new unmerited initiative of the grace of God. If we see resurrection as a completely new creation, then in fact something completely new takes place; God creates a new beginning and another being. In that case the creator no longer continues with the creation that has died — albeit in a completely new and different way. He simply creates another creature.

Theologians who see resurrection as a new creation and therefore death as total death not only introduce what I find to be an unacceptable distinction in the Godness of God, i.e. between his nature as creator and his nature as redeemer; they put the creator above or outside his creation. According to the conception which I am putting forward here, God is nowhere ever to be thought of apart from his creation, either in its origin or in its evolution and destiny. God's immanence is underestimated if we say that death is simply annihilation. The redemptive Christ event in which we saw the creator God at work shows us God in Jesus on a cross, dead in a grave, descending into the underworld. Revelation shows us that on the basis of this Christ event, God is in and with all men in the same way, even in the hell of their existence, even in their death. But because God was in the crucified and dead Jesus, this death did not have the last word. Jesus is risen and has been made Lord over everything and everyone. We may believe that the same Spirit which raised Jesus from the dead does the same for all who have died.

In the light of all this we can understand very well how an old Christian tradition was very anxious to take over the conception of an immortal soul from Greek philosophy. Despite all change, renewal, resurrection, glorification, new creation – i.e. despite all the discontinuity that develops between life on earth and glorified existence in God – this immortal soul could guarantee continuity. Through the immortal soul the subject of both forms of life remained the same. I need not repeat here again at length my objections to the continued use of the term soul. The word has become loaded through its use within a dualistic picture of humanity, and although it also seems appropriate for suggesting eternal life, as I said earlier, it makes it very difficult to conceive of a bodily resurrection, which is the real content of faith.

If, however, we want to use the term soul to denote the capacity by which human beings essentially exist in an indestructible openness, given freely by the creator God, in relationship to him,[26] then we need to remember that we are using this term in an unusual sense and outside its original climate. Soul has begun to turn into a philosophical and anthropological concept. So we may not interpret it directly in terms of a theology of creation. We must always respect the special character of the various levels of thought.

I am aware that in the second part of this discussion of resurrection I myself have adopted what theologians call an analogy of faith: that is, a method by which one seeks to clarify a particular understanding of faith with the help and by the analogy of another insight of faith. But I have done that only after producing arguments of a generally human and philosophical kind, in order to provide a basis for reflective belief in a resurrection within a constant questioning and searching 'until the dawn'.

IV

HEAVEN AS DESTINY

I think, then, that we may believe that the reciprocal relationship to God which came about in and through creation, and is restored and perfected in and through redemption, is experienced by the whole person in a different way after death. After death, human beings begin to live as human beings in another way.

1. Heaven as life

The dead live. We may believe that. They live as the same people that they were before their death. That implies a bodily resurrection at death. I have already argued that this is quite conceivable. It is not a question of reincarnation, nor of the resuscitation of a body, but of the recreation of a human being who has realized his or her humanity in and through an essential corporeality, with all that this implies in terms of mutual relationships with everything and everyone in the universe. The body rises in humanized form, not in its material character, its extent, but precisely to the degree in which it is human, a self-possession, a self-realization.

Of course it is very difficult to say anything meaningful about the resurrection life itself. It is a transcendent event in heaven. Naturally we are not to envisage this heaven as a sphere, as a place above the earth. Heaven is God himself. God's existence cannot be localized. God does not live somewhere. However, we human beings can only imagine existence, life, in spatial terms. Because we necessarily think of the life of the one, even of God, in connection with the life of others, we separate these modes of living in space and time. We simply cannot think of any relationships otherwise. Because God's innermost being does not coincide with our own — for all his immanence, God remains transcendent — we think of his existence as being above us, in heaven. If we constantly remember that this is a form of presentation which is indispensable, we can see that while we may not pursue this terminology further, we simply cannot get on without it.

So at death human beings come to God as human beings for their destiny. The life that was begun and sustained here on earth by the creator God and was already an event of love in and through the Spirit of the Son, is fully developed in heaven.

First of all I would like to stress quite emphatically that after death we find a life, the same eternal life, that we already know on earth in and through faith. All too often one gets the impression that at death people are encapsulated in their past, as though someone's past determined his or her future beyond death. Existence after death is not a matter of being frozen in the situation or condition in which one dies. There is no standstill, and in this sense there is no end either. The game is not played out. Men and women find life after death. Talk of eternal life puts the emphasis too exclusively on the concept of eternity and too little on the word life. This has perhaps been encouraged by the fact that the liturgy for the dead speaks of eternal life and eternal peace. In my view all this has to do with the conception of death as the separation of soul and body. Granted, on the basis of the tradition there is an affirmation of the survival of the immortal soul, but it is not at all easy to imagine the life of such a disembodied soul. Of course, it is asserted that the souls of the righteous achieve the blessed vision of God immediately after their death. However, from the beginning this concept became impenetrably obscure as a result of infinite and subtle discussions of a purely speculative kind: do the souls see God himself, his nature, or only his emanation, his glory? Do the souls see God's essence directly or is it mediated in some way? This and similar discussions which were carried on with acute perceptiveness for centuries were no help in making the blessed vision of God understandable as an abundance of true life.

In this climate, the saying 'That is eternal life, that they know thee, the only true God' (John 17.3) was also gradually watered down so that it became purely speculative knowledge of God. In John, the term 'know' has a much richer content. Knowing is the result of being one and becoming one in and through love. Love is a praxis, an event: 'And by this we may be sure that we know him, if we keep his commandments . . . No one who abides in God sins; no one who sins has either seen him or knows him . . . He who loves is born of God and knows God. He who does not love does not know God; for God is love' (I John 2.3; 3.6; 4.7f.). So knowing God here is not knowing about God in the intellectualist sense, nor is it seeing God in terms of observation. The knowledge of God can only be interpreted in terms of a mystical union, if this can stand the test of specific human love. 'In this is love perfected with us, that we may have confidence in the day of judgment, because as he is, so are we in this world' (I John 4.16). 'We know that we love the children of God, when we love God and obey his commandments' (I John 5.2).

So the blessed vision of God is not perfect knowledge, but a perfect life in and with God, as a gracious human event.

The content of this eternal life as event is the creator and redeemer God who gives himself. So future life may be thought of in terms of the present life of faith, though in the future eternal life, the eternal life that we now live in faith blossoms into a seeing. However, both in the life of faith now and in the future vision we have the same creator and redeemer God. Because this God always determines our present existence, because he himself creates the real content, meaning and ground of our existence, existence in the future cannot be different from our present existence. It is the same existence in another mode, experienced in another way. It is the crown and fulfilment of this existence, the coming to fruition of this life, so long as we do not understand all these concepts simply as lifeless conditions. Heaven is not an arsenal, a camping place, a place of rest. Heaven is the God who is eternally alive and who now gives himself definitively to humankind. Heaven begins on earth here and now to the degree to which we allow ourselves to be given God as unmerited grace, as he wills to give himself in his Son and in the Spirit, i.e. to the degree to which in this world we live after the model of Christ (cf. I John 4.17). Through this specific discipleship of Jesus of Nazareth we create in the power of his Spirit a piece of heaven for others on earth, like his personal love through which he now gives himself to us in his Spirit and fills our eternal life in faith. 'We are God's children now; it does not yet appear what we shall be, but we know that when he appears we shall be like him, for we shall see him as he is' (I John 3.2). Now already we are like him in and through discipleship. This is an often impossibly laborious way, a long way of the cross, following Jesus in his self-emptying, to become a servant, to become identified with the humiliated of society (cf. Phil.2.6-8), stumbling with a faith which cannot see, a struggle which hopes against all hope (cf. Rom.4.18). Now we are like him in and through the discipleship of a crucified one. But we are also like the risen and glorified one at the same time. If we become completely like him, by following him to his death, we shall also be conformed to his glorification (cf. Rom.6.5). Because we still live in faith, we see only in the fragments of a mirror.

One day we shall see him face to face: 'For now we see in a mirror dimly, but then face to face. Now I know in part; then I shall understand fully, even as I have been fully understood' (I Cor.13.12).

So it is clear that the future life can and must be thought of completely in terms of the present. Only in the light of the present can we say something meaningful about the future. However, the present cannot establish this future completely; that would not only be completely nonsensical, but in addition would not take enough account of the fact that in the future too, as in the present, we have to do with God. This God of our present faith and our future vision simply cannot be recognized finally in the present. He is and remains for us essentially unforeseeable in this life. That should make us extremely careful in talking about our future. Only in the light of revelation can we indicate this future with God. God is not mere future. He has given himself already as a gift, finally and irrefutably in Jesus of Nazareth, his redeeming word made man, which he never revokes. But precisely this man Jesus has shown us a God for whom we can never prescribe laws, who makes everything that we think of him spring up in and through the inconceivable, unpredictable inventiveness of his love for mankind. We must take constant account of this creativity of God's love for mankind, which transcends every concept and every conception, however responsibly we may talk about the future in terms of the past and the present. Paul's quotation of Isaiah remains true: 'What no eye has seen, nor ear heard, nor the heart of man conceived, what God has prepared for those who love him' (I Cor.2.9; Isa.64.4).

2. Heaven as community

God has created and redeemed us, as we are, as persons. He will fulfil us as persons. We shall live in a different way with God as the persons that we are now.

Following contemporary anthropology, I would understand personhood above all as openness, communication and relationship. We always achieve personhood along with others, through others, in community. If God brings us home to him, it is as persons, that is, together with others who have helped to determine and create our personhood, and also along with those whose personhood we ourselves have influenced actively, for good or ill. Our communication with others and our relationship to others are therefore not destroyed by death, since at the same time that would mean that our

personhood was broken off by death. This communication and relationship are of course experienced beyond death in a different way,
as is personhood itself. At all events it seems to me difficult to imagine how relationships can be maintained without any form of individuality. At death, for those of us who remain alive the person
who dies disappears in his or her individuality in so far as this can be
perceived and seen in and through his or her corporeality. The disappearance of this perceptible form of individuality also makes impossible and completely excludes any tangible contact between
living and dead, or better, between those who live on earth and those
who live with God. But this does not necessarily exclude the possibility of relationship and communication. For believers, relationship
with the essentially invisible God is not an aberration, an illusion, a
piece of self-deception, but it can become very clear in real experiences. Therefore it must also be possible to remain in communication
with people who live in and with God. However, I believe that this
communication presupposes the conception of the person as an individual. For it is a question of relationship and communication in
the service of love. I tried earlier to demonstrate how essential is the
individuality of the person in the experience of love. I cannot therefore imagine that a community of love can be realized beyond death
without any individuality. At all events, it is inconceivable without
the assumption of an abiding individuality.

If we go on thinking along these lines, I think that we can imagine
eternal life in heaven as a life of subjects, of persons who are and remain fully and completely themselves, in mutual surrender to God
and the whole of creation, in the glorified Christ. 'Love remains' (I
Cor.13.8). Love can be experienced only as a relationship between
free and conscious persons who do not give up, do not surrender
their uniqueness or individuality but give it to others, though in and
through this self-surrender they receive back themselves from others
as gift. 'Whoever loses his life for my sake will gain it' (Luke 9.24; cf.
Matt.16.25; Mark 8.35; John 12.25).

So eternal life in heaven is the free and final self-giving of the creator and redeemer God in the glorified Christ through which the human being, finally redeemed or glorified, achieves his or her full
self-identity. The glorified person may and can respond to the divine
self-giving through grace by giving himself or herself completely to
God. In this way a complete union in love comes into being. Through
this unhindered and complete union with the creator God in love the
glorified person remains in communication with the whole of divine

and creaturely reality. In and through communion with Christ, glorified human beings remain connected with the whole creation, whose head is Christ. In and with him they achieve the fulfilment of those who are still alive on earth. Because they already see this fulfilment of those who are still pilgrims on earth in their own participation in the glory of Christ, their participation in what happens on earth has to be called trust in the real sense. No hope, for they already see what awaits those who live on earth. They experience how those on earth are still on the way, but they already experience their final homecoming. In this sense we can still meaningfully claim that they too wait for the end of time, that is, for the event by which and in which God will be 'all in all' (I Cor.15.27). We cannot interpret this waiting as a particular form of suffering or want. They still see and experience in their unity with the glorified Christ the full glorification of mankind and the cosmos. United with the Spirit, they themselves help those still living on earth towards their final fulfilment.

3. Time and eternity

Living in eternity, risen and glorified human beings thus remain connected with what happens in time, in history.

Thinking about time and eternity makes the mind boggle. Since Kant, however, it is recognized that there is no such thing as time in itself, nor space either. Time has no independent existence. It is experienced by a thinking subject who is capable of conceiving of it as a succession of past, present and future, but who at the same time can see the successiveness of time as a unity. We could hardly find a clearer and apter comment than that of F. de Grijs: 'Space and time are not objects of sense experience. Everyone sees in space and no one has ever seen space. Time and space are not entities in which things take place or occur. Nothing is in space in the way that ink is in an inkwell. But space and time make possible relationships and connections between their contents. There must be space and time for anyone to establish a relationship between things, whether theoretically or in reality. But neither space nor time (which govern all entities) can be thought of or imagined. They do, however, make possible thought and imagination.'[1]

Time and space are categories in which and with which we think. We cannot get on without them. So time is irrevocably caught up with our way of thinking and imagining things. I therefore find it difficult to see why this should no longer be the case when human beings, as thinking subjects, as individuals, finally live with God. People never have timelessness, either in this life or in the one we must think of as coming afterwards. People never become eternal. That would be a contradiction in itself. So in my view eternal life is not simply timeless life. Eternity is only a characteristic of the divine mode of existence, and even in this eternal life of God the great question remains whether we can or may think away any real temporal dimensions.

In classical theology this last observation would simply have been condemned as blasphemy. That was because people thought that becoming – and the present *becomes future* – was essentially imperfection. We become what we not yet are, and to this degree becoming is a characteristic of the incomplete being; however, it must be decisively rejected in connection with the perfect God. In the meantime we have gained a rather different view of becoming. This no longer points towards incompleteness. Growth is not always a growth towards something that one is not yet or does not yet have. We need only think of growing in love. It is quite conceivable that two people are completely happy in their mutual love but that they grow in love as a result of a great many experiences. As we understand things now, becoming has a more positive connotation, suggesting dynamism, growth, development, life. Process theology has sought to apply this to thinking and talking about God from its own perspective.[2]

Thus time does not exist in itself, but is a matter of experience. And in this experience of time we can distinguish between knowing oneself to be subject to time and control of time. By the experience of being subject to time I mean, among other things, experience of guilt, repentance, conscience, any form of regret about missed chances and failures in the past; any suffering of collapse, or grief, or helplessness in the present; any insecurity, anxiety, doubt about the future. This experience of time as an overwhelming power through which time gains power over us as guilt, pain or threat, is inconceivable in eternal life. So we may imagine eternal life for human beings as meaning that the glorified man is lifted above time as the experience of guilt, impotence and anxiety. In fact any profound experience of time is always closely connected with human suffering. When one sits at the sick bed of someone undergoing untold suffering, one is asked every quarter of an hour what time it is. For such people, every minute lasts an hour. Boredom is also the experience of an infinite period of time. Alongside this we fortunately have other experiences. We can be caught up in something so intensively, can be so delighted, that we no longer have any experience, any awareness of time. We experience eternity here and now. Our language can make that clear. One can meaningfully speak of endless suffering, i.e. of suffering which lasts a disturbingly long time and with no end in sight. But it is impossible to speak of timeless suffering. However, one can speak of timeless joy and timeless happiness. In that case we are speaking of an experience by which we transcend time. However, we experience everything in time. Something was not there yesterday, and can be completely forgotten tomorrow. In that case may we not understand eternity as a kind of transcending of time? Eternity is therefore not the same as all time. Were that the case, then we could very well understand people who asked whether this constant vision of God would not ultimately become boring. Eternity is in no way a prolongation of time. Heaven is not worship that goes on for ever! Eternity is a particular kind, a particular mode of being by which we transcend time, i.e. are no longer subject to time.

On earth we all know such experiences of happiness, when we no longer have any sense of time. Here in our human history such an experience of eternity in time is what is ultimately offered as a possibility in faith. Whoever believes has eternal life, continually threatened by the essentially unforeseeable future, which is realized in and through human freedom. As a result, on earth eternity always remains the object of hope and trust. This unforeseeableness disappears in the beyond, and with it hope in the real sense of the word. But the eternity which is experienced there is not a fixation, is not immutability, a loss of the power to grow, a loss of dynamic.

Even in mediaeval theology, a particular form of time was associated with the eternal life of creatures, but this time from another perspective. A special concept was created for this, and people spoke of *aevum*, something which lay roughly between time and eternity as these concepts were thought of in the Middle Ages.[3] The *aevum* was distinguished from time because in it there was no earlier and later; nor was it eternity as such, because change and changeableness could still be experienced. We need only think back briefly to what Thomas said about the blessed vision of God by the disembodied soul. There he also spoke of a certain growth, usually understood intensively but sometimes understood extensively.[4]

By incorporating the category of time into participation in the eternal life of God by glorified humanity it is possible to maintain the distinction between individual and general eschatology and between particular and general judgment. As we saw, at a person's death something of human history was crowned by God. At his death, the human being who makes history comes before God. He has history completed by God. At his death man also has a piece of humanized matter, a piece of cosmos, glorified. In and through the death of individuals, a period of human history already comes to an end and a part of our earth is already newly made into what is really 'a new earth and a new heaven'. But human history and the world go on. I believe that the person who is glorified in Christ already experiences the completion of his or her own history, experiences the last day, and personally enters the new heaven and the new earth. I also believe that the person who is glorified in Christ already sees the perfect consummation of everything and everyone, in other words, sees the end of time and the last judgment. However, because he or she is essentially bound up with the creation and continues to be an indissoluble part of it, they still have a very real communion with what happens on earth and in history. They experience all this in the expectation that God will finally be all in all; that is, will also be experienced and responded to by all and in all.

So while I would see a real distinction between individual and general eschatology and would therefore claim that the last judgment on the last day has to mean something not only for the generation then living on earth but for all those who are already glorified, as the fulfilment of a living expectation, I do not want to go into further speculations about the last day and the end of the world. It is as hard to think of the end of the world and history as of their beginning. One can only talk meaningfully of the beginning if one has an awareness that beforehand there was nothing of the kind, and one can only talk of the end if one thinks that there will be nothing afterwards. So one necessarily thinks of beginning and end as events in time. 'Beginning and end are themselves categories of time which therefore cannot be put in a kind of super-time which is itself again time, and so on.'[5] We cannot continue to puzzle over this. However, there is just one thing more. If there is ever an end to our human history and to this world, of which we can speak in faith, then this end is God's sovereign initiative. And that is something that science cannot calculate, nor can it be foreseen in possible catastrophes which might happen to the world. We should have learned that from our investigation of apocalyptic. If the world were to be destroyed by nuclear weapons or some natural catastrophe, that would not be the end of the world and of history as spoken of by faith. Apocalyptic visions which chime in with the panic-like feelings of our time are quite alien to the gospel and muddy the clear spirit of hope which is given us, to continue to live and to work without anxiety.

4. Communion of saints

In tradition the participation of risen and glorified humanity in what happens on earth is expressed in the term communion of saints. This is a community which is formed by human beings in the Holy One, the holy event of redemption. In and through the community which comes about among human beings on the basis of their union in and through the glorified Christ, the boundary between death and life is destroyed within this community. In the kingdom of God there is no frontier between the living and the dead. There are only living beings, who here on earth together are on the way with God, and living beings who have been brought home in Christ to the Father. So beyond death they live in a communion of love which is stronger than death. In it they retain their significance for one another. That is realized in what we call prayer for the departed and the intercession of the saints – whose unceasing prayer is ready to help us.

Praying for the dead rightly plays a significant role in Catholic piety. This custom is almost as old as the church itself. Texts on old tombstones attest it, liturgical customs show it and at earlier councils guidelines and regulations were laid down for it.[6] Later the meaning and significance of this prayer and sacrifice for the dead was expressed above all in connection with the doctrine of purgatory. So in 1208 Innocent II required the following confession from the Waldensians: 'We believe that alms, sacrifice and other good works can be performed for the benefit of departed believers' (D 427). There was even a dogmatic definition of this at the First and Second Councils of Lyons (1245 and 1274: D 456, 464). In 1341 the Armenians were forbidden to pray for all the dead (D 535), a custom which had existed for centuries and which clearly bore witness to a dynamic view of life after death, for people in fact prayed for the saints and also for the Mother of God. Their starting point here was that happiness could be further increased by prayer on earth. The significance of praying for the dead was stressed again at the Council of Florence and in the same terms as at the Council of Lyons (D 693). The Council of Trent states that the mass gives satisfaction even for the departed (D 940; 950; 983; 998).

It is important to have a proper understanding of mutual prayer for and by the dead. God does not need this prayer. He does not wait for this prayer before he intervenes on behalf of men and women. Intercession does not exercise any pressure on God; it does not make him more well disposed; it does not cause him to change his mind; and it does not make his intervention speedier or more merciful. Unfortunately we still find such basically blasphemous conceptions in certain circles, where people delight in visions and appearances.

Intercession for one another fits in completely with God's mode of action. He incorporates people into his saving activity as people, in their freedom, their responsibility, their creativity. People *may* communicate God's salvation to one another. God as it were exercises his providence in conjunction with human beings. He allows human beings to pass on to others what they themselves have received from him. What Jesus said in his mission discourse applies to the whole ordinance of salvation: 'Freely have you received, freely give' (Matt.10.8). In this way we may contribute to the salvation of others in accordance with God's will. But we can do this only because God enables us to. We receive what we hand on. It is precisely this awareness of complete dependence, this radical orientation on the free gift of God, which enables us to be God's gift for others, which is deliberately expressed in intercessory prayer.[7]

Praying within the communion of saints may not remain limited to intercessory prayer. Those of us who live on earth are not just to pray for our departed but to our departed; together with them we may praise God, thank him, glorify him and worship him. So we live in prayer in the communion of saints and grow more intensively and deeply in unity around our glorified Lord. And our prayer means something for the saints, not by increasing their happiness but by showing them that we are growing into the community to which they belong.

V

PURIFICATION AND SATISFACTION – PURGATORY

I have already made a brief mention of purgatory. This dogma of Catholic faith really deserves a better reputation. However, all are agreed that the scriptural texts which are traditionally used to provide a biblical basis for the belief can only be interpreted in this direction with the greatest of good will.

1. The history of a dogma

In II Macc.12.43-45 it is clearly assumed that the living remain in solidarity with the dead and still can do and mean something for them.[1] Some people believe that it is possible to argue from Matt.12.32, where it says that there is no forgiveness for the sin against the Holy Spirit 'either in this world or in the world to come', that there is a possibility of forgiveness for other sins in the world to come. However, that is not historically the meaning of the saying. It means that a sin against the Holy Spirit will *never* be forgiven. And that is quite clear, simply because only the Holy Spirit gives forgiveness. Those who refuse faith in him, rule out the possibility of his work.

Traditionally I Cor 3.10-15 is always cited as a scriptural proof of the dogma of purgatory.[2] 'Each man's work will become manifest; for the day will disclose it, because it will be revealed with fire, and the fire will test what sort of work each man has done. If the work which any man has built on the foundation survives, he will receive a reward. If any man's work is burned up, he will suffer loss, though he himself will be saved, but only as through fire' (vv.13-15). This text is all too clearly concerned with 'that day', i.e. the day of judgment. Here fire has the symbolic significance which I mentioned explicitly, when we were discussing the day of Yahweh and the symbolism of judgment.[3]

II Maccabees 12.43-45 in fact talks about prayer for the dead, and as I said, this is a very old custom in the church.[4] To begin with, it came about without much reflection. It was above all Tertullian who developed the idea of a reconciling suffering after death. Remarkably enough, however, two great Greek theologians were to develop these ideas further, Clement of Alexandria and Origen, though the Eastern church was later to deny this particular aspect of expiation in suffering after death and to interpret suffering as purification.[5] In the Latin church Augustine and Gregory the Great above all made later thinking about purgatory possible and gave it direction. Augustine already speaks of purifying punishment before the last judgment, which possibly takes place through fire.[6]

The word *purgatorium*, place of purification, does not appear at all before the end of the twelfth century. However, before that there is already mention of a purifying fire, a purifying punishment, purifying pains and purifying suffering. Only at the end of the twelfth century is a special place for these created between heaven and earth.[7] I would like to point out that the souls in purgatory are rarely mentioned in thirteenth-century theology, which usually speaks of those who are in purgatory. This place is thought to be nearer to hell than to heaven, which is what the optimism of the first centuries assumed, when people spoke, with Tertullian, of a *refrigerium interim*, an intermediate period of refreshment.[8]

Mediaeval theology developed the doctrine of purgatory in detail. Generally speaking, it affirmed the necessity of purgatory for the expiation of sins already forgiven. That is connected with existing penitential practice in the church. Sins are not simply forgiven but must also be atoned for by undergoing punishment. We must attempt to understand the distinction between guilt and punishment in terms of this church practice. Thomas also holds this view, that in purgatory punishments are endured which have been incurred for sins past but already forgiven, but at the same time he also teaches that even venial sins are forgiven in purgatory (*In IV Sent.*, d.21, q,1, a.1, sol 1 and 4; ibid. a.2, sol 1). In recognizing this, Thomas accepts that there can be a free activity of love in purgatory, for only through the active affirmation of love are sins forgiven. Thus according to Thomas purgatory is at all events more than a place of chastisement and punishment.

In the second half of the thirteenth century we find for the first time that views about purgatory differ between Greek and Latin theologians. The Latins put all the stress on paying the penalty in order to make good violations of the divine majesty. The Greeks were afraid that this idea could be taken further, that it would be assumed that all sins could be blotted out by severe punishments, and that in the end there would be no need for hell. The doctrine of *apokatastasis* is still very much alive in the East, that doctrine which says that hell will simply disappear and at the end of time even the devil will be freed. We shall return to this question when we consider hell. This is an underlying fear of the Greeks, in that they refuse to believe in punishments which are supposed to bring final satisfaction for all sins and all sinners. They prefer to understand purgatory as a purifying suffering rather than as progressive divinization through grace. Of course those who are finally damned can never share in this.

Statements by the teaching office

Explicit statements by the teaching office about purgatory must be interpreted against the background of attempts at reunion with the Greek church and later of the polemic against the Christians of the Reformation.

At the First Council of Lyons in 1245 the Greeks were asked to take over the term purgatory because they had the same teaching about it as the Latin church (D 456). At the Second Council of Lyons in 1274 the question of fire was not allowed to come up. The term *purgatorium* was now also avoided. It was simply stated that after death there are purifying punishments for those who died penitently in love (D 464). At the Reunion Council of Florence (1438-1445) there is again no mention of fire, nor is there a close definition of precisely what is to be understood by the term 'purifying punishments'. Nor is there an examination of the distinction between sin-guilt and punishment-guilt. What is left as the content of the dogma is that anyone who dies in the love of God but has not yet given satisfaction for his actual sins or sins of omission must be purified after death by purifying punishments; merits of believers, their masses, their prayers, alms and good works aid the salvation of these souls in purgatory (D 693).

With the Council of Trent we find ourselves in quite a different context. The Reformers were allergic to all works of merit by which people could claim divine reward. They found it quite unacceptable that after death merit could be obtained through suffering which provided satisfaction. This fundamental perspective and the specific historical background of the sale of indulgences, corrupt practices with money for ransoming souls, and the like, explain the antipathy of the Reformation towards purgatory, all the more since there was not a single clear text in the Bible to support it. The Council of Trent dissociated itself from the basic Reformation view of merit. Against this background the Council formulated a doctrine of purgatory which to a large extent took over the views of the Council of Florence. However, the distinction between sin-guilt and sin-punishment was also taken up again. Purifying punishments were expressly defined as paying the penalty for remaining temporal sins. At the same time the Council of Trent made it clear that in purgatory there can be no question of a vision of God, much less of a heaven (D 840).

To sum all this up, we can say that it is defined as dogma that anyone who dies in a state of grace but is not yet completely purified (Lyons, Florence), and still has to undergo punishment in time for sins committed (Trent), must be further purified after death by purifying punishments before he or she can enjoy the blessed vision of God in heaven. In this process of purification the souls in purgatory can be aided by the merits of believers, above all by the sacrifice of the mass. The term fire has no binding character in dogma, nor has the teaching office anywhere made a statement about purgatory as a place of purification.[9]

I have given this short account of the history of purgatory to demonstrate convincingly how time-conditioned and contextual conciliar formulations can be. Expressions which were toned down or even omitted completely so as not to offend the Greeks and with an eye to reunion were taken up again and used against the Reformation. The teaching office sees no problem in taking over the anthropology with a dualistic orientation which was generally affirmed during these centuries. Hence all the difficulties which follow when one thinks for example about the kind of feeling of pain that fire could inflict on a disembodied soul.[10]

Insight into all this allows us to investigate the verbal formulations of these statements in the light of their specific historical context in order to discover their real meaning and purpose. So at all events one cannot claim that a departure from the letter of a conciliar document is a betrayal of its spirit.

2. Reconciliation and satisfaction

The development of the doctrine of purgatory in the Western church shows how markedly legalistic or juristic the thinking was in this church. All the emphasis is laid on paying the penalty for sins by undergoing punishments which provide satisfaction. In the East, for the reasons mentioned above, the leading idea was more one of purifying mercy.

Now it must be clearly recognized that Roman law thinking can make particularly good use of a widespread religious conception of God's *righteousness*. However, this conception was more strongly governed by human thought, above all in its primary form, than guided by God's action of revelation with his people and above all in Jesus of Nazareth. Although we cannot think of going into detail here about these important and significant problems, we must consider them briefly so as to look at the doctrines of purgatory and hell from a clearer Christian perspective than happened in the tradition.

Righteousness violated

Stress on the righteousness of God to some degree gives God himself into our hands. We can haggle. Through sin God is rightly hurt immeasurably. The harmony between God and mankind is put right out of joint, destroyed by sin. The holy God must react to that in anger by punishing the sinner. So it is essential that something be done. Men and women must seek to do everything possible to restore the right that has been violated, to satisfy the angry God whose rights have been infringed. God may, indeed must, punish. He owes it to his holiness and his righteousness.

Now what is more understandable than that people should look for means and methods of escaping the wrath of God and his punishment? Sacrificial practices and a sacrificial ritual were seen as a prime means of giving God satisfaction for his violated rights, the rights which humanity had infringed. In this way people hoped to be freed from further retribution and vengeance. That is all very clear. They sought to get God in their grasp and attempted to earn merit through voluntary sacrifice and the acceptance of punishment. Because of their personal achievement, people were no longer handed over without protection to a vengeful God. Through doing penance, through sacrifice, they could give God satisfaction and in so doing find peace: what had to be done was achieved, and righteousness was accomplished.

Beyond question this is the predominant view of God's righteousness in the Old Testament. In one particular tradition Yahweh leaves abundant traces of blood wherever he appears and he repeatedly calls for blood. Furthermore, if one polishes up this image of the God of righteousness and vengeance, sacrifice and satisfaction, and strips off its all too primitive colours, it corresponds completely with human thinking and even provides a basis for mutual human relationships and relationships between nations. Righteousness must be made a reality, guilt must be atoned for, anyone who behaves badly must repent. Punishment and penance seem indispensable for the sake of righteousness or even as a motive for moral action. Threats of vengeance in return indicate anxiety at guilty behaviour or neglect. In the last resort this is the same rational argument as is used to defend holding a balance of power in the world on the basis of the possession of weapons. Only the powerful threat contained in the possession of nuclear weapons deters aggression. One can in fact bring God in to justify all this. He wants to maintain the moral order by the threat of eternal hell fire.

Although such an image of God is never completely abandoned in the Old Testament, at a very early stage it is repeatedly tempered by expressions of a God who reveals himself, expressions which stand in direct contrast to the human portrait of a God who matches human ideas. God's mercy gradually becomes the revelation of the God-ness of God. There are countless texts about his mercy in the Bible, as there are countless occurrences of the adjectives with which it is described: God's mercy is boundless, eternal, full of compassion and pity, inventive and creative.

Here is a God who is quite different from the way in which people imagine him. He is a God of free grace which precedes every human merit and every achievement. He stresses mercy as an unconditional gift. He reveals himself as a God who always intervenes to save, on his own impulse, his own initiative. This God does not need to be assuaged by sacrifice. He does not keep his wrath and his vengeance ready, but only his goodness, his grace, his love and his faithful perseverance. He therefore asks only for trust, for faith in his unchangeable faithfulness to his covenant, to the word that he has given. As revelation progresses, sacrifices are recognized with increasing clarity as human works by which attempts are made to trade with God. Prophets criticize this misleading sacrificial cult in sharp terms (cf. e.g. Jer.7.21-23; Amos 5.21-25; Hos.10.1-15; Micah 6.6-8).

This true God, who calls only for faith and trust which consist in letting go and laying down all weapons which are kept in case of emergency, for self-defence and to ward off a God who sets out to fight in defence of his own honour and rights, is revealed in the Old Testament in the most unexpected and disconcerting way, in the suffering servant of Yahweh (Isa.42.1-4; 49.1-6; 50.4-11; 52.13-

53.12). This servant of Yahweh is smitten and mistreated quite unjustly. He does not strike back. He has no thought of vengeance and he does not bide his time. He takes the guilt of others on himself without saying a word. This servant of Yahweh is the image of Yahweh himself. The God of revelation is like that.

When we recognize how deeply the notion of retribution is rooted in all religious thought about God, even in Old Testament faith, we immediately see that in this defenceless, non-violent figure, something completely new is coming to light. Here is the revelation of something that is more than human. Here is a breakthrough in the closed circle of human thinking about righteousness, in which violated rights must be restored by punishment and repentance and restored to equilibrium, in which the principle that holds is an eye for an eye, a tooth for a tooth. Anyone who is struck and does not strike back, who does not repay in the same coin, anyone who offers unconditional forgiveness, anyone who does not call for satisfaction for harm suffered or rights violated, is not a human being. This conduct is no longer human. It is simply incomprehensible. Such a person, moreover, is extremely dangerous. In a criminal fashion he stands our legal order on its head.

Yet in this defenceless figure, in this attitude, God has revealed himself with the utmost profundity. God has taught his servant to react in this way: every morning God wakens his ear to hear as those who are taught (50.4-5). Therefore 'I gave my back to the smiters and my cheeks to those who pulled out the beard; I hid not my face from shame and spitting' (50.6). If evil is not answered with evil, the power and course of evil are finally broken. It cannot continue in new violence. It is consumed in unusual goodness and unhoped-for mercy. In this way God achieves justice and reveals the divine character of righteousness.

This revelation is first finally achieved with all its consequences in and through the person of Jesus of Nazareth. In his proclamation and his dealings with men he brought this boundless mercy to specific people, lost as they were. As a result of this he destroyed the order established on a divine basis. The merciful God of Jesus of Nazareth did not correspond to human thinking about this mercy. Speaking and acting as Jesus did went against any sound human common sense, against everything that people needed to secure themselves over against God. It was against the law. If God really was to be as Jesus revealed him, no one any longer had a claim on God and could no longer use religion as a guarantee for the existing order. In that case God's grace had to be enough, and as the image and likeness of this God, people had to be as gracious and merciful as he was himself. Away with him! Crucify him! God's righteousness demands the death penalty for his blasphemous talk and the implementation of a divine mercy. What else can one do? How else can one secure God's grace and faithfulness? Let us continue to earn our rest and security; punish us so that we experience that we are penitent enough to earn forgiveness.

This view of God's own righteousness as prevenient and boundless mercy[11] calls for a revision of a particular theology of sacrifice. It makes us think differently about punishment, suffering that gives satisfaction and pains that purify.

Mutuality in forgiveness

I want to make a brief investigation of this in connection with the real content of the doctrine of purgatory. That God should punish by way of retribution does not seem to me to correspond to the view of the true God which revelation makes possible. What one could describe as God's punishment is simply the experience of his absence. But this is always the consequence of a free human initiative which we call sin, as a result of which we do not accept God because we reject him in our unbelief. Where that happens everything has to be done by human beings in human terms. The place of revelation and the dependence of faith is now taken by absolute certainty that one is right; this makes it all too easy to regard understanding and respectability as one's own exclusive possession or that of a group or community. Trust is replaced by seeking security through achievement, power and possessions, by not being dependent on anyone else. Love, the chief art of which consists in allowing oneself be loved, is rejected as a relationship of intolerable dependence. All human relationships are reduced to the standard model of the commercial relationship *do ut des*, I give in order to get something. There is no longer room for nor experience of unmerited grace – the word has even become unknown – selfless goodness, sacrificial love, tender mercy, forgiveness and compassion. A fatalistic way of thinking dominates and governs society. When we see the evil consequences of all this it is impossible to speak of God's punishment; what we have is the experience of the absence of God. For where God comes, where man allows him to come in and through grace, everything changes.

It does not seem that punishment as a pedagogical method accords with the image of God offered us by revelation. Even if it did, the question would arise whether in our time we could still defend such an interpretation of punishment. Dostoievsky already wrote: 'All these sentences of hard labour in Siberian prisons, and formerly with flogging, too, do not reform anyone and, what's more, scarcely deter even one criminal, and, far from diminishing, the number of crimes are steadily increasing. You have to admit that. It therefore follows that society is not in the least protected, for though a harmful member is cut off automatically and exiled to some remote spot just to get rid of him, another criminal takes his place at once, and often two perhaps. If anything does protect society even today and indeed reforms the criminal himself and brings about his regeneration, it is, again, only the law of Christ, which reveals itself in the awareness of one's own conscience.'[12] A guilty person must be brought to conversion, to rebirth, to deliverance, to resurrection. The guilty person must leave his sinful way himself, on the testimony of his own conscience. That does not happen through compulsion or punishment but through the offer of grace, love, forgiveness and mercy. In the exalted love of the other the guilty person must recognize his or her own error and so come to conversion, to rebirth, from within.

I believe that this happens in the unveiled encounter with God which takes place at the resurrection from the dead. Then we see who God is and in the face of God we discover ourselves and achieve final self-knowledge. The unveiled revelation of the merciful love of God reveals to us our own lovelessness or lack of love, just as the revelation of the holiness of God at the same time confronts us with our own sinfulness. In the judgment of the Son of man God shows himself to risen humanity as pure grace, love and mercy. In and through this encounter we experience complete forgiveness. But this forgiveness is given by the Son of man to human beings.

The event of forgiveness brings about something within us, namely the will to begin the rebirth that has been granted, to integrate it in and through an event which offers satisfaction. This latter, satisfaction for sins, is not required by a righteous God. To put it in a trite way: it is not God who imposes punishments on men and women at the judgment, obliges them to repent and pay their last debts before he admits them to the glory of paradise. In the light of the merciful love of God, those who are risen seek to make amends out of self-respect, not in order to be worthy of the love of God but so that they may approach God with some self-respect. So God does not need this satisfaction, nor do we earn anything by it or have to gain anything from God. Paradise is already given without our deserving it. God does not require any more. But we can make sense of the fact that God still gives risen humanity a chance to do something which we feel obliged to do out of self-respect. In venturing to appear before God, we must dare to look at ourselves in the mirror and be able to stand the sight.

Perhaps an illustration will make clear what I mean. Suppose that you have hurt someone deeply. You have destroyed their life, have robbed them of all faith and trust in humanity and in God. This person knows that. He or she knows that it is your fault. He or she comes to you and says: 'Everything is forgiven and forgotten.' Can you simply accept this offer of forgiveness? Anyone who did that would show incredible immaturity, a complete lack of responsibility, not even a trace of self-respect. I must make good what I did wrong, try to put it right again. Not because the other person requires it, but because I owe it to myself as a mature person who does not want to escape responsibility. The other person who offers unconditional forgiveness must give me the chance to make some amends. That is the only way in which he or she can avoid treating me paternalistically, condescendingly, with an offer of forgiveness, and regard me as a free and responsible person. In this way one feels less humiliated and trapped than when nothing else is expected.

That is one way in which we could imagine purgatory. We need not be very disturbed that that way of thinking is more along the lines of Eastern than of Western theology, as this has been expressed in certain conciliar statements, since the Second Council of Lyons should remind us that this is more a matter of terminology. So we may see purgatory as an encounter with God in which God gives risen humanity the chance to make amends for wrongdoing towards him and creation; it is not just a demand of divine righteousness, a lack of mercy, but a revelation of his immensely great mercy. He wants to take people so seriously, to treat them so much as partners with full rights, that he allows them to fulfil a demand of human conscience, and achieve some self-respect. At all events that would fit in with the pattern of the human encounter with God. God never treats man like an immature child or a senile old person. God asks for our free surrender in love. In everything and at all times he respects the freedom that he himself gives us. We can and may mean something for him. He treats us as his image and likeness, as an equal partner in a loving relationship which presupposes that. However, this equality has nothing to do with merit; it is sheer, almost unbelievable, grace.

It is hard for us to have any specific picture of what I have called here the event of purgatory. It is not tied up with any single conception, much less with a place. It fits in very well with the approach I have favoured, namely of thinking of the resurrection as something which happens to the whole person at death. The resurrection as I have described it does not rob the distinction between eternity and time of all meaning. Although we obviously cannot measure the resurrection life by our earthly limited time, we can certainly not deny a degree of temporality if we want to say anything meaningful about glorified creatures. However, it is impossible to imagine this temporality. So it makes little sense to speak of purgatory as an event which takes place in a moment, for that too is an earthly conception of time, like speaking of the pains of purgatory in calculable concepts of days and years.

The conception of purgatory which I have presented here does not affect in any way what has been taught about the significance of prayer for the dead. However, the suspicions which I expressed earlier about the significance of such intercession remain. We can and may help those who are still alive to make amends to God, as they want to of their own accord, by virtue of the grace that they have received. As I have said repeatedly, the dead do not come before the judgment seat of the Son of man as solitary individuals but as persons, as members of a community, as members of a body. This awareness of faith is expressed through prayer and sacrifice for the dead. The mutual communion in which we mean something for one another before God and may do something for one another remains intact. I believe that this aspect of the communion of saints becomes clearer when we affirm the resurrection of men and women, of person as persons, directly at death, than if we speak in terms of souls. These are all too easily thought of in an atomistic way, which cannot be the case if we speak of persons, for persons exist only in and through a community of persons which is realized corporeally in history.

VI

EXISTENCE AS HELL

So far I have spoken of resurrection as the fulfilment of persons who at death are glorified by God as persons, and thus bring to completion a piece of human history and a part of earth. I have also tried to say something about purgatory. But what about hell?

First of all we must note that it emerges clearly from our historical survey that resurrection is almost always a concept with a positive content. Belief in resurrection arose as a hope and not in the perspective of retribution. The idea of a resurrection in which final punishments are assigned only appears at a later stage and remains at the periphery of what is essentially optimistic belief in the resurrection. We can even be aware that it still made good sense to think of a final annihilation of sinners by death when here and there people began to talk of an eternal punishment which was to consist in something other than disappearance for ever.

It also emerged from our historical investigation that the fire mentioned in connection with judgment, Gehenna and hell is to be understood symbolically and not literally. I also explained how Jesus' remarks about it are to be understood within the whole apocalyptic context of his ministry.

1. Comments on hell

The church fathers had little difficulty in accepting the existence of a hell and wrote crudely realistic passages about hell fire. Only the theologian Origen declared unequivocally that there is no hell as a pool of fire created by God, but that hell consists in the torments of the conscience of the sinner, who imagines that by his own guilt he has excluded himself from God's love. His teaching found approval, though by no means everywhere. Augustine and Gregory the Great added their authority in support of the traditional theory of a real punishment by fire. This is not the self-torment of the sinner but a penal act by the righteous God himself, a punishment in and with real fire.

To begin with, the eternity of hell was also taken for granted and unanimously affirmed. Clement of Alexandria was the first to show some doubts and hesitations in accepting this. Origen hoped for a final redemption of all things, a restoration of all in and through the triumph of Christ, the so-called *apocatastasis*. For him the basis of this hope is I Cor.15.25f. Christ rules until all his enemies are overcome. For Origen it does not seem inconceivable that even the devil will see heaven open for him at the end of time. Origen himself expresses all this hypothetically. He is followed in this hope e.g. by Gregory of Nyssa, Theodore of Mopsuestia and for a while even by Jerome.

Origen's pupils speak more apodeictically and therefore provoke more reactions. To some degree the West was influenced by Origenism, and while hell was said to be eternal it was also said that Christians who die in mortal sin are finally rescued from it because of the indelible mark of their baptism, by virtue of which they continue to belong to Christ. That is a hypothesis which was put forward by the so-called *Misericordes*. Augustine attacked it vigorously. In 543 we find a statement by Pope Vigilius: 'Anyone who says or believes that the punishment of evil spirits and godless men is only temporal and will end after a certain time or that evil spirits and godless men will be completely restored, let him be anathema' (D 211).

The influence of the *Misericordes* can be traced down to the Middle Ages, and in early Scholasticism there was a tendency to diminish the pains of hell, though the eternity of hell was never put in doubt. In high Scholasticism a stricter view was usually put forward and the fire was interpreted in a very realistic sense.

In the statements of the church's teaching office there is often mention of an eternal punishment in hell. In the so-called *Faith of Damasus* we read that the evil are punished for ever (D 16) and the Athanasian Creed says that those who have done evil are punished with eternal fire (D 40; see also D 160b, 228a). These texts are attempts to define the existence of the eternal punishment of hell in a biblical terminology which had become traditional.

At the Fourth Lateran Council of 1215 it is stated against the Albigensians that all will arise with their own bodies and will be judged in accordance with their works. Sinners receive an eternal punishment with the devil. The First Council of Lyons (1245) states, though not as a dogma: 'Anyone who dies in mortal sin without repentance will without doubt suffer the pains of eternal hell for ever' (D 457).

In statements by the Second Council of Lyons (D 464), Benedict

XII (D 531) and the Council of Florence (D 693), it is said that the damned suffer the essential pains of hell immediately after their death just as the blessed enjoy essential blessedness.

The feelings of pain, as distinct from real rejection, were never formally declared to be a dogma. However, they are part of the constant teaching of the tradition. Nor, of course, is there ever a dogmatic definition of the nature of these feelings of torment, though they are always called pains of fire in the tradition.

2. Religion and anxiety

As we already saw in the case of the doctrine of purgatory, these statements by the teaching office and the tradition must also be understood in the light of their own historical, cultural and religious context. For centuries God's righteousness was understood more in legalistic terms than as the justifying of sinners. For centuries God's righteousness was thought of along the lines of what humans understand by righteousness. Our investigation must have produced sufficient evidence to demonstrate how much this image of God is governed by anthropology. In a culture which took a different view of punishment from that generally current today, it was evidently also possible to talk of a God who punished. Punishment and anxiety about punishment took on a very positive value and were used with the most honest intentions with the aim of improving men, helping them, leading them to conversion and rebirth. People of our day may have little understanding of this, and it may be said quite emphatically that one should not do good in order to receive reward or escape punishment, but for the sake of the good itself, beause the good is worth striving for and achieving simply for its own sake. However, we cannot deny the insight into human nature contained in these words of Dostoievsky: 'He solemnly declared during an argument that there was absolutely nothing in the whole world to make men love their fellow-men, that there was no law in nature that man should love mankind, and that if love did exist on earth, it was not because of any natural law but solely because men believed in immortality. He added in parenthesis that all natural law consisted of that belief, and that if you were to destroy the belief in immortality in mankind, not only love but every living force on which the continuation of all life in the world depended, would dry up at once. Moreover, there would be nothing immoral then, everything would be permitted, even cannibalism. But that is not all: he wound up with the assertion that for every individual, like myself, for instance, who does not believe in God or in his own immortality, the moral laws of nature must at once be changed into the exact opposite of the former religious laws, and that self-interest, even if it were to lead to crime, must not only be permitted but even recognized as the necessary, the most rational, and practically the most honourable motive for a man in his position.'[1] If in 1879/80 Dostoievsky was able to attribute these sentiments to Ivan Karamazov as a particularly acute rationalist, we need not be very surprised to find a similar view among theologians and church leaders of earlier centuries.

I have not quoted this text because I personally subscribe to it but to demonstrate how people could once think about morality and religion, about the significance of eternal reward or eternal punishment.

There is no denying the fact that hell was often proclaimed in a shabby way and that preachers abused it by playing on primitive human fears of eternal damnation. Anxiety can also be healthy. However, it later became clear all round that this is not the ideal and that one cannot create morality and belief by playing on human fears. No one can deny that anxiety before God had too large a role in earlier religious upbringing. In fact many people were not gladdened but poisoned through God from their youth up.[2] Sociologically one can establish a clear connection between religious practice and anxiety in the Roman Catholic church. There is no longer such fearful preaching about hell and eternal damnation as in previous decades when mission preachers threatened it from the pulpit and described hell with such vividness that you would think that they had come straight from there, with the result that there were queues outside every confessional. Today people no longer talk of hell, and in the meantime not only have confessionals been taken down but whole churches remain empty. I mention this only as a demonstrable fact, not as a value judgment. No one should conclude from it that we should instil new fears into people to bring them to church. Now and then one hears the desperate comment: it only needs a new war and you will see people flocking back to church.

It is terrible so to misuse religion in order to instil anxiety, particularly the religion of love which Jesus made accessible and which from the beginning was expressed in phrases like: 'Fear not, for you have found favour with God' (Luke 1.30): 'Fear not, for I bring to you tidings of great joy which shall be to all the people: today there is born to you in the city of David the saviour, Christ; he is the messiah, the Lord' (Luke 2.11). 'Repent and believe in the good news' (Mark 1.15). The gospel really could be a different way from walking in the fear of the Lord. But religion was too exclusively reduced to morality, so that good news, the gospel, again became a law. And laws require sanctions. Anyone who can impose sanctions is feared and rarely loved. Could the development have gone otherwise? It is particularly difficult to pass fair judgment on the past in the light of the present. Be this as it may, the Christian churches must again proclaim the gospel as good news, as liberation. It is also liberation from the fear of God and eternal divine punishment. Everyone must be told what John wrote: 'There is no fear in love, but perfect love casts out fear. For fear has to do with punishment, and he who fears is not perfected in love' (I John 4.18).

3. Descended into hell

It is understandable that the idea of an eternal hell has continually met with unbelief and doubt. How could it be reconciled with God's infinite mercy, which goes beyond all our imagining and whose extent and limits no one can determine? Has Christ not in fact conquered all enemies (I Cor.15.25f.) and has God not wanted to reconcile the universe through him, making peace through the blood which was shed on the cross to reconcile all things in heaven and on earth (Col.1.20)? At the mention of his name must not every knee bow in heaven, on earth and under the earth, and every tongue confess that Jesus Christ is Lord to the glory of God the Father (Phil.2.10f.)? Has God not shown us his secret counsel, the decision which he made in Christ to realize the fullness of time: to bring the universe in Christ under one head, all that is in heaven and on earth (Eph.1.9f.)?

Do not all these and similar texts express a basic trust in the final victory of Christ over all evil? All power in heaven and on earth is given to Jesus of Nazareth, as we have come to know him (Matt.28.18). Can the supremacy of his love never finally break and overcome the power of evil?

There are Christians with deep faith who because of their trust in the glorified Christ have difficulty in finding a place for hell. They refuse to dream of eternal happiness for themselves which could not be experienced in universal solidarity with all creatures. It is often the most strongly committed religious thinkers who look for a key to open up hell. Here I want only to pause over an original attempt which was made by Hans Urs von Balthasar.[3] He interprets Christ's descent into hell as a kind of opening up of hell.[4] I shall leave him to clarify his view and motivation in his own words: 'Only when the very one who has our monstrous world on his conscience, who had the inconceivable power and fearful courage to unleash this monster, only when he had not merely joined in inflicting the most fearful torment but had subjected himself to it (for only God can know what it truly means to be forsaken by God), only when that maximum coincides with this minimum (both of which are beyond our comprehension), albeit not in indifference but in such a way that absolute power becomes one with absolute impotence in protective compassion, thus only when God is triune – the same God the Father and Creator of cosmos and mankind, who in the Godforsakenness of his Son concentrates in the cross every conceivable kind of abandonment, who together in a deeply intense love form the one Spirit, the Spirit of the Father and the Son, the Spirit of the strong and the weak, the Spirit of the same love – only then am I given a key which makes credible and tolerable to me a meaning of existence – though I may not understand him or it.'[5] This is indeed a particularly dense and difficult text, but it is worth reflecting on. Balthasar makes God himself in Christ share in all the emptiness, impotence, loneliness and even ill will which is part of human experience. The Son is abandoned by the Father. The Son allows himself willingly to be abandoned by the Father. The Spirit is the underlying factor which explains this attitude of both Father and Son, namely self-giving love. The nature of the trinitarian God is self-surrender.

In the light of this trinitarian view, which is rightly called 'theodramatic', Hans Urs von Balthasar can go on to say: 'In this finality of death the dead Son descends, no longer active, but stripped by the cross of all power and all initiative of his own, as the one who is utterly at the disposal of others, reduced to the purely material level, to the complete and indifferent obedience of a corpse, incapable of any active solidarity, much less of any "preaching" to the dead. Out of a last love he shares death with them.'[6] In this way God himself accepts the death of God which is required by sinners. He practises the death of God which these sinners demand. He respects human freedom which makes a definitive choice against God. But he does not give this choice any abiding significance. He shows his solidarity from outside with those who reject any solidarity with God and with human beings, and in this way he makes everything clear through absolute weakness.[7]

Difficult though the language is here, this is a grandiose and bold attempt to express Christian hope in connection with hell. In the Son, God himself shares in the hell of human existence and the existence of hell itself. But the Son is not annihilated by the annihilating will of the sinner. In his annihilation he is bound with the Father by the Spirit. The Spirit is the bond between these two extremes, between these two poles, the living God and the murdered God. The murderers of God, those who reject God, are saved through this solidarity of the Son with them.

According to Hans Urs von Balthasar, then, hell exists, but it is not final, thanks to God's solidarity, in and through his Son, with the sinners who reject him.

4. Information and summons

Not everyone will be able to cope with this profound, mystical attempt at an approach. Questions about hell seldom go so deep, and are usually in search of information. How can one reconcile the existence of an eternal hell with God's infinite mercy? Does hell exist? Do you believe that? Do you think that many people go to hell?

Before we try to discover how an eternal punishment could be reconciled with God's boundless mercy, we would first have to be sure that this was not a pseudo-problem. I have already given my views about God's punishment. God does not punish. What is described as punishment is the experience of his absence. It is very difficult to imagine 'eternal' punishment. From what I have said about time and eternity, we would have to conclude that eternal punishment also calls for eternal time. For sorrow and suffering produce an awareness and an experience of time. Eternity is never experienced as time, but is a transcending of time in and through an intense experience of happiness. To speak of eternal suffering is in any case an incorrect use of words. One can only suffer for all time, and be happy eternally.

But again: is it not a waste of time to bother about purely speculative problems? Is there a hell? Do many people go to hell?

These questions were already put to Jesus: ' "Lord, will those who are saved be few?" And he said to them, " Strive to enter by the narrow door; for many, I tell you, will seek to enter and will not be able" ' (Luke 13.23f.). So Jesus does not give a direct answer. Here he is asked for information, and that is not why he was sent by the Father. He knows that he is called to save the world and therefore he issues a summons to his hearers to strive to the utmost to belong to those who will be saved. Jesus does not speak to people about other people. He addresses them directly. He personally brings them a message, an offer, and he personally addresses an appeal to them. He turns to each of them with a call to be converted.

The whole of the Bible is written in what is referred to as an appellative or performative language. That is, it is written in a language which makes an appeal to us, a language which seeks to change something in us, a language which calls on us to repent. People still look to the Bible too much for information. But scripture is not written in such informative language, which only increases knowledge and satisfies curiosity. Here, too, Jesus provides no information about hell. But he does say repeatedly that people will fail to fulfil their destiny (see Matt.5.22,29; 10.28; 13.42,50; Mark 9.43; Luke 12.5; 13.28). So it is important for each of us to be watchful and strive to the utmost not to fall by the wayside and miss our destiny.

Everyone must take these warnings of Jesus seriously. Jesus never makes them hypothetical. He tells us quite seriously what is at stake. He says this to each one of us about our personal future. He puts that into our hands. He gives us his own Spirit in order to share with us the journey to our eternal salvation which he has already begun in us and which he himself wills to bring to completion. Of course we must allow ourselves to be guided by his Spirit. It is clearly within our power to maim the Spirit, to quench the Spirit (cf. I Thess.5.19). In that case we do not achieve anything.

Does that also happen in the case of people? There is no hint of information, but only a word to each of us, a summons.

No one can say whether or not there is a hell. At all events, it does not exist as a spatial pool of fire which God prepares from eternity in order to make the damned pay for their sins eternally. At all events God did not create a hell. If there is a hell, it is created by us. The existence of hell depends on us. Everyone creates his or her own hell.

Perhaps we might put it this way. If all that matters to us on earth is that by the grace of God we should help to realize something of heaven for others, what we do if we are really seeking to live as disciples of Jesus of Nazareth will be our heaven when we die. If we make life hell for others by our self-satisfaction, by egoism, lust for power, violence, hate, by the fact that we block out any view of heaven from others by our words and actions, then it is highly probable that we shall find this hell for ourselves even at our death. At our death we shall find what we sought during our life. It will be either

God and others as our heaven and eternal happiness, or only ourselves.

So with Karl Rahner we can say: heaven, purgatory and hell are not places; they are three different designations for God. Heaven is God who has finally become our own. Purgatory is God who goes through us to purify us. Hell is God as the opportunity we have lost.

EPILOGUE

Belief in eternal life is declining. I have mentioned three of the various reasons for it. There is no longer any need for this life. I have given my objections to such an attitude. I found a second reason in traditional conceptions of belief in an afterlife. We made a lengthy historical investigation of the conceptions and considered their real import in the light of their specific context, the cultural and religious climate in which they came into being. The result of this investigation allowed us to interpret the various conceptions very freely. That is what I have also done in the third part of this book. It is extremely important to do away with conceptions which make this belief difficult. The baby is all too often thrown out with the bath water. I hope that I have purged the basic content of our eschatological belief of the conceptions which obscure it, in order to make this belief itself more acceptable and to give reasons for it.

I think that a third, perhaps the most significant, reason why belief in the resurrection increasingly seems to be disappearing in our culture lies in the lack of experience of the resurrection and eternal life in the present. Faith can flourish only when it can strike roots in human experience. If that is not the case, then it remains an artificial construction which cannot endure. So it is desperately difficult to affirm the graciousness of God in a graceless society. If we talk of grace and people have to ask what we are talking about, then our message will not get through. We must be able to refer to real experiences.

If we are able to make the message of the resurrection and eternal life credible, we must be able to refer to experiences of love. Only experiences of love can make people see something of what is meant by concepts like resurrection and eternity. Love helps others to experience resurrection now, in their own life, in their history, here on earth.

When we consider the world around us, we might seem to be living in an enormous cemetery. We move between graves. Terms are chiselled on the tombstones. On one heavy stone, almost too heavy to lift, we have the word 'Indifference' written large as life. A large number of people have buried themselves under this stone, or have been buried under it by others, people who no longer care, people who no longer have any real concerns. They see no point in involvement. They regard everything as passé. They have only one desire – to be left in peace. They allow their existence to be celebrated in words which should resound only after their death: 'Lord, grant them eternal rest.' These people must be brought out from under this oppressive stone. We have to say to them, 'Get up, don't be so passive, open up the way, do something, get up, you're part of it, we need everyone, including you.'

On other tombstones we read the word 'Anxiety'. A great many people simply do not dare to live. They do nothing, in case they take a false step. Or they have suffered so much in life that they cower anxiously in a dark corner where no one will notice them, in case they are struck and hurt again. We must try to free such people from this understandable anxiety. We must make them realize that they are not the only ones to face it. We must give them strength, stretch out our hands to them and not let go. We must protect and defend them. We must bring them back to light, raise them.

On another tombstone we read, 'The past'. Under it are countless people who cannot forget. They keep opening old wounds. They cherish their own grief in boundless compassion for themselves. They live more with their own disappointments and misfortunes than with hope for the future. These living dead must also be taken out of the past in which they are buried. They must believe that for them, too, the future is much more important than the past. We must help them to let the past be past so that they can live for the future, help them to live with fewer memories and more wishes.

One could go on like this endlessly, There are so very many tombstones which need to be rolled away, now, today. There are so very many people who have to be brought up from the tomb, today. There are people who have to come to light, to be given new chances, to be reborn and created anew, today.

All this can come about only in an active love for these particular people. Only the love which makes us divert our attention from ourselves to others will see the need of others. Love provides the strength which others need to begin again, to rise. In and through love we must make belief in the resurrection possible and show it as future.

It is clear that no human being can offer this love or can persevere in this love unless they know themselves to be loved. They need to have personal experience of the fact that they too are constantly being given new chances, can constantly begin anew. God continually gives us this future, not just beyond death but beyond all boundaries. Faith is always resurrection faith, in all the movements of this believing existence. For faith is a refusal to be content with the facts. Faith means bearing witness that everything can be different. We attest this resurrection faith in the present by continually allowing ourselves to be raised by God and by raising others to new life by virtue of the resurrection of Christ. In the specific experience of love we have the strongest argument for eternal life. Dostoievsky makes an elder say this to a woman who finds it difficult to believe in eternal life: ' "It's something one cannot prove. One can be convinced of it, though." "How? In what way?" "By the experience of active love. Strive to love your neighbours actively and indefatigably. And the nearer you come to achieving this love, the more convinced you will become of the existence of God and the immortality of your soul. If you reach the point of complete selflessness in your love of your neighbours, you will most certainly regain your faith and no doubt can possibly enter your soul. This has been proved. This is certain." '[1]

The experience of love is itself an experience of eternity. I have already pointed this out often: eternity is to do wih the experience of happiness in and through which one transcends time. For human beings, the supreme experience of happiness consists in the experience of love. In this way love goes against time. One cannot meaningfully say, 'I love you for five years.' That won't do. One always says 'You're mine for ever.' Therefore God, too, is eternal because he is love. To the degree that we experience love we taste eternity. To return to Dostoievsky, love 'is the power behind the constant and unwearying confirmation of existence and the rejection of death.'[2] In love we say and experience the word of God which says, 'Continue to live, continue to live' (cf. Ezek.16.6).

We may spell out this divine word which gives life, which preserves life, which brings resurrection, is called love and is stronger than death (Song of Songs 8.6), and may make it credible to one another. This word can renew with us the face of the earth. The new earth and the new heaven begin here and now. We are challenged by the world to proclaim and describe our belief in an eternal life in a credible way, by helping to build God's dwelling among men on this earth by virtue of the resurrection of Jesus. For here God wills to come to dwell with them. They will be his people and he, God-with-them, will be their God. And he will wipe away all tears from their eyes, and death will be no more; there will be no more grief, nor tears, nor sorrow, for all that is old will have passed away (cf. Rev. 21.3f.).

We cannot do this with bitterness, but only with specific and active love. This does not work on a small scale, but it begins in a very small way, in an interpersonal way, between one individual and another. However, this relationship becomes so powerful an experience of eternity that in its power one can do wonders and make others, men and nations, rise.

In order to make belief in the resurrection and belief in eternal life acceptable, we need the experience of love. It is a well-tried means. It is absolutely true. Fons Jansen has expressed this in his distinctive way:

Would you live otherwise if there were nothing more?
Suppose that we should sleep for ever and that afterwards no one could even remember that they regarded you as a fool with your tales about another world . . .
Would that be a reason for living otherwise now?
In that case, would I trample down flowers or strike children?
Would I plan to hurt people or betray comrades?
Would I look with less reverence on the starry heaven?
Would I long less not to have to die?
I would only have sadness
that my longing for eternal life was self-deception,
That I could not rely on my heart's desires,
That my fantasy was not reliable
That the great religions of the world were a cheat.
But I would then share this deception with someone I loved.
We would weep over it together.
We would say,
'Our hearts are deceitful.
Let us support one another in this desperate plight.'
And we would do that.
And then the doubts would come.
For we would feel
that this love is not a deception.
It is not true that everything is untrue.
We feel, we sense, we taste immortality.
We shall die full of curiosity.[3]

Abbreviations

BZ	Biblische Zeitschrift
Coll.	Collationes. Vlaams Tijdschrift vor Theologie en Pastoraal
D	Denzinger, Enchiridion Symbolorum
ET	English translation
ETL	Ephemerides theologiae Lovanienses
EvTh	Evangelische Theologie
HUCA	Hebrew Union College Annual
IKZ	Internationale Katholische Zeitschrift
JSS	Journal of Semitic Studies
MS	Mysterium Salutis. Grundriss heilsgeschichtlicher Dogmatik, ed. J.Feiner and M.Löhrer
RB	Revue Biblique
RGG	Die Religion in Geschichte und Gegenwart
SBT	Studies in Biblical Theology
SVT	Supplements to Vetus Testamentum
TGL	Tijdschrift voor Geestelijk Leven
TvT	Tijdschrift voor Theologie
VT	Vetus Testamentum
ZKT	Zeitschrift für katholische Theologie
ZTK	Zeitschrift für Theologie und Kirche

Bibliography

PART TWO

A

C.Barth, *Die Errettung vom Tode in den individuellen Klage- und Dankliedern des Alten Testaments*, Zurich 1947; M.E.Boismard, 'Our Conquest of Death according to the Bible', *Concilium* 5, 1975, 72-9 (this was not in fact translated into English); J. D'Arc, *J'attends la résurrection*, Paris 1970; A.M.Dubarle, 'Immortality in the Old Testament and Judaism', *Concilium* 10.6, 1970, 34-45; P.Grelot, *De la mort à la vie éternelle*, Paris 1971; W.Herrmann, 'Das Todesgeschick als Problem in Altisrael', in *Mitteilungen des Instituts für Orientforschung* 16, 1970, 14-32; E.Kellermann, 'Überwindung des Todesgeschick in der alttestamentlichen Frömmigkeit vor und neben dem Auferstehungsglauben', *ZTK* 73, 1976, 273-90; O.Knoch, *Wirst Du an den toten Wunder wirken? Sterben, Tod und ewiges Leben im Zeugnis der Bibel*, Regensburg 1977; V.Maag, 'Tod und Jenseits nach dem Alten Testament', *STU* 34, 1964, 17-37; R. Martin-Achard, *De la mort à la résurrection d'après l'Ancien Testament*, Neuchâtel 1956; id., *Mort et Vie dans la Bible*, Cahiers Evangiles 29, September 1979; P.Müller, *Ursprünge und Strukturen alttestamentlicher Eschatologie*, Berlin 1969; J.T.Nelis, 'Het geloof in de verrijzenis in het Oude Testament', *TvT* 10, 1970, 362-81; H.D.Preuss (ed.), *Eschatologie im Alten Testament*, Darmstadt 1978; G. von Rad, 'Alttestamentliche Glaubensaussagen von Leben und Tod', in *Gottes Wirken in Israel*, Neukirchen 1974, 250-67; L.Ruppert, 'Erhöhungsvorstellungen im Alten Testament', *BZ* 22, 1978, 119-220; A.Schmitt, *Entrückung. Aufnahme. Himmelfahrt. Untersuchungen zu einem Vorstellungsbereich im Alten Testament*, Stuttgart 1973; J.Schreiner, 'Alttestamentliche Vorstellungen von Tod und Unsterblichkeit', in *Stichwort:Tod*, Frankfurt 1979, 117-37; G.Sternberger, 'Das Problem der Auferstehung im Alten Testament', *Kairos* 14,

1972, 273-90; E.Sutcliffe, *The Old Testament and the Future Life*, Oxford 1946; S.Talmon, 'Eschatologie und Geschichte im biblischen Judentum', in R.Schnackenburg (ed.), *Zukunft. Zur Eschatologie bei Juden und Christen*, Düsseldorf 1980, 13-50; L.Waechter, *Der Tod im Alten Testament*, Stuttgart 1967.

B

R.H.Charles, 'Critical History of the Doctrine of a Future Life in Israel', in *Judaism and Christianity*, London 1899; id., *Religious Development between the Old and the New Testament*, London 1914; J.Coppens, 'L'Apocalyptique. Son dossier. Ses critères. Ses éléments constitutifs. Sa portée néotestamentaire', *ETL* 53, 1977, 1-13; M.Delcor, 'Le milieu d'origine et le développement de l'apocalypse juîve', in W.C. van Unnik, *La littérature juîve entre Tenach et Mischna*, Leiden 1974, 101-17; id., 'Bilan des études sur l'apocalyptique', in *Apocalypses et théologie de l'espérance*, Paris 1977, 27-42; A.Denis, *Introduction aux pseudépigraphes grecs d'Ancien Testament*, Louvain 1970; P. Grelot, *L'espérance juîve à l'heure de Jésus*, Paris 1978; K. Koch, *The Rediscovery of Apocalyptic*, SBT II 22, London 1972; J.Maier and J.Schreiner, *Literatur und Religion des Frühjudentums*, Würzburg 1973; J.Maier and K.Schubert, *Die Qumran-Essener. Texte der Schriftrollen und Lebensbild der Gemeinde*, Munich 1973; K.Müller, 'Die jüdische Apokalyptik', *TRE* III, Berlin 1979, 201-51; P. van den Osten-Sacken, *Die Apokalyptik in ihrem Verhältnis zu Prophetie und Weisheit*, Munich 1969; H.H.Rowley, *The Relevance of Apocalyptic*, London 1943; D.S.Russell, *The Method and Message of Jewish Apocalyptic*, London 1964; id., *Between the Testaments*, London 1963; J.M.Schmidt, *Die jüdische Apokalyptik. Die Geschichte ihrer Erforschung von den Anfängen bis zu den Textfunden von Qumran*, Neukirchen 1969; W.Schmithals, *Die Apokalyptik*, Göttingen 1973; J.Schreiner, *Alttestamentlich-jüdische Apokalyptik*, Munich 1969; T.C.Vriezen and A.S.van der Woude, *Literatuur van Oud-Israel*, Katwijk 1980; J.Willi-Plein, 'Das Geheimnis der Apokalyptik', *VT* 27, 1977, 62-81.

C

(a) **General**. M.E.Boismard, 'Our Conquest of Death according to the Bible' (see A above); O.Cullmann, 'Die Hoffnung auf die Wiederkunft Christi nach dem Neuen Testament', in *Vorträge und Aufsätze*, Tübingen 1966, 378-402; id., 'Das wahre durch die ausgebliebene Parusie gestellte Problem', ibid., 414-26; id., 'Parusieverzögerung und Urchristentum. Der gegenwärtige Stand der Diskussion', ibid., 427-44; J.Gnilka, 'Contemporary Exegetical Understanding of "the Resurrection of the Body"', *Concilium* 10.6, 1970, 129-41; E.Grässer, *Die Naherwartung Jesu*, Stuttgart 1973; P. Grelot, *De la mort à la vie éternelle*, Paris 1971; G.Greschake, *Auferstehung der Toten*, Essen 1969; G.Kegel, *Auferstehung Jesu. Auferstehung der Toten. Eine traditionsgeschichtliche Untersuchung zum Neuen Testament*, Gütersloh 1970; W.G.Kümmel, *Promise and Fulfilment*, SBT 23, London 1957; id., 'Die Naherwartung in der Verkündigung Jesu', in *Zeit und Geschichte*, Bultmann Festschrift, Tübingen 1964, 31-46; J.Lambrecht, 'Het leven na de dood volgens de Schrift', *TGL* 30, 1974, 363-89, 461-83; X.Léon-Dufour, *Face à la mort. Jésus et Paul*, Paris 1979; H.M.Matter, *Wederkomst en wereldeinde. De zin van de parousie in het Nieuwe Testament*, Kampen 1980; E.Schillebeeckx, *Jesus*, London 1979; id., *Christ*, London 1980; H.Schlier, 'Das Ende der Zeit', in *Das Ende der Zeit. Exegetische Aufsätze und Vorträge*, Freiburg 1971, 67-84; id., 'Tod und Auferstehung', in *Der Geist und die Kirche. Exegetische Aufsätze und Vorträge*, Freiburg 1980, 33-55; id., 'Der Tod im urchristlichen Denken', ibid., 101-16; J.Schmid, 'Der Begriff der Seele im Neuen Testament', in H.Fries and K.Ratzinger (eds.), *Einsicht und Glaube*, Freiburg 1962, 112-31; R.Schnackenburg, *God's Rule and Kingdom*, London and New York 1963; A.Vögtle, *Das Neue Testament und die Zukunft des Kosmos*, Düsseldorf 1970; id., 'Theologie und Eschatologie in der Verkündigung Jesu', in *NT und Kirche*, Schnackenburg Festschrift, Freiburg 1974, 371-98; H.Wenz, *Die Ankunft unseres Herrn am Ende der Welt*, Stuttgart 1965.

(b) **Synoptics**. F.Mussner, 'The Teaching of Jesus about the Life to Come according to the Synoptics', *Concilium* 10.6, 1970, 692-5; G.Bornkamm, 'End-expectation and Church in Matthew', in G.Bornkamm, G.Barth & H.J.Held, *Tradition and Interpretation in Matthew*, London 1963, 15-51; M.Punge, *Eschatologie und Heilsgeschichte bei Matthäus*, in J.Rohde, *Rediscovering the Teaching of the Evangelists*, London 1968, 107-12; G.R.Beasley-Murray, *Jesus and the Future. An Examination of the Criticism of the Eschatological Discourse Mark 13 with Special Reference to the Little Apocalypse Theory*, London 1954; J.Lambrecht, *Die Redaktion der*

Markus-Apokalypse. Literarische Analyse und Struktur-untersuchung, Rome 1967; D.A.Koch, 'Zum Verhältnis von Christologie und Eschatologie im Markusevangelium', in *Jesus Christus in Historie und Theologie*, Conzelmann Festschrift, Tübingen 1975, 395-408; W.Marxsen, 'Mark's topical Eschatology', in Rohde, op.cit., 113-39; R.Pesch, *Naherwartung, Tradition und Redaktion in Mk 13*, Düsseldorf 1968; id., 'Markus 13', in J. Lambrecht (ed.), *L'apocalypse johannique et l'Apocalyptique dans le Nouveau Testament*, Louvain 1980, 355-68; Neirynck, 'Marc 13. Examen critique de l'interprétation de R.Pesch', ibid., 369-401; W.Bösen, *Jesusmahl. Eucharistisches Mahl. Endzeitmahl. Ein Beitrag zur Theologie des Lukas*, Stuttgart 1980; J.Dupont, 'L'après-mort dans l'oeuvre de Luc', *RTL* 3, 1972, 3-21; E.E.Ellis, 'Die Funktion der Eschatologie im Lukasevangelium', *ZTK* 66, 1969, 387-402; J.Ernst, *Herr der Geschichte. Perspektiven der lukanischen Eschatologie*, Stuttgart 1978; H.Flender, *St Luke: Theologian of Redemptive History*, London 1967; R.Geiger, *Die lukanischen Endzeitreden. Studien zur Eschatologie des Lukas-Evangeliums*, Frankfurt 1973.

(c) **John.** J.Blank, 'Die Gegenwartseschatologie des Johannesevangeliums', in K.Schubert, *Vom Messias zu Christus. Die Fülle der Zeit in religionsgeschichtlicher und theologischer Sicht*, Freiburg 1964, 279-314; M.E.Boismard, 'Evolution du thème eschatologique dans les traditions johanniques', *RB* 68, 1961, 508-24; R.Bultmann, 'The Eschatology of the Gospel of John', in *Faith and Understanding*, ET London and New York 1969, 165-83; M. de Jonge, *L'évangile de Jean. Sources, rédaction, théologie*, Louvain 1977; G.Richter, 'Präsentische und futurische Eschatologie im vierten Evangelium', in P.Fiedler and D.Zeller, *Gegenwart und kommendes Reich*, Stuttgart 1975, 117-52; K.Romaniuk, ' "I am the Resurrection and the Life" (John 11.25)', in *Concilium* 10.6, 1970, 68-77; R.Schnackenburg, 'Das eschatologische Denken im Johannes-Evangelium', in *Johannes Evangelium* IV/2, Freiburg 1971, 530-44; F.Cromphout, *Hoelang nog? Een pas door de apokalyps*, Louvain 1969; id., *De sluier opgelicht? Apokalyptiek in oud en nieuw testament*, Louvain 1979; J.Lambrecht (ed.), *L'Apocalyptique johannique et l'Apocalyptique dans le nouveau testament*, Louvain 1980.

(d) **Paul.** J.Baumgarten, *Paulus und die Apokalyptik*, Neukirchen 1975; J.Becker, *Auferstehung der Toten im Urchristentum*, Stuttgart 1976; H.Biedermann, *Die Erlösung der Schöpfung beim Apostel*

Paulus. Ein Beitrag zur Klärung der religionsgeschichtlichen Stellung der paulinischen Erlösungslehre, Würzburg 1940; H.C.Cavallin, *Life after Death. Paul's Argument for the Resurrection of the Dead in I Cor.15. Part I. A Enquiry into the Jewish Background*, Lund 1974; F.Froitsheim, *Christologie und Eschatologie bei Paulus*, Würzburg 1979; P.Hoffmann, *Die Toten in Christus. Eine religionsgeschichtliche und exegetische Untersuchung zur paulinischen Eschatologie*, Munster 1966; G.Klein, 'Apokalyptische Naherwartung bei Paulus', in *Neues Testament und christliche Existenz*, Festschrift H.Braun, Tübingen 1973, 241-62; J.Kremer, 'Paul: The Resurrection of Jesus: the Cause and Exemplar of our Resurrection', *Concilium* 10.6, 1970, 78-91; P.E.Langevin, *Jésus Seigneur et l'eschatologie. Éxégèse de textes prépauliniens*, Bruges 1967; A. Lindemann, *Die Aufhebung der Zeit. Geschichtsverständnis und Eschatologie im Epheserbrief*, Gütersloh 1975; H.Schlier, 'Das, worauf alles wartet. Eine Auslegung von Römer 8,18-30', in *Das Ende der Zeit*, Freiburg 1971, 250-70.

PART THREE

M.Amigues, *Le chrétien devant le refus de la mort*, Paris 1981; P.Aries, *L'homme devant la mort*, Paris 1977; G.Bachl, *Über den Tod und das Leben danach*, Graz 1980; H.U.von Balthasar, 'Umrisse der Eschatologie', in *Verbum Caro. Skizzen zur Theologie* I, Einsiedeln 1960, 276-300; id., 'Eschatologie im Umriss', in *Pneuma und Institution, Skizzen* IV, Einsiedeln 1974, 410-55; J.Boonen, 'Denkmodellen van leven na de dood', *Coll.* 20, 1974, 36-54; H.Bourgeois, *Je crois à la résurrection du corps*, Paris 1981; G.J.F.Bouritijs et al., *Omtrent de dood*, Roermond 1971; W.Breuning, 'Entfaltung der eschatologischen Aussagen', in *Mysterium Salutis* V, Zurich 1976, 779-890; F. de Grijs, *Brieven aan de parelvisser. Over tijd en eeuwigheid, leven en sterven, heden en toekomst*, Baarn 1980; P.Grelot, *Le monde à venir*, Paris 1974; G.Greshake, *Auferstehung der Toten*, Essen 1969; id., *Starker als der Tod*, Mainz 1976; id., 'Tod und Auferstehung', in *Christlicher Glaube in moderner Gesellschaft* V, Freiburg 1980, 63-130; G.Greshake and G.Lohfink, *Naherwartung, Auferstehung, Unsterblichkeit*, Freiburg 1978; J.Hick, *Death and Eternal Life*, London 1976; A. Holl, *De laatste vraag. Wat komt er na de dood?*, Bilthoven 1973; K.Lehmann et al., *Vollendung des Lebens. Hoffnung auf Herrlichkeit*, Mainz 1979; G.Maertens, 'Neen, niet Amen en uit. Nadenken over voortbestaan', *Coll.* 23, 1977,

387-412; H.A.R.Mourits et al., *Dood doet leven*, Tielt-Utrecht 1972; J.Pohier, *Quand je dis Dieu*, Paris 1977; K.Rahner, 'The Hermeneutics of Eschatological Assertions', *Theological Investigations* 4, London 1966, 323-46; id., 'The Inexhaustible Transcendence of God and our Concern for the Future', *Theological Investigations* 20, London 1981, 173-86; J.Ratzinger, *Eschatologie. Tod und ewiges Leben*, Regensburg 1977; E.Schillebeeckx, 'Thoughts on the Interpretation of Eschatology', *Concilium* 5.1, 1969, 22-9; R.Schulte, 'Leib und Seele', in *Christliche Glaube in moderner Gesellschaft* V, Freiburg 1980, 6-61; C.Schütz, 'Allgemeine Grundlegung der Eschatologie', *Mysterium Salutis* V, Zurich 1966, 553-700; H.Smeets, *Zo zie ik de dood. Leven, sterven, eeuwigheid*, Hilversum 1974; T.F.Torrance, *Space, Time and Resurrection*, Edinburgh 1976; R.Troisfontaines, *Ik sterf niet. Een filosofie van dood en leven*, Tielt – The Hague 1963; id., *Ik treed het leven binnen. Onze verwachtingen van het hiernamaals*, Den Haag 1966; W. van Soom, *Zie het licht. Een verantwoording van de christelijke hoop*, Bruges 1976; H.Vorgrimler, *Der Tod im Denken und Leben der Christen*, Düsseldorf 1978; id., *Hoffnung auf Vollendung. Aufriss der Eschatologie*, Freiburg 1980; E. van Waelderen, 'Nieuwsgierig zullen wij sterven', *Sacerdos* 39, 1972, 133-42; id., 'De onverwoestbare levenswil van de mens', ibid., 142-9; D.Widerkehr, *Perspektiven der Eschatologie*, Einsiedeln 1974.

The following issues of journals are completely devoted to the question; *Communio* 5, 1980, no.3: *Wenn ich einmal sterben werde; Concilium* 5.1, 1969: *Eschatology; Concilium* 10.6, 1970: *Immortality and Resurrection; Concilium* 11.5, 1975: *The Longing for Immortality; Concilium* 128, 1979: *Heaven; Tijdschrift voor Theologie* 10, 1970, 4: *Leven ondanks de dood.*

Notes

PART ONE

1. L.Tolstoy, 'The Death of Ivan Ilyich', in *The Cossacks*, Harmondsworth 1960, 107f.

2. Maarten 't Hart, *De aansprekers*, Amsterdam 1979, 92f.

3. L.Tolstoy, op.cit., 137.

4. Bernard Shaw, *Back to Methuselah*, Harmondsworth 1971, 65.

5. M.Yourcenar, *L'Oeuvre du Noir*, Paris 1968, 375.

5a. M. Yourcenar, *Memoirs of Hadrian*, London 1974, 209.

6. Jacques Pohier, *Quand je dis Dieu*, Paris 1977.

7. G.Lohfink, 'Was kommt nach dem Tod?', in G.Greshake and G.Lohfink, *Naherwartung, Auferstehung, Unsterblichkeit*, Freiburg 1978, (185-200) 186.

8. P.Delooz, 'Qui croit à l'au-delà?', in *Mort en présence*, Brussels 1971, 17-38.

9. A. Greeley, 'Public Opinion and Life after Death', *Concilium*, 1975, 5, 6-18 (the English edition did not appear during this period).

10. G.Zeegers, G.Dekker and J.Peters, *God in Nederland, Statistisch onderzoek naar godsdienst en kerkelijkheid*, Amsterdam 1967, 124f.; W.Goddijn, H.Smets and G. van Tillo, *Opnieuw: God in Nederland. Onderzoek naar godsdienst en kerkelijkheid ingesteld in opdracht van KRO en weekblad De Tijd*, Amsterdam 1979, 34-8.

11. R.Masure and N.Molisse, *Arbeider en Godsdienst*, Brussels 1974, 48-50.

12. Cf. E.Schillebeeckx, 'Kritische Beschouwingen over het Secularisatiebegrip in verband met allerlei thema's van het Pastoraal Concilie', in *Pastoraal Concilie van de Nederlandse Kerkprovincie* Iv, Amersfoort 1969, 114-39.

13. W.F.Hermans, 'Het oude kanon. Verhaal', in *Cultureel Supplement* 538 of *NRC Handelsblad*, 13 February 1981.

14. J.J.M.Stieger, 'Op de kern af', in *Benediktiner Tijdschrift* 31, 1970, 29.

15. H.Fortmann, 'Latijnse Uitvaart', in *Hoogtijd en andere beschouwingen*, Baarn 1978, 72.

16. See here in detail H.Fortmann, *Als ziende de onzienlijke* I, Hilversum 1974.

17. R.Garaudy, *Het hart op de tong*, Baarn 1976, 41.

18. E.Bloch, *Das Prinzip Hoffnung*, Frankfurt 1959, 1378.

19. W.F.Hermans, op.cit.

20. See J.Ellul, *La foi au prix du doute*, Paris 1980, 34-72.

21. H.Arts, *Met heel uw ziel. Over de christelijke godservaring*, Antwerp 1978, 24.

22. Ad den Besten, 'Verlies van het transcendente', in *Rondom het Woord* 21.4, 32.

23. Ibid., 30f.

24. 'Leven na de dood', in *Archief der Kerken* 34, 1979, col. (813-16) 814.

25. Ibid., col.815.

26. R.Guardini, *The Last Things*, Slough 1957, 31f.

PART TWO

A

1. Cf. H.M.Kuitert, 'Mens en lichaam in de heilige Schrift', in *Om en Om. Een bundel theologie en geloofs bezinning*, Kampen 1972, 15-38.

2. Cf. L.Ruppert, 'Erhöhungsvorstellungen im Alten Testament', *Biblische Zeitschrift* 22, 1978, 119-220.

3. Cf. particularly the commentary with translation and notes on Job and Ecclesiastes by P.O.Drijvers and P.Hawinkel, Baarn 1971.

4. Exegetes do not agree here. Belief in the resurrection is found here by e.g. O.Kaiser, *Tod und Leben*, Stuttgart 1977; H.J.Kraus, *Psalmen* I, Neukirchen 1960; A.Weiser, *The Psalms*, Old Testament Library, London and Philadelphia 1964; this interpretation is rejected by e.g. E.Würthwein, 'Erwägungen zu Psalm 73', in *Wort und Existenz*, Göttingen 1970, 170ff.

5. Thus G. von Rad, *Old Testament Theology* 1, London 1975, 404ff.; M.Dahood, *Psalms* 1, New York 1973, 301; with some qualifications, A.Weiser, op.cit., 389. This view is completely rejected by C.Barth, *Die Errettung vom Tode in den individuellen Klage- und Dankliedern des Alten Testaments*, Zollikon 1947, 158; R.Tournay, 'L'eschatologie individuelle dans les psaumes', *RB*, 1949, 481-506.

6. The Bible contains *canonical* books. This means that the community of faith recognizes its own belief in certain writings and also allows itself to be governed by these writings (canon means norm, rule, guideline). As far as the Old Testament is concerned (the Jews call it Tanach), these canonical books were established after a long-drawn-out process, in a number of phases. The Jewish Tanach took on definitive significance at the time of a rabbinic synod in Jamnia about AD 100. The earliest Greek translation of the Old Testament, the Septuagint, made for Greek-speaking Jews in the Diaspora who no longer knew Hebrew, contained a number of writings which do not occur in the Tanach, e.g. Baruch, I and II Maccabees, Judith, Tobit, Sirach, Wisdom. In order to indicate the different character of these

books, the Catholic tradition talks of deutero-canonical books; in Protestantism they are called *apocryphal* books. Apocryphal means hidden, out of sight. To begin with, this was also meant literally; these were books which were not suitable for public reading in worship and which were not to be circulated. Later the word acquired negative connotations and virtually came to signify heretical.

In addition, there are writings which belong neither to the Tanach nor to the Septuagint but which, being composed between about 200 BC and AD 100, played a major role in the life of Jews and Christians. The Catholics called these books Apocrypha whereas the Protestants spoke here of Pseudepigrapha, as it were writings presented under the name of a particular person who had nothing to do with their origin but whose name was used to give greater authority to the works.

7. Scholars are far from being unanimous over this interpretation in which Daniel is seen as being in perfect continuity with traditional Jewish prophecy. The divergent view sees this book as being a clear exponent of apocalyptic dualism. For my own interpretation I rely on what seem to me to be convincing arguments in M.Hengel, *Judaism and Hellenism* I, London 1974, 181; G.W.E.Nickelsburg, *Resurrection, Immortality and Eternal Life in Intertestamental Judaism*, Cambridge 1972, 23; P.Grelot, 'Histoire et eschatologie dans le livre de Daniel', in *Apocalypses et théologie de l'espérance*, Paris 1977, 63-109; the last-mentioned author presented his view at an earlier stage in his book *De la mort à la vie eternelle*, Paris 1971.

8. B.Alfrink, 'L'idée de résurrection d'après Daniel 12.1-2', *Biblicum* 40, 1959, 355-71.

9. D.Aerenhoevel, 'Die Hoffnung auf die Auferstehung. Eine Auslegung von 2 Makk 7', *Bibel und Leben* 5, 1964, 36-42; U.Kellermann, *Auferstanden in den Himmel. 2 Makkabäer 7 und die Auferstehung der Märtyrer*, Stuttgart 1979.

10. I use this term, as opposed to the earlier terminology which spoke of *late* Judaism, to refer to the period from about 200 BC, in which rabbinic Judaism began to play a decisive role and the rabbis were to be concerned about the stability of what was now a stateless people.

11. Cf. G.Wied, *Der Auferstehungsglaube des späten Israel in seiner Bedeutung für das Verhältnis von Apokalyptik und Weisheit*, Bonn 1967, 101.

12. Cf. K.Lehmann, *Auferweckt am dritten Tag nach der Schrift*, Freiburg 1968.

13. The mentality expressed in these chapters shows clearly that it is impossible that this could be a text from the time of Isaiah. What we have here is a text of which neither the literary unity nor the date of origin can be established. These chapters may consist of various revisions which in approach date from the fifth to the third century BC. Thus A. Vermeylen, 'La composition littéraire de l'Apocalypse d'Isaias', *ETL*, 1954, 5ff.

14. Thus R.Bourke, 'Le jour de Yahvé dans Joël', *RB* 66, 1959, 121-212; L.Cerny, *The Day of Yahweh and some relevant Problems*, Prague 1948;

W.S.McCullough, 'Israel's Eschatology from Amos to Daniel', in J.M.Wevers and D.B.Redford, *Studies on the Ancient Palestinian World*, Toronto 1972, 66-101; A.Gelin, 'Jours de Yahvé et Jour de Yahvé', *Lumière et Vie*, September 1953, 39-52; K.D.Schunck, 'Strukturlinien in der Entwicklung der Vorstellung vom Tag Yahwehs', *VT* 14, 1964, 319-30; G.von Rad, 'The Origin of the Concept of the Day of Yahweh', *JSS*, 1959, 97-108. According to other exegetes, Amos introduced this term as an innovation and found an echo only in prophetic circles, thus e.g. M.Weiss, 'The Origin of the Day of the Lord Reconsidered', *HUCA* 37, 1966, 29-71.

15. In this approach I am obviously dependent on the thorough and detailed study by A. Vögtle, *Das Neue Testament und die Zukunft des Kosmos*, Düsseldorf 1970.

B

1. Cf. A n.7. Here I shall mention some of the apocryphal or pseudepigraphical books which are important for our theme; I have also given the approximate dates of origin and the way in which they are usually referred to.

Ethiopian Enoch (c.164 BC = I Enoch); the Book of Jubilees (c.150 BC = Jub.); The Testament of the Twelve Patriarchs (140-110 BC = TestXII Pat.); The Ascension of Moses (AD 7-28 = AssMos); The Testament of Abraham (AD 1-50 = TestAb); Apocalypse of Abraham (AD 70-100 = Apoc.Ab.); Syrian Apocalypse of Baruch (AD 50-100 = IIBar); IV Ezra (AD 96-100); *Liber Antiquitatum Biblicarum* (first century AD = LAB). Perhaps all these works were composed within Palestinian Judaism. I must also mention two works of Hellenistic origin: The Sibylline Oracles (150-120 BC) and the Slavonic Book of Enoch (AD 1-50 = II Enoch). In this section I shall also be introducing the Qumran writings. I shall refer to most of these in the customary way: the figure gives the cave in which the work was found, the letter the nature of the writing, thus e.g. 1QS (Community Rule); 1QH Thanksgiving Psalms); 1QM (War Rule); Dam (Damascus Document).

2. R.Bultmann, 'Is Exegesis without Presuppositions Possible?', in *Existence and Faith*, ed. S.M.Ogden, Cleveland and New York 1960, 289-96.

3. Thus e.g. R.H.Charles, *Religious Development between the Old and the New Testament*, London 1914; H.H.Rowley, *The Relevance of Apocalyptic*, London 1943; D.S.Roessler, *Gesetz und Geschichte. Untersuchungen zur Theologie der jüdische Apokalyptik und der pharisäischen Orthodoxie*, Göttingen 1960; P.D.Hanson, 'Jewish Apocalyptic Against its Near Eastern Environment', *RB* 78, 1971, 31-58; E.Jacob, 'Aux sources bibliques de l'Apocalyptique', in *Apocalypses et théologie de l'espérance*, Paris 1977, 43-62.

4.Cf. J. Stiassny, 'L'occulation de l'apocalyptique dans la rabbinisme', in

Apocalypses et théologie de l'Espérance, Paris 1977, 179-203. The influence
of the parallelism with apocalyptic ideas in rabbinism comes through over-
whelmingly in the large number of texts collected in the gigantic work by
H.L.Strack and P.Billerbeck, *Kommentar zum Neuen Testament aus Tal-
mud und Midrasch*, 6 vols, Munich 1965.

5. Cf. e.g. H.D.Betz, 'Zum Problem der religionsgeschichtlichen Verständnis der Apokalyptik', *ZTK* 63, 1966, 391-409; 'Das Verständnis der
Apokalyptik in der Theologie der Pannenberg Gruppe', *ZTK* 65, 1966,
257-70; W.Murdock, 'History and Revelation in Jewish Apocalypticism',
Interpretation 21, 1967, 167-87; G. von Rad adopts a distinctive position in
his *Old Testament Theology* II, London 1975, and sees apocalyptic as an
eschatologizing of Jewish wisdom literature. This theory is advanced with
some qualifications by H.P.Müller, 'Mantische Weisheit und Apokalyptik',
in *SVT* 22, 268-93; it is fiercely attacked by P. van den Osten-Sacken, *Die
Apokalyptik in ihrem Verhältnis zu Prophetie und Weisheit*, Munich 1969.

6. Cf. G.Kittel, *Die Probleme des palästinensischen Spätjudentums und
das Urchristentum*, Tübingen 1926. Here it is said that apocalyptic is simply
a subsidiary phenomenon of Jewish belief and that we should see it as the
piety of the time, to be compared with someone who might study Christianity from the perspective of the Christian sects (p.14). This view determines the climate of Kittel's *Theological Dictionary of the New Testament*,
which more than any other standard work has influenced generations of exegetes and theologians.

7. This has happened above all under the impetus of U.Wilckens, 'Die Be-
kehrung des Paulus als religionsgeschichtliches Problem', *ZTK* 56, 1959,
273-93; id., 'The Understanding of Revelation within Primitive Christianity', in W.Pannenberg (ed.), *Revelation as History*, London 1969, 55-122;
and by E.Käsemann, 'The Beginnings of Christian Theology', in *New Testament Questions of Today*, London and Philadelphia 1969, 82-107; id.,
'On the Subject of Primitive Christian Apocalyptic', in ibid., 108-37; id.,
'Konsequente Traditionsgeschichte?', *ZTK* 62, 1965, 137-523. These authors argue for the connection between Old Testament prophecy and apocalyptic. In a phrase which has become famous Käsemann even calls
apocalyptic 'the mother of all Christian theology', 'Beginnings', 100. Käsemann's view is developed further by his pupil P.Stuhlmacher, *Gerechtigkeit
Gottes bei Paulus*, Stuttgart 1965, and by A.Strobel, *Kerygma und Apokalyptik*, Göttingen 1967. In systematic theology the significance of apocalyptic for the New Testament has been stressed particularly strongly by
theologians like Pannenberg and Moltmann and by G.Sauter in his *Zukunft
und Verheissung*, Zurich 1965.

This theory has been attacked by G.Ebeling, 'Der Grund christlicher
Theologie', *ZTK* 58, 1961, 227-44. He sees apocalyptic simply as a suspect
symptom of a heretical trend. Käsemann is also attacked by E.Fuchs, 'Über
die Aufgabe einer christlichen Theologie', *ZTK* 58, 1961, 245-67. Even
Käsemann's teacher, Bultmann, cannot follow his pupil here, cf. 'Ist die

Apokalyptik die Mutter der christlichen Theologie?', *Exegetica*, Tübingen 1967, 467-82.

8. Of course P.Lagrange had shown the importance of apocalyptic and pointed to the affinity between prophecy and apocalyptic and to the influence of this latter trend on the New Testament. However, he did not study apocalyptic for its own sake because he was convinced of the dominant influence of Pharisaism, in which the law is more influential than apocalyptic, cf. his *Le Judaïsme avant Jésus Christ*, Paris 1931. J.Bonsirven, *Le Judaïsme Palestinien au temps de Jésus Christ*, Paris 1935, sees authentic Pharisaic traits in apocalyptic, including reverence of oral tradition. Moreover it is not inconceivable that the Pharisees, who were theological innovators e.g. in the sphere of messianism, the hereafter, the doctrine of angels and demons, were strongly influenced by Persian religion. Bonsirven inclines – albeit with important reservations – to accept apocalyptic as an offshoot of prophetism.

9. Cf. M.Delcor, 'Bilan des études sur l'apocalyptique', in *Apocalypses et théologies de l'espérance*, Paris 1977, 27-42; E.Jacob, 'Aux sources bibliques de l'Apocalyptique', ibid., 43-61.

10. For the apocryphal and pseudepigraphical literature the classic study has long been R.H.Charles, *Apocrypha and Pseudepigrapha of the Old Testament*, Oxford 1913; it is now likely to be superseded by J.H.Charlesworth, *The Old Testament Pseudepigrapha*, London and New York 1983.

11. Cf. J.Maier and K.Schubert, *Die Qumran-Essener*, 79-98.

12. This at least is the interpretation of e.g P.Volz, *Die Eschatologie der jüdischen Gemeinde im neutestamentlichen Zeitalter*, Tübingen 1934, 261; cf. also W.D.Davies, *Paul and Rabbinic Judaism. Some Rabbinic Elements in Pauline Theology*, London 1955, 317.

13. H.L.Strack and P.Billerbeck, *Kommentar zum Neuen Testament*, 31: 'Scheol, Gehinnom und Gan Eden', IV/2, 1012-1165.

14. Cf. 'Das Weltverständnis in der jüdischen Apokalyptik, dargestellt am äthiopischen Henoch und am IV Ezra', *ZTK* 73, 1976, 283-305.

C

1. *Theology of the New Testament*, London and New York 1955, 2f. Bultmann finds this view, which had already been advocated strongly by J.Weiss and A.Schweitzer, so obvious that he does not once seek to justify it.

2. A more developed view of this can be found in my earlier book *Verlost tot vrijheid*, Averbode 1979.

3. Cf. L.Oberlinner, 'Die Stellung der "Terminworte" in der eschatologischen Verkündigung des Neuen Testaments', in P.Fiedler and D. Zeller, *Gegenwart und kommendes Reich*, Festschrift A.Vögtle, Stuttgart 1975, 51-66.

4. Cf. W.G.Kümmel, *Promise and Fulfilment*, SBT 23,London 1957; id., 'Die Naherwartung in der Verkündigung Jesu', *Zeit und Geschichte*, Bultmann Festschrift, Tübingen 1964, 31-46; E.Grässer, *Die Naherwartung*

Jesu, Stuttgart 1973; G.Lohfink, 'Zur Möglichkeit christlicher Naherwartung', in G.Greshake and G.Lohfink, *Naherwartung, Auferstehung, Unsterblichkeit*, Freiburg 1978, 38-81; A.Vögtle, 'Theologie und Eschatologie in der Verkündigung Jesu', in *Neues Testament und Kirche*, Festschrift R.Schnackenburg, Freiburg 1974, 371-98; P.Fiedler and D.Zeller, et al. (see n.3), in I.Maisch, *Die Botschaft Jesu von der Gottesherrschaft*, 27-41; P.Wolf, *Gericht und Reich Gottes bei Johannes und Jesus*, 43-49; L.Oberlinner, op.cit.

5. Cf. E.Sjöberg, *Der Menschensohn im äthiopischen Henochbuch*, Lund 1946.

6. Cf. W.Kasper, *Jesus the Christ*, London 1976, 74-8; in his *Jesus*, London and New York 1979, E.Schillebeeckx hesitates to reduce Jesus to the level of the apocalyptic circles which expected an imminent end of the world (154f.). He goes on to say: 'And that for him (the historical Jesus) the end-event was very near, despite various distictions that have to be made, can hardly be denied either' (177). When asked for an explanation of this at his conversation in Rome, Schillebeeckx said: 'By that I mean that he (Jesus) was well aware of the nearness of the eschatological kingdom, not of the apocalyptic consummation (e.g. in the same way as John the Baptist). Jesus must be put in an eschatological and not in an apocalyptic context', cf. T.Schoof, *De Zaak Schillebeeckx, Officiële stukken*, Bloemendaal 1980, 175.

7. Cf. J.Dupont, 'La parabole du figuier qui bourgeonne, Mk 13, 28-29', *RB* 75, 1968, 526-48.

8. Cf. A.Strobel, *Kerygma und Apokalyptik*, Göttingen 1967, 85; see also G.A.Wewers, *Geheimnis und Geheimhaltung im rabbinischen Judentum*, Berlin 1975, 235-7.

9. Q stands for Quelle, the German word for source. As a common source for their Gospels in addition to Mark, Matthew and Luke used a second source, so-called Q, which consists of a collection of sayings of Jesus. In his *Jesus*, Schillebeeckx thinks it not improbable that a certain Christian community expressed its own view of the Jesus event in this Q. In connection with the problem that concerns us he writes of the Q community: it 'was a withdrawn one, waiting as it was upon God, as upon the approach of the heavenly Jesus'(412).

10. Since H.Conzelmann, in his *The Theology of St Luke*, ET London and Philadelphia 1960, reissued 1982, tried to show that Luke had deliberately given up the eschatological expectation of an imminent end to the world in favour of a life of Christians and the church within history, determined by the Spirit, this argument has commanded increasing assent; cf. G.Schneider, *Parusiegleichnisse im Lukas-Evangelium*, Stuttgart 1975, with extensive bibliography. However, it seems to me difficult to deny that the Third Evangelist and author of Acts still reckons with an imminent parousia; cf. J.Ernst, *Herr der Geschichte. Perspektiven der lukanischen Eschatologie*, Stuttgart 1978. For example, Luke is the only one who in his version of what hap-

pened at the last supper twice alludes to the connection between Jesus' death and the fulfilment of the kingdom of God (22.16,18); here he makes Jesus see this fulfilment not only for himself but also for the disciples: 'As my Father appointed a kingdom for me, so do I appoint for you that you may eat and drink at my table, (22.29f.); cf. W.Boesen, *Jesusmahl, Eucharistisches Mahl, Endzeitmahl. Ein Beitrag zur Theologie des Lukas*, Stuttgart 1980, 33-6, 75-7, 134-9.

11. Cf. W.Thüsing, *Erhöhungsvorstellung und Parusie-Erwartung in der ältesten nachösterlichen Christologie*, Stuttgart 1969, 91.

12. See above all J.Dupont, *Syn Christoi, L'Union avec le Christ suivant saint Paul*, Paris 1952.

13. Cf. A.Vögtle, 'Röm.13,11-14 und die "Nah"-Erwartung', in J.Friedrich, W.Poehlmann and P.Stuhlmacher, *Rechtfertigung*, Festschrift H.Braun, Tübingen 1976, 557-73; M.Rese, 'Die Rolle Israels im apokalyptischen Denken des Paulus', in J.Lambrecht, *L'Apocalypse Johannique et l'Apocalyptique dans le Nouveau Testament*, Louvain 1980, 311-16.

14. See J.Coppens, 'Les deux obstacles au retour glorieux du Sauveur', *ETL* 46, 1970, 383-9.

15. M.Rese, op.cit.

16. Thus G.Theissen, *Untersuchungen zum Hebräerbrief*, Gütersloh 1969; cf. also B.Klappert, *Die Eschatologie des Hebräerbriefs*, Munich 1969. There is a warning against this all-too-crude judgment e.g. by F.Laub, *Bekenntnis und Auslegung. Die paränetische Funktion der Christologie im Hebräerbrief*, Regensburg 1980, 224-8.

17. E.Lohmeyer, *Die Offenbarung des Johannes*, Tübingen 1953, 202.

18. In speaking of an 'apocalyptic stimulus' which was necessary for persistence in being a disciple of Jesus, as he understands this discipleship, albeit very exactly and specifically for this time, J.B.Metz, *Zeit der Orden? Zur Mystik und Politik der Nachfolge*, Freiburg 1977, at all events uses the term apocalyptic in a sense which cannot be established historically.

19. See R.Bultmann, 'The Eschatology of the Gospel of John', in *Faith and Understanding*, ET London and New York 1969, 165-83.

20. Cf. M.E.Boismard, 'Evolution du thème eschatologique dans les traditions johanniques', *RB* 68, 1961, 507-24; G.Richter, 'Präsentische und futurische Eschatologie im 4. Evangelium', in P. Fiedler and D.Zeller, *Gegenwart und kommendes Reich* (see n.3 above), 117-52 with bibliography.

21. The whole context is clearly about physical living and dying. Here it is said by Jesus that belief is on another level and happens where physical living and dying as such reach their limits.

22. From this E.Käsemann draws the conclusion that in fact the future perspective of eschatology is eliminated. This is connected with his view of Johannine christology, which he interprets in a docetic way. The Word which exists before all time in the glory of the Father descends to this earth, where it experiences the same glory within a world which rebels against

God. The glory is experienced precisely in the form of lowliness. At death, which is regarded as conquest and liberation, the Word returns to untrammelled experience of the glory of the Father as it already knew this before the incarnation. See *The Testament of Jesus*, London and Philadelphia 1968.

23. See p. 81.

24. Cf. H.M.Matter, *Wederkomst en wereldeinde. De zin van de parousia in het Nieuwe Testament*, Kampen 1980, 9ff.

25. R.Bultmann, *The Gospel of John*, ET Oxford and Philadelphia, 519f.

26. R.Pesch gives overwhelming arguments in favour of this authenticity in his commentary *Das Markusevangelium* II, Freiburg 1977, 235ff.

27. The word *psyche*, soul, also has this meaning in other New Testament texts, e.g. Mark 8.36; Matt.6.25; Luke 21.19; James 1.21; 5.20; I Peter 1.9,22; 2.25.

28. See pp. 83ff.

29. See p. 87.

30. See J.Ernst, *Herr der Geschichte* (n.10), 75-77, 86.

31. See G.Schneider, *Parusiegleichnisse* (n.10), 82.

32. Thus e.g. W.Bousset, *Die Offenbarung Johannis*, Göttingen 1906, 271, with reference to I Enoch 62.15 and II Enoch 28.8; *Assumptio Jeremiae* 9,2; see also E.Lohmeyer, *Die Offenbarung des Johannes*, Tübingen 1963, 64.

33. See J.Lambrecht, 'Apokalypse 11,1-14', in *De sluier opgelicht? Apokalyptik in oud- en nieuw testament*, Louvain 1979, 62-79.

34. See pp. 87f.

35. See G.Bouwman, 'Als Christus niet verrezen is', in *Schrift* 60, 1976, 227-33. Thus also P.Hoffmann, *Die Toten in Christus*, 241ff.

36. Cf. W.Schrage, 'Leid, Kreuz und Eschaton. Die Peristasenkataloge als Merkmale paulinischer *theologia crucis* und Eschatologie', *EvTh* 34, 1974, 141-75.

37. See A.Feuillet, 'Exégèse de 2 Cor.5.1-10 et contribution à l'étude des fondements de l'eschatologie paulinienne', *RSR* 44, 1956, 161-92, 360-402; cf. X.Léon-Dufour, *Face à la mort. Jésus et Paul*, 262-8.

38. The arguments for and against are discussed in detail in the works mentioned above by P.Hoffmann, *Die Toten in Christus*, and H.H.Schade, *Apokalyptische Christologie bei Paulus. Studien zum Zusammenhang von Christologie und Eschatologie in den Paulusbriefen*, Göttingen 1981.

39. See W.Beinert, *Christus und der Kosmos. Perspektiven zu einer Theologie der Schöpfung*, Freiburg 1974; see also F.Mussner, *Christus, das All und die Kirche*, Trier 1955; id.,'Die Schopfung in Christus', in *MS* II, Einsiedeln 1967, 455-61.

40. See J.Lambrecht, *Die Redaktion der Markus-Apokalypse*, 177-9. According to this author this imagery is above all taken from Joel 2.10f.; 3.4; 4.15f., rather than from Isa.13.10; 34.4, as is usually asserted.

41. Thus F.Hahn, 'Die Rede von der Parusie des Menschensohnes. Markus 13', in *Jesus und der Menschensohn*, Festschrift A. Vögtle, Freiburg

1975, 240-66, against A.Vögtle, *Das Neue Testament und die Zukunft des Kosmos*. R. Pesch, who earlier shared Vögtle's metaphorical interpretation, was convinced by Hahn's arguments, cf. *Das Markusevangelium* II, Freiburg 1977, 264-305.

42. J. Dupont, 'La ruine du temple et la fin des temps dans le discours de Marc 13', in *Apocalypses et théologie de l'espérance*, 207-69, has produced a particularly good study of Mark 13. In it he does not interpret the cosmological phenomena in conjunction with a judgment but as accompanying the appearance of God in person, as a theophany (250f.). F.Neyrinck seems to endorse this, see 'Marc 13. Examen critique de l'interprétation de R.Pesch', in *L'Apocalypse johannique et l'Apocalyptique dans le Nouveau Testament*, (369-401) 378. There is a particularly attractive interpretation of Mark in L.Geysels, *De sluier opgelicht?* (n.33), 95-111.

43. See F.Laub, *Bekenntnis und Auslegung* (n.16), 155f.

44. H.Wiersinga, *Je kunt beter geloven. Het geloofsmodel in de brief aan de Hebreeën*, Baarn 1978. This is a book which I can particularly recommend on what is a very difficult letter.

45. See the clear exposition by F.Cromphout, *Hoelang nog? Een pad door de apokalyps*, Louvain 1979.

46. See e.g. IV Ezra 7.11: 'I have created the world for the sake of mankind, but when Adam transgressed my commandments, the creation was condemned.'.

47. Here one can partly follow the interpretation by A.Vögtle, 'Röm. 8,19-22: eine schöpfungstheologische oder anthropologisch-soteriologische Aussage?', in A.Descamps and A. de Holleux, *Mélanges bibliques en hommage à Béda Rigaux*, Gembloux 1970, 351. Here he goes deeper into the thesis which he already defended in his monograph *Das Neue Testament und die Zukunft des Kosmos*, 183-208. With many other exegetes I believe that in this text Paul shows the cosmic consequences of the Christ event.

48. Here I follow the interpretation of e.g. H.Schlier, 'Das warauf alles wartet. Eine Auslegung von Römer 8,18-30', in *Das Ende der Zeit. Exegetische Aufsätze und Vorträge*, Freiburg 1971, 271-96; see also his commentary, *Der Römerbrief*, Freiburg 1977, 256-64. See also G.Bouwman, *Paulus aan de Romeinen*, Averbode 1980, 258-62.

49. See J.Gnilka, *Der Kolosserbrief*, Freiburg 1980, 51-76, with an extensive bibliography. See above all Excursus 1: 'Die theologiegeschichtliche Bedeutung des Christusliedes', 77-87; see also F.J.Steinmetz, *Protologische Heilszuversicht. Die Strukturen des soteriologischen und christologischen Denkens im Kolosser- und Epheserbrief*, Frankfurt 1969.

PART THREE

Chapter II

1. For the origin and evolution of this view see H.H.Berger, 'Het Rijk van de Vrijheid', in G.J.F.Bouritius, *Omtrent de dood*, Roermond 1971, 58-101.

2. See J.Baur, 'Platos Wort zu Seele und Unsterblichkeit', in *Einsicht und Glaube*, Göttingen 1978, 18-25; also 'Zum christlichen Verständnis der platonischen Theologie', 10-18; 'Unsterblichkeit der Seele und Auferstehung von den Toten', 25-50.

3. M.Yourcenar, *Memoirs of Hadrian*, 207f.

4. The texts are cited in J.J.Thierry, *Opstandingsgeloof in de vroegchristlijke kerk*, Amsterdam 1978; see H.E.Mertens, 'De relativiteit van de traditionele beelden', *TvT* 10, 1970, 382-404.

5. See H.Zeller, '*Corpora Sanctorum*', *ZKT* 71, 1949, 385-465; A.Stuiber, *Refrigerium Interim. Die Vorstellungen vom Zwischenzustand und die frühchristliche Grabeskunst*, Bonn 1957; G.Greshake, *Auferstehung der Toten*, Essen 1969.

6. See K.E.Boerresen, 'Augustin, interprète du dogme de la résurrection', *StTh* 23, 1969, 153f.

7. This aspect is illuminated in the article by A.Pattin, 'Onze Ziel na de dood volgens St Thomas van Aquino', *TGL* 29, 1973, 665-75.

8. See H.E.Mertens, op.cit., 389-91.

9. See F.P.Fiorenza and J.B.Metz, *Der Mensch als Einheit von Leib und Seele*, MS II, Einsiedeln 1967, 614-32.

10. See M.Dyckmanns, *Les Sermons de Jean XXII sur la vision béatifique*, Rome 1973.

11. K.Barth, *Die Auferstehung der Toten*, Zurich 1953, 112.

12. E.g. R.Bultmann and E.Brunner, *Das Ewige als Zukunft und Gegenwart*, Munich 1965; O.Cullmann, *Immortality of the Soul or Resurrection of the Dead*, London 1958; E.Jüngel, *Tod*, Stuttgart 1971; J.Moltmann, *Umkehr zur Zukunft*, Munich 1970; P.J.van Leeuwen, *Het christelijk onsterfelijkheidsgeloof*, The Hague 1955; G. van der Leeuw, *Onsterfelijkheid of opstanding?*, Kampen 1947; G. van Niftrik, *Kleine Dogmatiek*, Kampen 1947; G.C.Berkouwer, *De Wederkomst van Christus* I, Kampen 1961, 35-79; H.Berkhof, *Gegronde verwachting*, Nijkerk 1967, though this last author has some qualifications. There are also qualifications in P.Althaus, 'Der Mensch und sein Tod. Zu H.Thielickes "Tod und Leben"', *Universitas* 3, 1948, 385-94; id., *Die Christliche Wahrheit* 2, Gütersloh 1948, 475-93. Paul Tillich accepts the possibility of talking of both immortality and resurrection: both are symbols of equal value which seek to express the eschatological unity of man with God as the most authentic depth-dimension of being. For all this see above all H.Wohlgschaft, *Hoffnung angesichts des Todes. Das Todesproblem bei Karl Barth und in der zeitgenössischen Theologie des deutschen Sprachraums*, Munich 1977.

13. K.Barth, *Church Dogmatics*, III/2, Edinburgh 1960, 370.

14. This is the case for P.Althaus and E.Brunner according to the interpretation by G.Greshake, 'Das Verhältnis "Unsterblichkeit der Seele" und "Auferstehung des Leibes" in problemgeschichtlicher Sicht', in G.Greshake and G.Lohfink, *Naherwartung*, 103.

15. E. Jüngel, *Tod*, 115.

16. K. Barth, *Church Dogmatics*, III/2, 639.

17. This is the interpretation by H. Wohlgschaft, op.cit. 85, 99-102.

18. J. Moltmann, *Die Sprache der Befreiung*, Munich 1972.

19. See P.Althaus, 'Auferstehung', *RGG* 1, 698; O. Cullmann, op.cit.

20. H.Ott, *Eschatologie*, Zurich 1958; W.Elert, *Der christliche Glaube*, Berlin 1941; H. von Campenhausen, in J.Schlemmer (ed.), *Was ist der Tod?*, Munich 1969; *Tod, Unsterblichkeit und Auferstehung*, in E.Schlink and H.Volk (eds.), *Pro Veritate*, Munich 1963, 195ff.

21. See J.B.Cobb and D.R.Griffin, *Process Theology: An Introductory Exposition*, Philadelphia 1976; J. van der Veken, ' "Liefde heerst niet, is niet onbewogen", Kennismaking met het procesdenken van A.N.Whitehead en C. Hartshorne', *Coll.* 8, 1978, 5-22; 'God iedere morgen nieuw: Het proces-denken van A.N.Whitehead en C.Hartshorne', *TvT* 18, 1978, 361-89 and further literature there.

22. C.Hartshorne, *The Logic of Perfection and Other Essays in Neo-classical Metaphysics*, La Salle, Illinois 1962, 252f.

23. *TvT*, 382-3.

24. *The Tragic Sense of Life*(1931), quoted by John Hick, *Death and Eternal Life*, London 1976, 215.

Chapter III

1. I cannot venture on even a limited bibliography. I mention only the books by W.Luijpen, *Existentiële fenomenologie*, Utrecht-Antwerp 1959; *Fenomenologie en Atheisme*, Utrecht-Antwerp 1953; and the standard work by N.M.Wildiers, *Wereldbeeld en theologie. Van de middeleeuwen totvandaag*, Antwerp-Amsterdam 1977.

2. A.Vergote, *Het huis is nooit af*, Antwerp 1974, 121.

3. E.g. J.Auer, 'Auferstehung des Fleisches. Was kann mit dieser Aussage heute gemeint sein?', *MTZ* 26, 1975, 17-37; W.Breuning (see bibliography); G.Greshake (bibliography); I.Kremer, . . . *Want zij zullen leven. Dood, Verrijzenis en nieuw leven*, Bruges-Boxtel 1973; J.Moingt, 'Immortalité de l'âme et/ou résurrection', *Lumière et Vie*, 1972, 65-78; K.Rahner, 'The Intermediate State', *Theological Investigations* 17, London 1981, 114-24; C.Schütz, 'Vollendung', in J.Feiner and L.Vischer (eds.), *Neues Glaubensbuch*, Freiburg 1973, 526-44; see also the exegetical study by P.Benoit, 'Resurrection: At the end of time or immediately after death', *Concilium* 10.6, 1970, 103-14. See also *The New Catechism*, London 1967, 467-87.

4. J.Ratzinger, 'Zwischen Tod und Auferstehung', *IKZ* 9, 1980, 209-26, decidedly sees ghosts when he claims here that Catholic theologians who deny the continuation of the human soul do this because of an antipathy to tradition and on the basis of biblical fundamentalism (sic!). As to the latter, it can only be good news that contemporary thought, on the basis of anthropology, is coming so close to the biblical view of humanity that we can rec-

oncile the insights which are being achieved by modern science with a biblical basis.

5. See e.g. K.Rahner, 'The Comfort of Time', *Theological Investigations* 3, London 1967, 141-57.

6. D.de Petter 'Dood en Onsterfelijkheid', in *Begrip en Werkelijkheid. Aan de overzijde van het conceptualisme*, Hilversum-Antwerp 1964, 217-33.

7. Ibid., 223f.

8. There is a good and critical survey of many of these arguments with a personal view in A. de Cock, 'Over de Onsterfelijkheid. Een filosofische ver-handeling', *Algemeen Nederlands Tijdschrift voor Wijsbegeerte en Psychologie* 61, 1969, 112-36.

9. R.Michiels, 'De theologie van Rahner', *Coll.* 8, 1978, 264-92, is a very thorough study offering insights into Rahner's difficult and encyclopaedic theological work. The same issue also has Rahner's theological testament, 342-58.

10. See e.g. K.Rahner, *On the Theology of Death*, New York 1961, and a good summary view of his thought on these problems in K.Rahner and H.Vorgrimler, *Kleines theologisches Wörterbuch*, Freiburg 1980, 411ff.

11. See pp. 111ff.

12. See pp. 129ff.

13. L.Boros, *The Moment of Truth: Mysterium Mortis*, ET London 1965; *God is with Us*, ET London 1967; *Living in Hope*, ET London 1971; 'Has Life a Meaning?', *Concilium* 10.6, 1970, 11-20.

14. J.Ratzinger, who supports Rahner, also has a positive attitude to this approach by Boros; see *Eschatologie*, 157-60.

15. L.Bakker, 'Geloven in verrijzenis', *Bijdragen* 28, 1967, 294-318; A.J.Thiadens and L.A.Bakker, *Doodgaan is nog geen sterven*, Baarn 1972.

16. *The Brothers Karamazov*, Harmondsworth 1958, 62f.

17. See M.Trowitzsch, 'Einkehr ins Unendliche, Individualität und Un-sterblichkeit beim jungen Schleiermacher', *ZTK* 77, 1980, 412-34.

18. W.F.Hermans, *Uit talloos veel miljoenen*, Amsterdam 1981, 84f.

19. E.Schillebeeckx, 'Leven ondanks de dood in heden en toekomst', *TvT* 10, 1970, (418-51) 423.

20. Ibid., 437.

21. Ibid., 441.

22. Ibid., 441f.

23. E.Schillebeeckx, *Jesus*, London and New York 1979, 632.

24. J.Pohier, *Quand je dis Dieu*, Paris 1977, esp. 83-132; id., 'A Case of post-Freudian belief in the Resurrection?', *Concilium* 11, 5, 1975, 91-106 (not in the English edition). See my review in 'Als ik God zeg', *TGL* 36, 1980, 313-22.

25. E.Schillebeeckx, 'Leven ondanks de dood', 444.

26. J.Ratzinger uses the term 'soul' in this creaturely context as a concept of faith. See *Eschatologie*, 130. This was already the case in *De Kern van ons*

geloof, Tielt-Utrecht 1970, 296-9, and in his articles 'Jenseits des Todes', *IKZ* 1, 1972, 293-304; 'Zwischen Tod und Auferstehung', *IKZ* 9, 1980, 209-26. That is quite obviously right, but in that case he should not continue to criticize Catholic theologians who find the term soul unusable for philosophical and anthropological reasons.

Chapter IV

1. F. de Grijs, *Brieven aan de parelvisser*, Baarn 1980, 16.
2. See ch.III n.2 above.
3. See G.Lohfink, 'Zur Möglichkeit christlicher Naherwartung', in G.Greshake and G.Lohfink, op.cit., 64-70.
4. See p. 156.
5. F. de Grijs, op.cit., 20.
6. See Hefele-Leclercq, *Histoire des conciles*, Paris 1911: Council of Vaison (422), ibid., 2, 445; Council of Arles (443 or 452), 466; Council of Orleans (533), 1135; Council of Braga (563), 3, 178-80; Council of Auxerre (578), 219.
7. See e.g. G.Greshake and G.Lohfink, *Bittgebet. Testfall des Glaubens*, Mainz 1978; H.Schaller, *Das Bittgebet. Eine theologische Skizze*, Einsiedeln 1979.

Chapter V

1. See p. 60.
2. See J.Gnilka, *Ist I Kor 3,10-15 ein Schriftzeugnis für das Fegfeuer?*, Düsseldorf 1955.
3. See pp. 68ff.
4. See A.Stuiber,*Refrigerium interim*; C.Pietri, 'La mort en Occident dans l'épigraphie latine: de l'épigraphie païenne à l'épigraphie chrétienne, 3ᵉ-6ᵉ siècles', *Maison Dieu* 144, 1980, 25-48; P.Aries, 'La liturgie ancienne des funérailles', ibid., 49-59; P.C.J.van Dael, 'De dode in de oud-christelijke grafkunst', *Communio* 5, 1980, 215-25.
5. See H.G.Beck, *Die Byzantiner und ihr Jenseits. Zur Entstehungsgeschichte einer Mentalität*, Munich 1979.
6. *De civitate Dei* 21, 16 and 28.
7. See J. le Goff, 'Le purgatoire entre l'enfer et le paradis', *Maison-Dieu* 144, 1980, 103-38.
8. See A.Stuiber, *Refrigerium interim*.
9. See K.Lehmann, 'Was bleibt vom Fegfeuer?', *IKZ* 9, 1980, 236-43.
10. See e.g. Thomas, *in IV Sent.* d. 44 q.3, a.3, sol 3; *CG IV*, 20; *De Ver.*, 1.26 a.1.
11. I found an extended and convincing argument for this approach in the magisterial works of R.Girard, *La violence et le sacré*, Paris 1972; *Des*

choses cachées depuis la fondation du monde, Paris 1978. The theological validity of his thesis within Jewish Christian thought is confirmed in the study by R.Schwager, *Brauchen wir einen Sündebock? Gewalt in den biblischen Schriften*, Munich 1978. I gave a short account of Girard's first book in 'Een teken zijn op aarde', *Getuigenis* 23, 1978-79, 73-78. Girard's view was very much criticized, though in a way which I did not find convincing, by H.U.von Balthasar, *Theodramatik* III, Einsiedeln 1980, 176-91.

12. *The Brothers Karamazov*, 71.

Chapter VI

1. *The Brothers Karamazov*, 77.

2. See T.Moser, *Gottesvergiftung*, Frankfurt am Main 1976. I cannot follow the author in everything, but he makes some very important points.

3. It is not my purpose to suggest that H.U.von Balthasar is arguing for the *apocatastasis*. I leave the reader to interpret him and pass judgment.

4. A particularly attractive and informative thesis on the interpretation of this article of faith in the course of history has been written by W.Maas, *Gott und die Hölle. Studien zum Descensus Christi*, Einsiedeln 1969.

5. H.U.von Balthasar, *Einfaltungen. Auf Wegen christlicher Einigung*, Munich 1969, 130.

6. Id., 'Pneuma und Institution', *Skizzen zur Theologie* IV, Einsiedeln 1974, 387, 400.

7. Ibid., 396. See W.Maas, op.cit., 246-56.

Epilogue

1. *The Brothers Karamazov*, 61.

2. *The Devils*, Harmondsworth 1953, 280.

3. In G 3, 15, 1962, 268.

Indexes

Index of Biblical References

Old Testament

New Testament

258 *Index of Biblical References*

Index of Names